Recycling Cities for People

Cahners Books International, Inc.

221 Columbus Avenue
Boston, Massachusetts 02116

Recycling Cities for People
The Urban Design Process

Laurence Stephan Cutler, AIA, RIBA   Sherrie Stephens Cutler, AIA, RIBA

International Standard Book Number: 0-8436-0153-1
Library of Congress Catalogue Card Number: 76-14969

Printed in the United States of America

Designed by Lauri Rosser

Illustrations on pages 25 and 26 (*right*): George Braziller, Inc. from
The Future of the Future by John McHale; reprinted with permission
of the publisher. Copyright © 1969 by John McHale.

Illustrations on page 11: reprinted from *The Image of the City* by
Kevin Lynch by permission of The M.I.T. Press, Cambridge,
Massachusetts. Copyright © M.I.T. Press, 1960.

Illustrations on page 14: reprinted from *Cities* by Lawrence Halprin
by permission of The M.I.T. Press, Cambridge, Massachusetts.
Copyright © M.I.T. Press, 1972.

Illustrations on pages 50, 52, and 73: have been reproduced
with the permission of The American Institute of Architects. Further
reproduction is not authorized.

Illustrations on page 18: from *London Bridge is Falling Down,*
copyright © 1967 by Peter Spier, Illustrator. Reprinted by permission of Doubleday & Co., Inc. British Empire rights by permission
of Worlds Work, London.

Library of Congress Cataloging in Publication Data
Cutler, Laurence S
 Recycling cities for people.
 Bibliography: p.
 Includes index.
 1. Cities and towns—Planning—United States.
I. Cutler, Sherrie Stephens, joint author. II. Title.
HT167.C88   309.2′62′0973   76-14969
ISBN 0-8436-0153-1

To the memory of E. David Lukashok

Contents

Foreword

If our cities are hard on people, and they clearly are, then a pivotal question comes up as to why people are so very, very hard on themselves.

Laurence and Sherrie Cutler's book, or textbook to be more precise, is a timely attempt to put people in touch with some answers to that question. A strategy for recycling the physical increments of which our surroundings are composed is, for them, nothing less than a strategy for reinstating human values as the underpinnings of urban structure and experience.

In a time when society frequently behaves, and builds, as if no values are possible, this transcendentalist couple—a kind of Ralph Waldo Emerson and Margaret Fuller—have evoked an enduring conscience, characteristic of New England, even if their practice of architecture and urban design, centered in Cambridge, is taking them to places as disparate as Nigeria and Pawtucket, Rhode Island, as Micronesia and Gardiner, Maine. Yet there is nothing of the presumptuous piety of missionaries here, just an easy-going importing of perception, a saunter through the lessons that their own professional experiences have suggested, and an affable grab at the elbow of increased environmental concern. Perhaps it is because their work has drawn upon practically every discipline under the sun that they have realized that there is, truly, nothing new under it. Thus the evidence of the past, as they view it in the context of present day trends, is not so much worn out heirloom luggage to be carted along, generation after generation, but a vital resource to which a self-comprehending culture should be naturally accountable.

So while the Cutlers illustrate how to recycle cities, the practical reasons for public perception of and involvement in the process provides the connecting tissue—an ethic holding their diverse examples together. This book, then, is simply, refreshingly, a kind of offering, not a cast-in place altar, encrusted with so-called truths. Without ostentation, the Cutlers familiarize us with the books and the structures that have moved them and we are taken through the process by which they have come to terms with their own projects. Never are we asked to believe anything outright except, perhaps, to believe in beliefs. In this sense, their book is an armature of questions over which to weave our own identification with the day-to-day environment.

Basic to this approach is their sneaking assumption about, rather than the typically sneaking suspicion of, the worst of such public identification with planning decision. Not only are everyday people inadequately informed about the actions and events that shape their surroundings, they are also unconvinced that being informed will do any good. There are encouraging exceptions to this, of course, but generally speaking, a communal throwing up of hands has become one of our democracy's few predictable rituals.

Like most of humanity's technological and institutional extensions, conceived to stretch the spectrum of its ability, the city, in which such extensions are concentrated, has coiled back upon and hung a noose around the things it was meant to strengthen. "There is no way out, around, or through," as Sartre described the prepackaged ennui of contemporary existence.

If unseemly demeanor or abrasive manners can be ascribed to the way buildings relate to each other along our streets, this is in part expressive of the kind of torturous internal aggressions building up inside of people themselves as, steadily, the forces that actually determine the rhythm of our lives move farther from their control.

Dr. Edward T. Hall, the anthropologist, writes in his book *Beyond Culture,* "One of the most devastating and damaging things that can happen to anyone is to fail to fulfill his potential. A kind of gnawing emptiness, longing, frustration, and displaced anger is turned inward on the self or outward toward others. Yet, how man evolved with such an incredible reservoir of talent and such fantastic diversity is not completely understood. Man is not anywhere nearly enough in awe of himself, possibly because he knows so little and has nothing to measure himself against."

Self-image, self-respect or, as Dr. Hall writes, self-awe, none of these can really be blamed for the jagged-edged, emotion-scraping configuration of most urban environments, in which buildings are little more than cut-rate icons intended to symbolize established institutions. It is precisely the absence of introspective qualities that has allowed wholesale desolation in the name of urban planning. If we are to develop an introspective environment, facilitating cultural expression as well as functional needs, we have to create, more than buildings, loci for encounters between people and activities, between people and varied times of the day, between people and different periods of their communities' history. Comprehension of the "incredible reservoir of talent," of the "fantastic diversity" of which Dr. Hall writes, is finally the most practical and utilitarian function that a well-rounded community environment can serve. Regenerating a sense of control over events will only come about when, out of everyday experience, people can sense something of themselves and their history along the streets and within the structures which line and define their lives. It is for such regeneration that this book is both an appeal and a well-documented primer.

William Marlin

Associate Editor, *Architectural Record*
Architecture and Design critic, for
The Christian Science Monitor

Preface

We are going to find each other—we who are searching for the right way of living the truth and the peaceful way of harmony with each other and with nature . . . We are all part of it, we cannot break away from it.

—T. Banyacya, a Hopi

New and meaningful juxtaposing of seemingly diverse and unrelated elements has historically been the key capability of the imaginative mind. In this era of specialization and categorization, there is an acute need for this ability and for the person who possesses it—let us call that person a generalist/specialist.

The generalist was at one time a singular total individual, the so-called Renaissance man. Now, although great creative capability must still be a singular effort, there exists the need for a team approach to problem solving. "The generalist" who would organize new functions of the human environment today must, in fact, be a part of such a team—perhaps made up of specialists, but with the ability to merge into the *creative communal mind* of the committee, the Professional firm, the department, the corporation. All of these must all be capable of this "communal genius" if they are to be successful in the creative task, which has always been to "put it all together."

Acknowledgments

That this book has two authors does not mean that the task of writing it has been any easier than if there had been only one. The debt we owe to others seems especially great, because much of what we have included herein is a result of work we have not only done together, but with other members of ECODESIGN, our professional firm in Cambridge, Massachusetts. We owe a debt of gratitude to these comrades at ECODESIGN for their specific contributions: David Lennon Smith and James Hobart Piatt, as well as, Gretchen Bath, Paula J. Behrens, Robert Mays, Y. T. Morikawa, Joan E. Ramer, Daphne Allen Rice, Gunars Viksnins, and George Grant, an ECODESIGN comrade in spirit.

We would also like to acknowledge the following professional firms: CE Maguire, Inc., Nelson, Haley, Patterson & Quirk, and Thomas Griffin Associates Company; these governmental agencies: The Newburyport Redevelopment Authority, the Pawtucket Redevelopment Agency, the Regional Transportation District of Denver, Colorado, as well as the cities of Cambridge, Massachusetts; Denver, Colorado; Gardiner, Maine; Newburyport, Massachusetts; and Pawtucket, Rhode Island.

We owe a special debt to some others whose influence as teachers and friends contributed to us personally and have taught us through their own thinking and philosophies: Gordon Bronson, Peter Garland, Eduard Sekler, Jose Luis Sert, Albert Szabo, the late Joe Thompson, and the late Norman Waxman.

We have tried very hard to document and acknowledge anything that we have used from the work of others, but for any inadvertent oversights, we apologize and extend our gratitude to those we may have missed here.

A note of thanks to Professor Eric Techolz of Harvard's Laboratory for Computer Graphics, and a final note of thanks to Michael Hamilton and Walter Cahners, who instigated, prodded, and harassed us until we finally put pen to paper and produced the pages you are about to read.

Laurence Stephan Cutler, AIA, RIBA
Sherrie Stephens Cutler, AIA, RIBA

Cambridge, Massachusetts

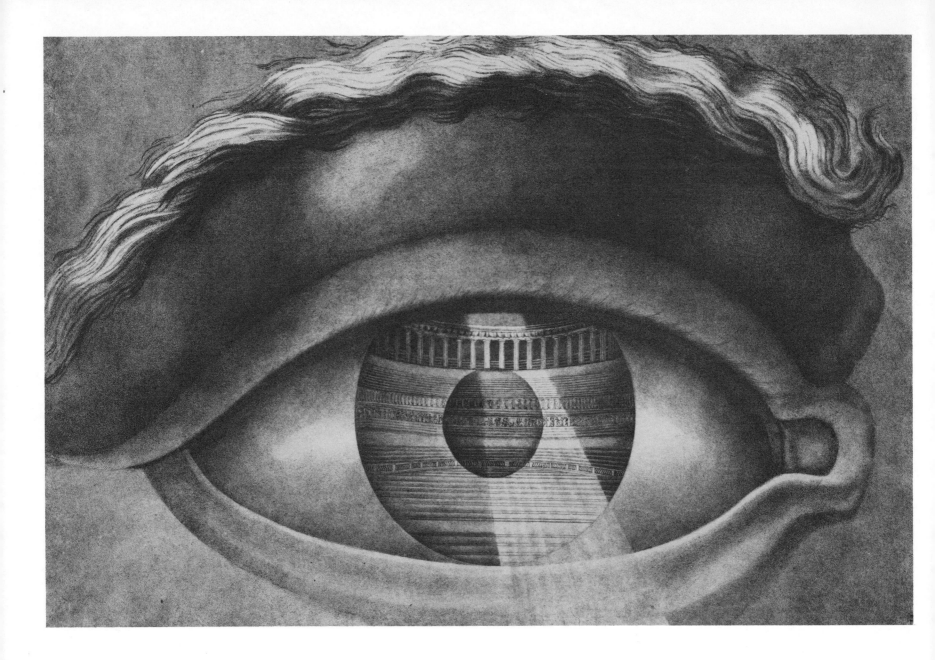

Symbolic juxtaposition. As seen through the pupil of an eye, by Claude-Nicholas Ledoux (late eighteenth century).

The State
of the Art

1

Designing for Cities

Don't walk in front of me,
                I may not follow;
Don't walk behind me I may not lead;
Walk beside me and be my friend.

—Camus

The layperson and city design

The involvement of the layperson in the design of a city is not a new role. When the earliest settlements began to evolve from a cluster of dwellings into a village, into a town, and then into a city, the inhabitants' involvement in the process was what, in actual fact, forced the adaptations. Settlements have always had to conform to the new and changing needs of the dwellers. In the more primitive forms of urbanization, this involvement was as simple and rational as the town meeting form of government. But now more complex urban forms have complicated the layperson's requirement for the design of his cities and the more structured forms of government necessary to operate the city have obscured the individual's role in its design.

A camel is a horse designed by a committee

On occasions when citizen involvement has been built into the political system, it has been in such capacities as planning commissions or building committees where an individual's effectiveness is fragmented by the special interests and "related professions" of the other members.

The planning commission form of civic design has often failed because neither the commission members (nor their constituents) have been adequately prepared to deal with the prime duty of their position—*to view the city as an integrated whole*. The members—usually a real estate broker, a general contractor, an engineer, a developer, and an environmentalist/activist—see their duties as simply protecting and advising conservatively. Additionally, they feel responsible for actions taken that reflect on their own fragmented and isolated area of special interest or expertise. Such worries about personal accountability and concerns for what is personally unfamiliar, tend to have a stultifying effect that restricts the communal imagination and derring-do of committees and commissions. Lack of familiarity also impedes commissions in working with their constituents in obtaining the understanding necessary for approvals of innovative approaches.

Our citizens, whether "policy makers" or constituents, have simply never been educated to see their own roles, professions, businesses, and so on as innate parts of the city as a whole. Nor have they the tools to weight the importance of an urban element with respect to other factors, to propose areas of compromise, to understand the major interfaces of activities within the city, or to devise and implement innovative urban concepts.

Body: Home of the individual human

City: Home of the communal human

A high-school education includes biology, botany, chemistry, physics—all directed toward an understanding of the natural systems. The human body is studied: its evolution from earlier forms, its structural/skeletal framework, the materials transfer and removal functions of its circulation systems, the communicative functions of the nervous system, and the regenerative function of its reproductive systems. The sixth-grade biology student studying the human organism realizes that to study these functions independent of each other would be impossible and meaningless. But the city, which is as much the home of the communal human as the body is of the individual human is studied only as fragmented activities—if it is studied at all by the end of high school.

In college one never studies the city unless the student himself so chooses, and that choice usually is because of prerequisites for city planning or architectural courses leading to professional degrees. And in those courses, the notion of the city having regenerative functions is as little broached as sex education was in the 1950s.

The question now arises as to whether there is a textbook available to reeducate the layperson who would be directly involved in the design of cities. Where can the student of the city be provided with the background in order to see his city in its proper perspective?

The state of the art of designing for cities as it exists in current literature is comprehensive but suffers as well from fragmentation. The existing works related to the design and understanding of cities fall into three major categories: historical, analytical, and elemental, while a fourth—synthesis—remains virtually unpublished except in the literature of proposals, reports, and implementation plans prepared for particular cities. We have selected some classic examples in each category to give the reader insights into the existing literature and the state of the art of designing for cities.

The historical works are the tomes of the methodical "greats" capable of imparting the historical *overview* of cities necessary in order to sense major new directions, modes of change, and to cite important precedents:

1

Historical Context of Cities—Lewis Mumford, *The City in History*

2

Historical Analysis of Cities—Edmund N. Bacon, *The Design of Cities*

3

Historical Overview of Cities—Christopher Tunnard, *The City of Man*

The analytical works are philosophical theses by the *imaginative* few who see the city in their own unique way—as a work of art or a hieroglyphic tablet capable of being "read" in different ways by different people:

1

How to Read a City—Grady Clay, *Close-Up: How to Read the American City*

2

The City and Its Image—Kevin Lynch, *The Image of the City*

3

The City as a Work of Art—Le Corbusier, *Creation is a Patient Search*

The elemental works have proliferated as the city is catalogued by various urban *specialties*. They are essential because they are the building blocks and the tools with which the urbanists must work. But so often the synthesis, putting the elements together, is not there. The books that fall into the "elemental" category are numerous and individually they cover just about every possible dimension and element of the city. They can provide a comprehensive and solid textbook base, but how the elements are used together, how and whether new formulas are tried, depends on the creativity of the chemist. For the sake of brevity, only the first three books herein are discussed; this list is ever expanding and is more completely covered in the bibliography.

1

Elements of the City—Lawrence Halprin, *Cities*

2

The Spaces of Cities—Gordon Cullen, *Townscape*

3

The Law & the Preservation of the City—John J. Costonis, *Space Adrift*

4

The City as Public Policy—Jonathon Barnett, *Urban Designs as Public Policy*

5

The City as a New Town—London County Council, *The Planning of a New Town*

6

The Architecture of the City—Paul Spreiregen, *The Architecture of the City*

7

The Words of the City—Charles Abrams, *The Language of Cities*

8

The Landscape of Cities—Edited by Cliff Tandy, *Handbook of Urban Landscape*

9

Models & Systems for Use in the City—Edited by Jean Perraton and Richard Baxter, *Models, Evaluations, & Information Systems for Planners*

10

The Ecological Economics of the City—Walter Isard, *Ecological-Economic Analysis for Regional Development*

11

The Psychology in Cities—Edward T. Hall, *The Hidden Dimension*

12

The Sociology in Cities—Jane Jacobs, *The Death & Life of Great American Cities*

The synthesis is, as yet, unpublished as a textbook type for studying city design. It exists more in the literature of proposals, reports, renewal plans, action plans, and brochures. It also exists in the experience of the participants of these plans—client, contractor, designer, and users. Outstanding is the team that possesses collectively not only the abilities to determine the problems, but also to propose solutions that pull disparate pieces together, to explain the proposal so that it is understood, to resolve conflicts, use opposition positively, and finally, to implement a creative concept in the city.

Urban designs or "city works" evolved in this way have always represented the ability of the human species to work together creatively in the same way that the artist or the writer works independently. The creative process of the participants in these collective city works is perhaps not any more explicable than those of the singular creative artist, but it is a freedom of thinking, an optimism and openness of mind—a solution orientation.

What is the question?

How can we save our dying cities? As a dying Gertrude Stein replied when Alice B. Toklas asked, "Gertrude, Gertrude—What is the answer?" (referring, of course, to the meaning of life), "My dear Alice, what is the question?" Design synthesis in the city is the phrasing and answering of some of the questions:

☐
What is worth saving?
☐
Can we create a more human urban environment?
☐
What can we do about the city and why?

☐
Ideally what could happen?
☐
What's happening here now?
☐
What are the city's assets?
☐
What are the city's liabilities?
☐
What immediate action should we take?
☐
How do we go about doing it?
☐
Who does what?
☐
How can the community participate?
☐
Are our goals mutual goals?
☐
What elements or factors are involved?
☐
What are the recurring problems?
☐
How can we think about old problems in new ways?
☐
How can we clarify and systematize the urban functions?
☐
How can we reinforce a city's urban frame and reorganize its components?
☐
How can urban elements be juxtaposed to form new concepts?
☐
Can we make new concepts public and make them understandable?
☐
How can we implement tasks and work together?

No book can phrase all the questions and give the answers. This can only happen through the participation in the process; this book can only introduce a newcomer to that process and show the reader what may be important now and in the future.

The Historical

Historical Context of Cities—Lewis Mumford's
The City in History

Lewis Mumford traces the history of urban culture from its ancestral forms and patterns to suburbia and the megalopolis—from the emergence of urban settlements as simple sanctuary to village and stronghold to the period in history that marked the passage from village to city. According to Mumford, this happened in the late neolithic culture, when "the more developed villages at some natural meeting point between regions may have gained in population and arable land . . . not the numbers of people in a limited area alone, but the number that can be brought under unified control to form a highly differentiated community, serving purposes that transcend nurture and survival that have decisive urban significance."

An understanding of the rich relics in art and technics, the signs of institutional life, and the significance of assemblages of building materials are the resources with which we track our urban history. The past gives us the notion that our age of automation and urban expansion has displaced the humanistic goals urbanization was supposed to serve. Mumford states that the needs today are similar to those of the past, yet the scale is the whole planet rather than a river valley, and that man's prime need is to "contrive channels for excessive energies." If this is not done, then the entire ecological system on which man's own life depends will disappear in a posthistoric era.

Mumford contends that these insights into the future come from an analysis of the rules of the Bronze Age, and that: "The final mission of the city is to further man's conscious participation in the cosmic

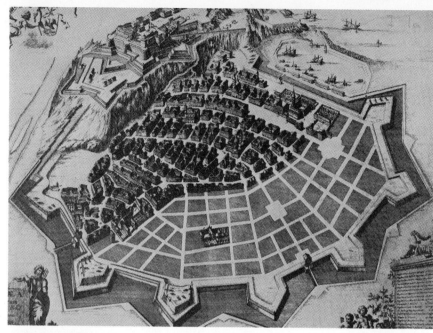

Classic stages of town building. The plan of Nice shows the three classic stages: 1) the castle on the hill, 2) block extension of a port community, 3) more orderly radial street layout.

A civic opportunity. Naarden in the Netherlands was originally a military extravaganza converted into a civilian community.

and the historic process." The magnification of all the dimensions of life is the supreme reason for the place of the city in history.

Historical Analysis of Cities—Edmund N. Bacon's
Design of Cities

Edmund Bacon presents a number of accounts of the historical or, rather, morphological development of the city ranging from ancient Athens to the new Brazilian city of Brasilia. He also examines the work of such great urbanists as Vitruvius, Sixtus V, John Nash, and Sir Christopher Wren, illustrating how their great works have influenced subsequent development around them.

Although Bacon is not an historian by training he states that his own particular role as "a participator in the recent history of the rebirth of Philadelphia" gives him the experience to synthesize the rich ideas of many planners that are applicable to all cities.

Bacon's basic belief is that there are universal parallels in the currents of history and that city planners and urbanists should draw upon them. His thesis is that one should explore the nature of decisions as they have occurred throughout history, as well as the context within which these decisions were made. To understand the development of the city through time is what Bacon states as the most fundamental need: to understand the deeper forces at play that actually form the spaces and structure of a great city is to comprehend the basic principles in city design.

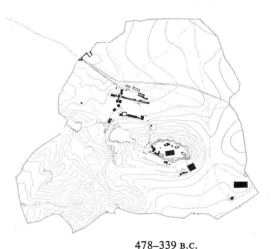

600–479 B.C.

478–339 B.C.

338–86 B.C.

86 B.C.–287 A.D.

The evolution of the form.
Athens from 600 BC to 287 AD.

Historical Overview of Cities—Christopher Tunnard's—*The City of Man*

Christopher Tunnard defines the city as a place that can only be experienced as a constantly changing fact of life influenced by particular schools of thought. He predicts rapidly increasing urbanization in the future and traces his visions of the New Urbanism back to their origins and the historic trends and schools in architecture and planning. Among these trends in particular were the industrial company towns that were developed along river edges because the mills were usually powered by water. The next period of history was captured by the romantic mood, which fully embraced the notion that God has made the country and man the town. This was the early nineteenth-century era of Herman Melville, the Hudson River school, gothic libraries, and Garden City on Long Island.

Tunnard quotes the famous aphorism, ''Architecture is the decoration of construction'' and goes on to make a strong case for the need of art in civic design. He feels that the goal of beauty is the unifying principle for city planning. The planning profession would be healthier if artists participated in the creation of urban form. In the United States there is a tendency to admire the picturesque wherever it can be found. Since there is very little beauty to admire in the mass, the emphasis is either on the ''quaint'' or the ''spectacular''—''old'' Williamsburg or the ''skyline of New York.''

Tunnard presents the historical reasons for the loss of a sense of value for esthetics in our constructions and in our urban lifestyles. The traditions that enabled the design and construction of fine buildings and cities with style have been maligned by the

The City of Man being destroyed by devils. The City of Rome was for St. Augustine the symbol of vanity in all material things. ''The City of Man has its stories, yes, even its virtues, and we should not be so concerned about our environment if it were not also a symbol of our aspirations here on earth.''

advent of community participation in the design process, by economics and by pure functional requirements.

He challenges professionals to work toward the day when architecture and city planning are united in a total approach to the city that can be titled ''The Grand Design.'' The new creative designer will be a ''visual expert, an artist in the form of cities, aware of the contribution which others must make if we are to live in communities which achieve an integration of art and life.''

Tradition is the key to begin—historical roots in an ever-evolving series of schools of thought is the direction, according to Tunnard.

The Analytical

How to Read a City—Grady Clay's *Close-Up: How to Read the American City*

Grady Clay translates an urban situation to its visitors or inhabitants in a manner that enables them to discover what the city is really about. It also enables one to perceive and to examine what the city is becoming.

In essence, Clay observes, the sizes of changes in the American city, the imprints of the past and the footprints for the future are out there shifting about, more or less ready to be found. Strange objects heave themselves into view and give off odd signals; familiar actors change costumes and shift roles; the action moves; the tempo changes. Cities, in short, are forever rewriting their repertoires.

Clues exist throughout our cities indicating a change in direction the city is about to make in contrast to its traditional growth through history. Clay proposes new nomenclature (a word game) for the elements of a city so as to come to "grips with city life—a playful, watchful approach, open-minded both to words and to their referents." Actually, one could invent his own word game simply by looking at the elements of the city and selecting something commonplace that would give it a different meaning because of its new name. This, Clay asserts, would also give it a label with new understandings of both the social and physical interactions.

Clay illustrates his points with aspects of our familiar environment that we all seem to ignore, such as his "epitome districts": shopping centers in classic suburban settings and street grid systems and their "breaks" (changes in the direction of movement), and strip development with ever-pulsating, ever-shifting corners of activity.

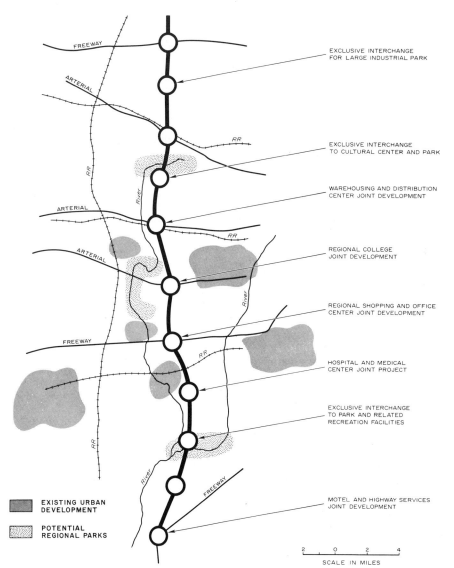

Joint development along a strip.

EXCLUSIVE INTERCHANGE
FOR LARGE INDUSTRIAL PARK

EXCLUSIVE INTERCHANGE
TO CULTURAL CENTER AND PARK

WAREHOUSING AND DISTRIBUTION
CENTER JOINT DEVELOPMENT

REGIONAL COLLEGE
JOINT DEVELOPMENT

REGIONAL SHOPPING AND OFFICE
CENTER JOINT DEVELOPMENT

HOSPITAL AND MEDICAL
CENTER JOINT PROJECT

EXCLUSIVE INTERCHANGE
TO PARK AND RELATED
RECREATION FACILITIES

MOTEL AND HIGHWAY SERVICES
JOINT DEVELOPMENT

EXISTING URBAN
DEVELOPMENT

POTENTIAL
REGIONAL PARKS

FREEWAY ARTERIAL RR River

2 0 2 4
SCALE IN MILES

10

"As evidence about the environment accumulates, as data pours into the well-financed centers, it grows more complex and often more abstract. This is why it must be tested all the more ruthlessly at every step against ordinary, everyday experience. The gap between the power of experts to manage data and that of the ordinary citizen to have access to it must be narrowed."

The linear/levee city.
Strip development may be reorganized into clusters or nodes at intersections, or continue to string along existing highways, settling down into specialized districts.

A dynamic polynuclear city system.

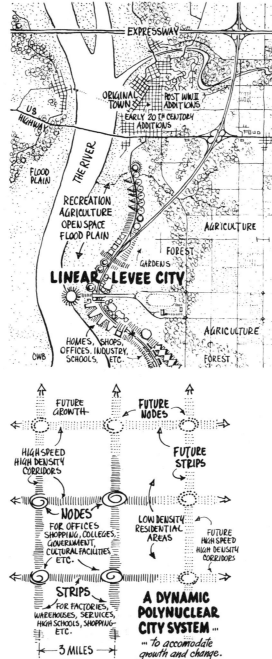

The City and Its Image—Kevin Lynch's *The Image of the City*

Kevin Lynch has examined the form of the city and what that form means to the city's inhabitants. The urban landscape as a composite becomes the "look of cities," a personification of the city as a whole.

For Lynch, the creation of a city means to give visual form to a place and he suggests a means whereby the urban designer might begin to deal with visual form at the urban scale, and he also offers some basic principles of civic design.

"In discussing design by element types, there is a tendency to skim over the interrelation of the parts into the whole. In such a whole, paths would expose and prepare for the districts, and link together the various nodes. The nodes would joint and mark off the paths, while the edges would bound off the districts, and the landmarks would indicate their cores. It is total orchestration of these units which would knit together a dense and visual image, and sustain it over areas of metropolitan scale."

Lynch suggests that the single most important aspect for enjoying a city and using a city is its vividness and sense of coherence. The image the city projects is a process between the observer and the observed, it can be controlled through an understanding of the elements that make it what it is *by design*. The elements Lynch has identified as the most significant are paths, edges, districts, nodes, and landmarks. Through field reconnaissance these elements can be reinforced toward "a future synthesis of city form considered as a whole pattern."

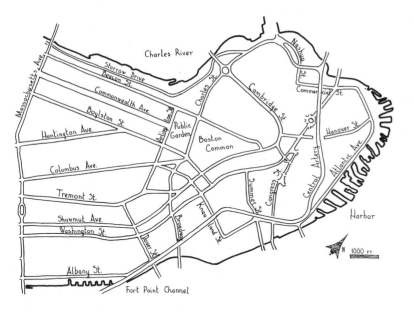

Outline map of the Boston peninsula.

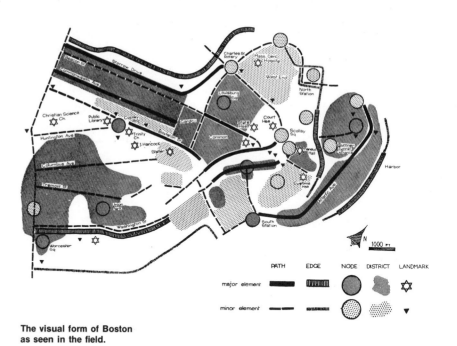

The visual form of Boston as seen in the field.

PATH   EDGE   NODE   DISTRICT   LANDMARK

major element

minor element

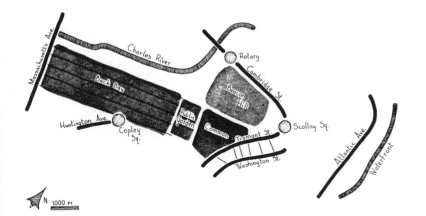

The Boston that everyone knows.

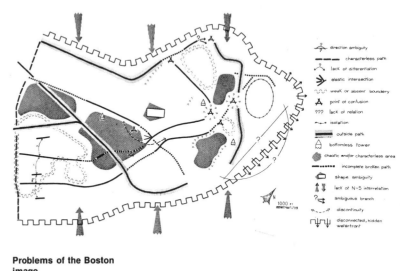

Problems of the Boston image.

direction ambiguity
characterless path
lack of differentiation
elastic intersection
weak or absent boundary
point of confusion
??? lack of relation
isolation
outside path
bottomless tower
chaotic and/or characterless area
incomplete broken path
shape ambiguity
lack of N–S interrelation
ambiguous branch
discontinuity
disconnected, hidden waterfront

The City as a Work of Art—Le Corbusier's
Creation Is a Patient Search

Le Corbusier, in 1922 at the Salon d'Antonine, posed the question "What is town planning?" and quickly answered his own question by "Well, it's a sort of street art. . . . It includes such things as the glass knobs on the stair ramp of houses. . . . I will do you a monumental fountain, and behind it I will put a town of three million inhabitants."

Le Corbusier's architecture and urbanism projects were significant because of his early days as an art student; his development as a professional architect was essentially an artistic development. His unique concepts were each originally conceived first as art works. He looked into his drawings and invented, and then created visual solutions to physical problems.

In 1935, Le Corbusier coined the phrase "La Ville Radieuse," which he claimed was not possible to translate into English. But the central philosophical statement implicit in all of his work was that architecture and urbanism are a single problem demanding only one solution.

"My cities are green cities.
  My houses give: Sun
                    Space
                    and Green. . . .
You must take 2000 people together, build a big house with only one entrance only for 2000 people."

Although Le Corbusier flaunted his rather simplistic and emotional statements as complex interpretations of complex problems, the actual forms he created have elevated the art of urbanism to the highest levels.

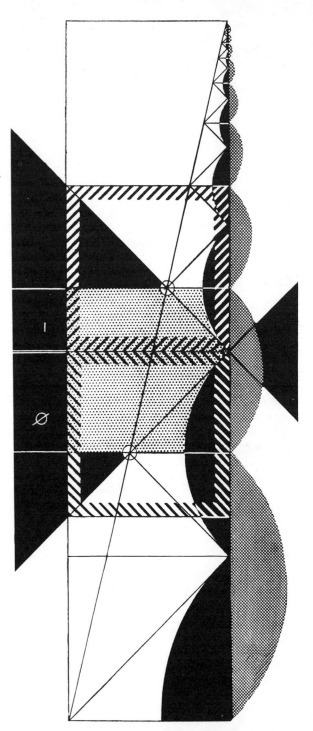

Creation is a patient search.
Le Modulor is a means of classifying dimensions based on the human figure and man's movement in a system of proportions that can be applied to the design of a whole city.

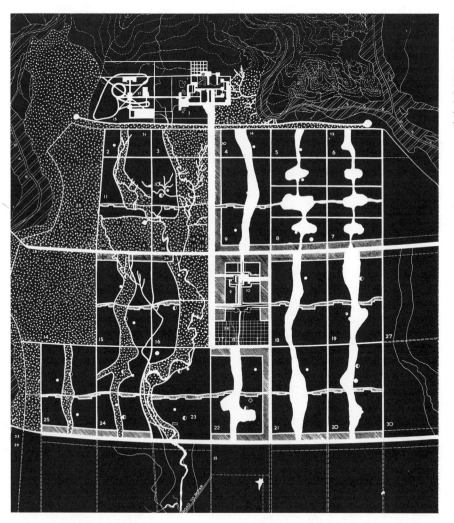

In the late 1950's, Le Corbusier designed the new capital city of the Punjab (India) at Chandigarh. The essential feature of the plan is the application of Le Modulor to Urban Sectors (800 x 1200 meters) each of which embraced the daily twenty-four hour life cycle of the contained population.

The Elemental

Elements of the City—Lawrence Halprin, *Cities*

Lawrence Halprin has concerned himself with the problem of how our growing cities can provide man's basic environmental needs: open space, air, light, and the opportunity for social and emotional fulfillment.

"The ultimate purpose of a city in our times is to provide a creative environment for people to live in." In order to identify the conditions required to be a "creative environment," Halprin has attempted to describe the basic materials that make up the character of the city. He examines the elements starting with urban open spaces, which he as a landscape architect considers the most important, for these are the "spaces within which its life takes place." The whole hierarchical range of public open spaces—the streets, the plazas, the parks—and the private living spaces—the small gardens and yards—are explored. Then he looks at the more specific urban materials such as water, paving, textures, street furniture, and the elements of the third dimension such as trees, steps, ramps, bollards, fences, and walls.

"A city is a natural phenomenon as well as a work of art in the environment. Form in nature is not a result of preconceived order. It evolves as it grows or happens, as mountains develop by upthrusting, boulders by glacier dropping. An art form to me is the result of the inherent nature of materials and the process of putting them together."

Trees for all seasons. There are specific and difficult conditions the tree in the city faces that are opposite to the conditions in its natural environment.

The floor of the city can be like a rich rug underfoot. Round river stones, brought up from the local river bed and dumped at random on the floor of the street, form the simplest paving, as in this Spanish city.

The Spaces of Cities—Gordon Cullen's *Townscape*

Gordon Cullen coined the word "townscape" to mean the art that can transform a group of buildings from something meaningless into a meaningful composition; or a complete city or town from an urban designer's diagram on a piece of paper into a satisfying three-dimensional environment for human beings. The basic ingredients of townscape are such things as the floor, street lighting, the wall, closure, squares, mystery, change of level, immediacy, place, serial vision, content, as well as many others.

"Within a commonly accepted framework—one that produces lucidity and not anarchy—we can manipulate the nuances of scale and style, of texture and colour and of character and individuality, juxtaposing them in order to create collective benefits."

Really what Cullen looks for through his dissection of the city is the art of the environment, for he quite enjoys the increasing possibilities of new relationships of forms that come from groupings of buildings. Joining the elements of the townscape together into patterns is the means with which the city becomes a place of vitality with warmth and power—"the home of man."

Changing with elegance. The sloping plane that joins two levels, being unusable, is generally regarded as a dead spot, but a direct solution can achieve a monumental dignity.

Mystery around the corner. From the matter-of-fact pavement of the busy world we glimpse the unknown, the mystery of a city where anything could happen.

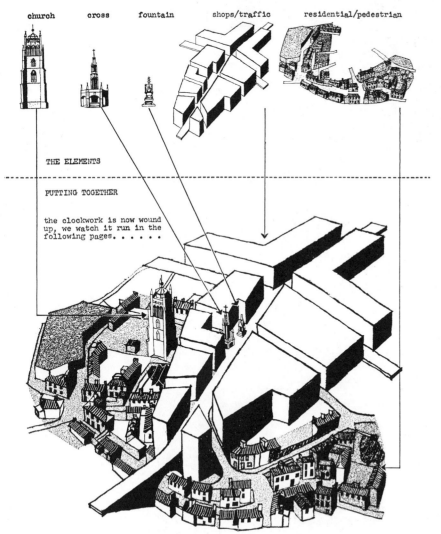

church   cross   fountain   shops/traffic   residential/pedestrian

THE ELEMENTS

PUTTING TOGETHER

the clockwork is now wound
up, we watch it run in the
following pages. . . . . .

Putting it all together. In town design and town appreciation, there are also two worlds, the animal world of self-preservation, or marginal sight, and the civilized, or magic, world of beholding.

The Law and the Preservation of the City—
John J. Costonis's *Space Adrift*

John Costonis, decrying the increasing rate that historic buildings and whole segments of American cities are being demolished or are falling into hopeless disrepair has seized upon the bicentennial fervor to awaken the public to the problem and propose solutions from the legal point of view.

The crux of the problem lies in the economies of old buildings because private developers cannot pay the ever-increasing costs of rehabilitation and restoration and the government will not assist in constructive restoration projects of non–national landmark sites. Costonis has provided a plan labeled *"Development Rights Transfer."* With this plan the owners of important buildings who can't take advantage of the full potential of the sites as now zoned, can sell or transfer these rights to owners of other nearby sites. As an example, if the owner of a ten-story historic building is not realizing the full value of his investment and he wishes, therefore, to demolish the building and replace it with a twenty-story building, he has the alternative of selling the development rights to the ten-stories above his building at fair market price. The air space above the historic building would be sold to developers who want to build more than current zoning permits on their own lots. In this manner, the owner of the historic structure would be compensated and motivated to retain and restore his local landmark building. The new developer would be able to take full advantage of his site and the increased taxes that his property would generate would offset the low taxes of the landmark property (this is real estate tax reduction).

There also would be established a Development Rights Bank and revolving fund where unused rights would be deposited and later sold under the guidance of the city government. Costonis seeks preservation restriction—a property interest conveyed by the landmark owner to the obligating owners to retain the property in its landmark status.

If one realizes that more than one-third of the 16,000 buildings listed in the Historic American Buildings Survey, begun by the federal government only forty years ago, have already been demolished, then it can easily be seen that such practical, implementation-oriented ideas are necessary if the heritage of our cities' historic structures is to be preserved.

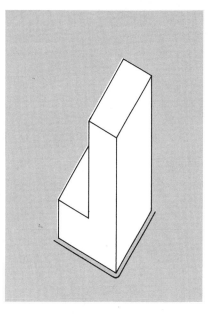

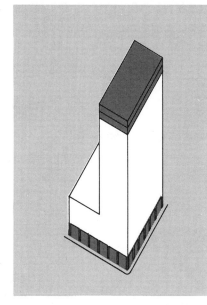

Maximum use of zoning allowances. An office building utilizing maximum Floor Area Ratio with no bonus space.

A typical zoning bonus. An office building with an amenity (arcade) for which a zoning bonus of additional floor area is awarded.

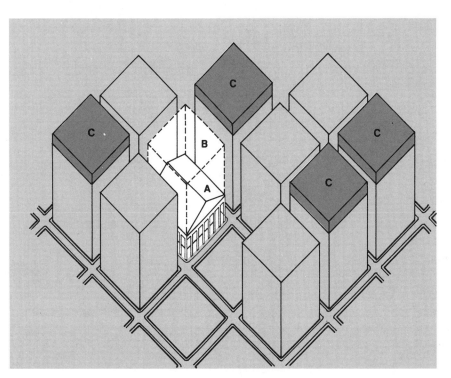

Development rights transfer. The landmark building (A) utilizes only a fraction of the development rights of the site, the remainder of which (B) are transferred to various other sites within a transfer district and appear as additional bulk (C) on neighboring buildings.

The Synthesis

The ''synthesis'' may be the unpublished symphony of the state of the art, but existing urban designs or ''city works'' stand as testimony to its categorical existence as the primary force in city design. The Old London Bridge, Rockefeller Center, the Brooklyn Heights Promenade are all city works, and these and others are examples of creative group synthesis, courage, and ''can-do'' in the city.

Megastructure and Mixed Land Use, Circa 1176

London Bridge is broken down,
    Dance o'er my Lady Lea;
London Bridge is broken down,
    With a gay lady . . .
Build it up with stone so strong
    Dance o'er my Lady Lea,
Huzza, 'twill last for ages long,
    With a gay lady.

It was not renowned for its beauty or even for its flawless engineering—why then does the Old London Bridge still live in nursery rhymes of children and the imagination of historians years after its demolition?

Perhaps because the unprecedented chutzpah and fortitude of those who built the Old London Bridge in the face of overwhelming political, economic, and technological obstacles presents a model of socioeconomic and city planning genius. Or perhaps because the multileveled mix of land uses incorporated in the bridge—commercial, residential, office, religious, defense, transportation and energy production—stands today as a formula for vigor beside our contemporary two-dimensional ''planning-by-strips-and-zones'' land use.

London Bridge going up, going up, going up. . . . The stormy political history of this project was matched by the engineering feats it demanded. Construction of the closely spaced piers required driving piles inside cofferdams by primitive means while battling the swift tides of a sixteen foot tidal range.

Perhaps the first ''Air Rights'' project, the old bridge offered all the modern conveniences and rent control. By the end of the fourteenth century, houses and shops—gabled, chimneyed, multi-storied—occupied both sides of the roadway, as well as above it, and projected out over the river, haphazardly braced from the spandrel walls and the cutwaters.

The bridge was built pier by pier, year by year as money was available and politics made it expedient. The bridge was worked across the 900-foot river crossing—sometimes neglected for entire reigns (Richard the Lion-Hearted), but finally completed (under John of the Magna Carta) by three London merchants and a French engineer.

Not one aspect of the bridge was totally functional or acceptable in today's terms. The buildings were badly constructed fire hazards, the roadway was crowded and narrow, boat passage was dangerous, and the invention of the "Toll Collection" was an unpopular, although resourceful, approach to the financial problem. Nevertheless, the daring technology of the construction, the many-leveled integration of the multimodal circulation system, the maximization of the bridge as an urban asset, the reinforcing of this important city connection as a "commercial node," the first use of tidal power as an energy source—any or each of these innovations, whether intended as solutions to problems or accidents of convenience, are lessons for today. Most outstanding, however, is the creativity and courage of the individuals who brought these concepts into being.

The Thames River in 1616— a water resource, a sewer system and an energy source. In the seventeenth century the bridge became a favorite residential street, partly because the river afforded both water supply and sewage disposal, two conveniences lacking in the rest of London. The tides were harnessed energy by waterwheels placed between the piers.

20

Enlightened Private Enterprise as the Shaper of Cities, Circa 1930

Big Business and all that makes New York City "the Big Apple" come together to compose Rockefeller Center. Its assembly of corporate towers, its plaza, and its chromatic relief structures are reminiscent of the personal monuments and subsidized civic art of the political family compounds of renaissance Italy. The goals were the same: corporate bravado and civic pride—with enlightened private enterprise as the shaper of cities.

With Rockefeller Center, as with the Old London Bridge, the fact was the fearlessness with which so many were able to agree and pull together so many diverse and innovative solutions to complex problems in a single city project. A new scale of city planning was assumed for the first time in a developing "high-rise" city and pursued boldly on twelve acres of burgeoning Manhattan. The organization was that of an independent "complex" while still working within the system of the city's circulation and zoning gridiron.

No lesser a goal was the humanizing of the dark gothic skyscraper technology with light and air and the humanizing of sterile skyscraper office usage with the inclusion of new and various activities and events.

The combination of leisure, entertainment, theater, night clubs, international trade offices, journalism, undercover shopping, and the convenience of a built-in parking garage may have begun merely as a formula of private enterprise devised to assure a balance of cost and returns but, whether accident

The corporate giants behind Prometheus. The Concourse below grade has direct access to the subway mezzanine, and relates to Rockefeller Center's twenty-one buildings as well as three additional blocks. This is consistent with the center's Promethean task in achieving intercorporate, interagency cooperation for a convenient urban lifestyle.

Can this many major corporations find happiness together in an underground world of convenience? Rockefeller Center's underground concourse system has nearly two miles of below-street passageways. It is lined with more than one hundred shops, restaurants, and stores, as well as subway exchanges, all of which provide a variety of services creating a virtual city-beneath-a-city.

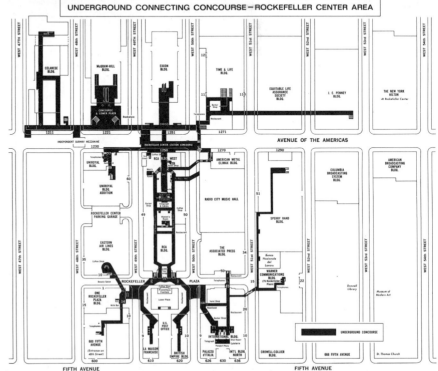

UNDERGROUND CONNECTING CONCOURSE—ROCKEFELLER CENTER AREA

or enlightenment, the seeds of a contemporary urban quality of life were planted.

The underground concourse system has grown with deceptive ease as Rockefeller Center has expanded, with each new building connecting into the original concourse. But in 1958, for example, in order to provide a link with the center's Time & Life Building rising across the Avenue of the Americas, Rockefeller Center leased the north end of the Sixth Avenue Subway mezzanine from the New York City Transit Authority—such a lease was an urban innovation in itself.

The evolution of the center's design concepts and its use program is clearly traceable from the technical, economic, and humanistic considerations and goals. The urban design of New York City during its development in the 1930s needed a rational, yet human, new direction. Unfortunately, although the formula was now known and proven, it was not often used, and New York City is now suffering the consequences. On occasions when the ambitious new larger scale of planning was present, the civic and commercial land use mixes and their resultant amenities or the flexibility for change were not there—nor was the gift of public art and public space.

A quality of life: recognizing the changing seasons. Skaters whirl on the Rockefeller Plaza Outdoor Ice Skating Pond set among the skyscrapers of Rockefeller Center, the world's largest city-within-a-city. Diners in the promenade cafés flanking the pond view the skaters through large panorama windows. During the summer, the skating area is transformed into a colorful outdoor café. Works of art are incorporated throughout, but highlighted by Paul Manship's Prometheus statue.

| **Formula for City Works** | = | **Clear Response** | × | **Technical Economic Humanistic** } | **Goals** |

Is a clear response to technical, economic and humanistic goals the formula for successful "city works"? It was for the Old London Bridge, Rockefeller Center, and other urban designs.

The Brooklyn–Queens Expressway presented an incredible series of seemingly unsolvable and contradictory technical, topographical, historical, economic, and social problems: 1) insufficient space for the multilane highway without expensive land taking, 2) difficult interface between the residential and the waterfront shipping activities, 3) community reaction against destruction of historic homes and relocation, 4) reaction against the destruction of the steep land form—the visual backdrop of Columbia Heights, and 5) the creation of highway noise in a quiet residential area.

Again, only the participants know for sure whether the solution was an accident of economic necessity and logical thinking, or an enlightened intent to provide humanistic elements. Regardless, the boldness of the three-level cantilevered engineering solution solved far more than the land/cost problem. No park was originally planned with the expressway, but the steep bank had to be retained and the traffic noise had to be controlled—the result was a third tier, which became the beautiful promenade. This single, straightforward decking concept simultaneously maximized land values by the layering of traffic and promenade, preserved the historic old homes on the Heights, eliminated displacement and relocation, and reinforced some of the most dynamic views and vistas of New York City and the harbor from both the highway and Heights.

Clear, dramatic definition of city edge. How the urban uses and functions come together, how the transitions are made and the connection established—these are the challenging issues in urban design.

A many leveled solution to a multimodal problem. Shipping, docking, cargo transfer, trucking, auto, bus, subway, pedestrian are the transportation functions handled here on many levels—cantilevered design for the six-lane freeway plus service road required only fifty feet in addition to the existing street to provide the right of way.

Again, the formula led to a solution that created a uniquely urban quality of life by an amazing combination of land uses—civic, shipping, industrial, transportation, residential, recreation, and a multi-level, multimodal approach to circulation. Again, the solution provides public space and amenity at a special intersection of the city.

Another innovative precedent. The inclusion of the freeway structure itself in the historic preservation district of Brooklyn Heights is an important recognition of the equal importance of exterior space and relationship of non-building urban elements to buildings in determining urban quality and historic significance—all these are ultimately inseparable.

2

The State of
the Environment:
A Sampler
of Trends

The new American revolution

There are five revolutions that must take place either simultaneously or not at all: a political revolution; a social revolution; a technological and scientific revolution; a revolution in culture, values and standards; and a revolution in international and interracial relations. The United States is the only country, so far as I can see, where these five revolutions are simultaneously in progress and are organically linked in such a way as to constitute a single revolution. In all other countries, either all five revolutions are missing, which settles the problem, or one or two or three of them are lacking which relegates revolution to the level of wishful thinking.

—Jean François Revel, *Without Marx or Jesus: The New American Revolution*

Adaptation and control

Why is the human special? His development has been based on adaptation and on the ability to control his environment. He distinguished himself by adaptation; and his revolutions and technology are simply a manifestation of this trait. Now he must apply adaptation to the hybrid world of man/nature that his technology has created. This adaptative evolution must be universally and studiously planned within a new perception of man's history and a defined vision of his future.

Planned evolution

These natural revolutions, when guided by forethought and controlled by enlightened afterthought, could be transformed into "planned evolution," which is as logical and innately human a concept as planned parenthood.

The environment within which we, as well as our cities, must either evolve, decline, or be recycled is the "historical space" described by the historian, S. Giedeon: "Historical space has many dimensions. It is many-sided. It does not permit the observer a single point of reference by which to interpret its phenomena. There appears—as in modern physics— no exact causality, no determination. Identical causes do not lead absolutely to identical effects."

Preparedness for uncertainty

This state of semicausality means that an individual's involvement in this evolutionary process can permit no preestablished point of view. Constantly changing, our cities require a preparedness for the uncertainty that is both inherent in that state and inevitable in the lack of any foolproof "formula" for city revitalization. In spite of the existence of successful models for regenerating segments of cities the only constant apparent in these precedents is a simultaneous consideration for all things great and small—an awareness of many facets of human life that make for a more human environment.

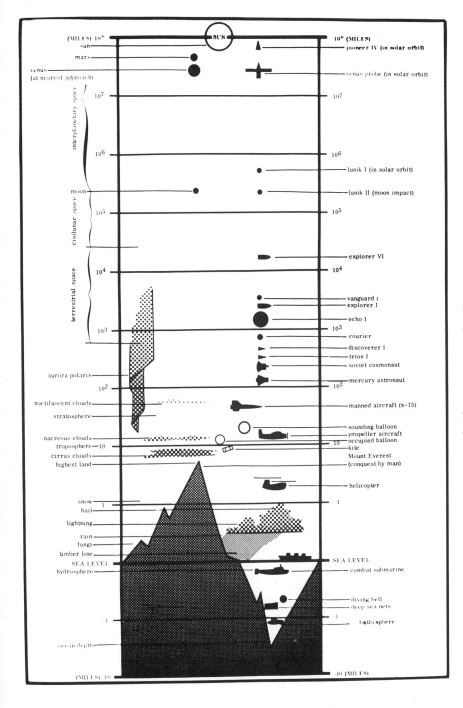

Vertical mobility.

The human environment is no longer limited to the surface crust of the earth. Technology has increased man's vertical mobility and expanded both his real life cycle and his perceived time span. Psychological realms are just beginning to be explored while the social and political exist in flux. Complexity and change are the only consistency in the contemporary human environment and in the forseeable future.

Consciousness

If man's predominance and his evolutionary survival have been because he excelled at adaptation to and control of his environment, then he must now learn to apply himself consciously and systematically to an adaptive process that has previously been a largely unconscious one.

The global eco-system

The process must be a studious and continuous adaptation to the "global ecosystem," which is the totality that man must either adapt to or of which he must become a part. The global ecosystem is the interacting of the *human* systems—biological, social, technological—and the *environmental* systems— atmospheric, terrestrial, and oceanic. This global ecosystem has even been diagrammed by John McHale in *Future of the Future,* and the author's caption can be interpreted as describing the weakness in mankind's present adaptive process: "We need to extend the physical and biological concepts of ecology to include the social behaviors of man— as critical factors in the maintenance of his dynamic ecological balance. Nature is not only modified by human action as manifested in science and technology—through physical transformations of the earth to economic purpose—but also by those factors, less amenable to direct perception and measure, which are political-ethical systems, education, needs for social contiguity and communication, art,

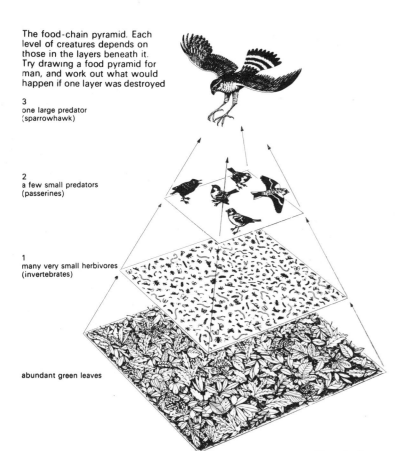

The food-chain pyramid. Each level of creatures depends on those in the layers beneath it. Try drawing a food pyramid for man, and work out what would happen if one layer was destroyed

3
one large predator
(sparrowhawk)

2
a few small predators
(passerines)

1
many very small herbivores
(invertebrates)

abundant green leaves

The adaptive process has previously been a largely unconscious one.

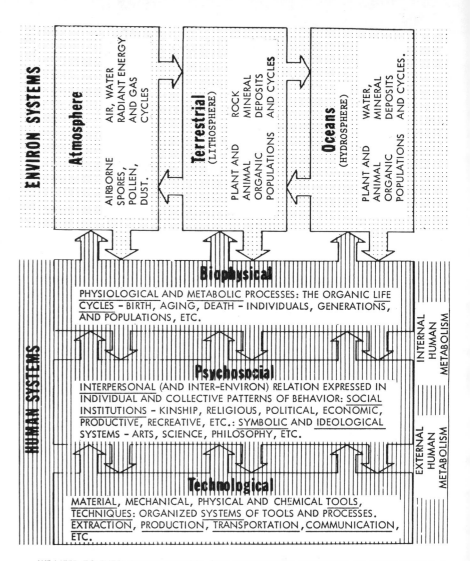

WE NEED TO EXTEND THE PHYSICAL AND BIOLOGICAL CONCEPTS OF ECOLOGY TO INCLUDE THE SOCIAL BEHAVIORS OF MAN--AS CRITICAL FACTORS IN THE MAINTE-NANCE OF HIS DYNAMIC ECOLOGICAL BALANCE. NATURE IS NOT ONLY MODIFIED BY HUMAN ACTION AS MANIFESTED IN SCIENCE AND TECHNOLOGY--THROUGH PHYSICAL TRANSFORMATIONS OF THE EARTH TO ECONOMIC PURPOSE--BUT ALSO BY THOSE FACTORS, LESS AMENABLE TO DIRECT PERCEPTION AND MEASURE, WHICH ARE POLITICAL--ETHICAL SYSTEMS, EDUCATION, NEEDS FOR SOCIAL CONTIGUITY AND COMMUNICATION, ART, RELIGION, ETC. SUCH 'SOCIO-CULTURAL' FACTORS HAVE PLAYED AND WILL INCREASINGLY CONTINUE TO PLAY A CONSIDERABLE ROLE IN MAN'S FORWARD EVOLUTIONARY TRENDING AND ITS EFFECTS ON THE OVERALL ECOLOGY OF THE EARTH.

The global ecosystem.

religion, etc. Such 'socio-cultural' factors have played and will increasingly continue to play a considerable role in man's forward evolutionary trending and its effects on the overall ecology of the earth.''

Other seers of the future have, even earlier, signaled for the balance of intellectual, emotional, and political cultures which was the source of the creative powers of the Golden Ages of the great nations.

The fallacy: "Let's keep personal feeling out of this."

We must proceed more humbly. Before demanding in a disorganized world such a unity of emotional, intellectual, and political culture, we must first understand how far the emotional and intellectual are today interrelated, how nearly we have approached that vital preconception of every culture: the affinity between its methods of thinking and of feeling. . . .

The influence of feeling on practical decisions is often regarded as unimportant, but it inevitably permeates and underlies the decision of men. The chaos of our cities, from Soviet Russia to the U.S., cannot be explained as a result of social and economic conditions alone. In the rebuilding of Moscow, in the slum clearance of New York, there is the same lack of scale, the same schism between retrogressive feeling and advanced technical means. Actions are released by social and economic impulses, but every human act is affected, is formed unconsciously, by a specific emotional background.*

No "gadget fix" for our worldly ills

Until now technology has been the master of man's adaptive process and technological revolution created the cities. But the adjustments to the problems of the cities in the next era will not be what Dan Brand calls the ''gadget fix,'' nor, as

*S. Giedeon, *Space, Time and Architecture*, p. 760-1.

H. Wentworth Eldredge describes, will it be "complexes of ziggurats springing up, nor people coming up from these underwater cities for a quick look at the obscured sunshine from time to time." No futurist now believes that gadgeting can cure our urban ills.

Need for social inventions

"The years ahead may be like a war in which the main enemies are our own ignorance and confusion about what to do for the good of us all"—this was John Platt's expressed concern in *Perceptions and Change: Projections for Survival.* Our only protection against the enemies of ignorance and confusion is to determine—for the world, for our settlements, and for ourselves as individuals—first, what are the real priorities of our many problems and then to establish a set of mutual and progressive goals. These goals will only be valid within a context of free information and with clear and open paths of communications. Then perhaps our ills can be treated with new "social inventions" that can be adapted early enough and universally enough to be effective.

Determining new priorities for mutual goals.

Classifying World Problems

Grade	Estimated Crisis Intensity (number affected times degree of effect)	Estimated Time to Crisis (if no major effort at anticipatory solution)		
		1–5 Years	5–20 Years	20–50 Years
1.	10^{10} *Total Annihilation*	*Nuclear or RCBW Escalation*	*Nuclear or RCBW Escalation*	✝ (Solved or dead)
2.	10^9 *Great Destruction or Change (Physical, Biological, or Political)*	(too soon)	Famines Eco-balance Development Failures Local Wars Rich-Poor Gap	Economic Structure and Political Theory Population and Eco-balance Patterns of Living Universal Education Communications-Integration Management of World Integrative Philosophy
3.	10^8 *Widespread Almost Unbearable Tension*	Administrative Management Need for Participation Group and Race Conflict Poverty-Rising Expectations Environmental Degradation	Poverty Pollution Race Wars Political Rigidity Strong Dictatorships	?
4.	10^7 *Large-Scale Distress*	Transportation Diseases Loss of old cultures	Housing Education Independence of Big Powers Communications Gap	?
5.	10^6 *Tension Producing Responsive Change*	Regional Organization Water Supplies	?	?
6.	*Other Problems —Important, but Adequately Researched*	Technical Development Design Intelligent Monetary Design		
7.	*Exaggerated Dangers and Hopes*			Eugenics Melting of Ice Caps
8.	*Non-Crisis Problems Being "Overstudied"*	Man in Space Most Basic Science		

Feeling:
The Psychosocial
Environment

Changes in belief systems

Changes in belief systems are required if mankind is to survive in the coming decades successfully. John Platt of the Mental Health Research Institute at the University of Michigan has enumerated four components that he believes have scientific validity and fit together as "four legs on a table," in forming a more humane society.*

1
Ecological Ethics. This is the belief in the web of nature and the need to protect it from damage, pollution, and overpopulation.

2
Human Potential Concepts. We need to live in clusters where we support each other psychologically through love and transactional relationships and provide for and reinforce the fullest possible development of every human being.

3
Existential Responsibility. We bear personal responsibility at every instant for our beliefs and how we act on them. It is ultimately how the individual has chosen out of the many opinions and options presented to him, not fate, which determines the future.

4
Cybernetic Working-Through. We must proceed ahead by a steering process that is continually evaluating, choosing, and acting with feedback—monitoring for adjustment in our course, which should be cited for improvement in every sector and is not fractional.

Can man continue his adaptation—physically, socially, and psychologically—to this increasingly hybrid world? Can he cope within the framework identified above? These questions are poignant when one considers that there are major energy

*John Platt, "World Transformation: Changes in Belief Systems," *The Futurist,* June 1974.

imbalances between the oil-consuming and oil-producing nations, that scientific advances bring hazards of mass destruction through more powerful weapons, that new machines to relieve labor bring unemployment problems, that satisfaction of basic needs brings revolutions of rising expectations, that advances in communication and transportation bring increased pollution and "information overload" to society. *Each apparent technological success has brought new and greater social problems.*

Directing our human energies

Up to now the priorities of the American Dream have dictated that technology be oriented toward goals of increased production and expanded wealth. These priorities are the incentives that have guided the technology. On the other hand, one could contemplate the role of technology if given a more social orientation to its problem-solving capabilities. If the critical problems are the use of resources, water and food sources, health, destruction of the biosphere, and so on, only a change in priorities based on a worldwide change in belief systems can alter the direction of our technological energies.

And what of our political energies? What's happened to the creation of leaders in our time? How do you explain the fact that we are not very innovative politically today? Historian Henry Steele Commager has posed answers to these questions.

"Talent grows in whatever channels are available and are popular."

Every major institution of a political, Constitutional nature was invented and developed before 1800, and Americans since then have made no major contribution to the principle or the practice of politics . . . a number of things have happened, I think, to explain the decline of leadership, the decline of creativity. One thing is that talent grows in whatever channels are available and are popular.

Reconsidering our goals.

Wanted: New Technology

The suggestion is often made that there is too much technology already, but anyone who tries to solve a human problem is likely to wish for some new technology.

Problem	Examples of Desired Technology
Poverty	More efficient ways to build houses and grow food.
Health	An effective means of destroying cancer cells without harming non-cancerous tissue, or an immunizing agent against cancer.
Age	Drugs that would retard the aging process.
Alcoholism	A drug that would enable people to have a "high" yet be harmless.
Divorce	A better way to match people who would make compatible mates, perhaps through highly accurate personality tests and computerized matching system.
War	Apparatus for detecting rising tensions among nations, and appropriate social technology for mediating quarrels.
Racism	New techniques to help people change their appearance, so that "racial features" become a matter of choice rather than biological necessity.
Unhappiness	An electrical or chemical method that would stimulate the pleasure centers of the brain, without causing adverse effects.
Pollution	Materials that disintegrate rapidly and safely after use. Economic ways to recycle automobile tires.

"Public enterprise was prized and rewarded."

There were very few channels for talent in the Eighteenth Century. There were not great financiers, great merchant princes, great artists, great musicians, great courtiers—all of the things that you found a place for in France, in Germany, and in Britain at the time. And theology was on the decline, and talent all went into law and public service. That is one explanation of the Eighteenth Century.

Now there's enormous, innumerable areas for talent. And on the whole, talent goes where the public rewards are ostentatious—not just financial, but in prestige.

In the Eighteenth Century in Salzburg, in Vienna, it was music. In the Nineteenth and Twentieth Century America, the great rewards went to the railroad builders, to the titans of industry—to the Rockefellers, and the Carnegies, and the Schwabs, and scores of others whose names are familiar—to the J. P. Morgans—and others, who could master the economy of the country—not to the statesmen. And it went, in other words, to private enterprise, not to public enterprise.

The greatest distinction between the Eighteenth Century and the Twentieth is that in the Eighteenth Century it was public enterprise that was prized and rewarded. Rewarded not financially—heaven knows, they all went bankrupt in their country's service—but rewarded in prestige and in satisfaction. In the Twentieth Century, it was private enterprise that is rewarded. And even those in public enterprise usually see to it, as Mr. Nixon does, and as others do—they get the private rewards as well.

"The concept of the public welfare is broad and inclusive. The values it represents are spiritual as well as physical, aesthetic as well as monetary. It is within the power of the legislature to determine that the community should be beautiful as well as healthy, spacious as well as clean, well-balanced as well as carefully patrolled."

United States Supreme Court, 1954

Berman vs. Parker, 348 US 26, 75 Supreme Court 98, Ed. 27 (1954)

"Public servants have forgotten they were servants."

This is rather a new development in American public life—that public servants have forgotten they were servants. They think they're masters. If there's any basic principle in American life, it is that the civil servant is indeed the servant of the people. The people are masters. And people have the right to exact certain things from their civil servants.*

A renaissance of the public ethic, of public commitment is the trend that defines the necessary changes in our belief systems. A renaissance that would change the mood of the country or the world, that would revive the flagging spirits, revive the popularity of characteristics of integrity, and co-operation and the belief in the capabilities of political systems. Dr. Commager is optimistic about the existence of the trend.

There are enough prospects, if only they'd attract the great minds—the prospects of great international problems—problems that glare, not upon the United States, but the whole of the globe—population, the destruction of resources, the destruction of the ocean, the danger of the atomic bomb, the danger of militarism. . . . Oh, it's very demanding— it was even in 1776 or 87. It's now on a global scale. Perhaps this is devastating. Perhaps this discourages individuals who think they can make a contribution. The situation in the 1770's was manageable, in a sense. It could be done in the American context. Now it is very difficult to manage a global situation. Nevertheless, the demands on the public arena are tremendous and I'm happy to see that the young are responding to this. The young medical students don't want to practice medicine.

*"A Conversation with Henry Steele Commager," © 1974. Educational Broadcasting Corporation. *Bill Moyers' Journal*, WNET/13 (New York), March 26, 1975.

Sensing: The Biophysical Environment

They want to be research doctors. They don't want to practice being law students, they want to be welfare lawyers and poverty lawyers and environmental lawyers. They don't want to go to a Wall Street firm.*

Only a social will to implement change will cause that to happen.

What Revel as an outsider sees as simultaneous, multifaceted revolutions already beginning in America is what Commager predicts as "the great revolution of our time." All this is taking place within the psychosocial environment. No design or physical ingenuity will bring change or solutions, only a social will to change will cause that to happen within this environment. The biophysical and technological revolutions have had their day and the social adjustments have been violent. Psychologically our individual transformation in beliefs should be a personal and pacifying process.

*"A Conversation with Henry Steele Commager," © Educational Broadcasting Corporation, 1974. *Bill Moyers' Journal,* WNET/13 (New York), March 26, 1975.

The physical and biological functions of the human body and other physical bodies also effect the total environment.
☐
The physical structure of the ecosystem
☐
Organic life cycles
☐
Body dimensions and needs
☐
Changing generations and adaptations
☐
Birth/aging/death
☐
Individuals/communities/populations/race
☐
Physiological and metabolic processes
☐
Male/female/sex roles
☐
Environmental diseases:
Overcrowding
Heart attacks
Influenza
Urban violence

Change in Man's Age

The bio-physical framework of time and space within which we live and evolve has already changed rapidly and continues to change:

When the three-year-old in Des Moines, Iowa, who today watches Sesame Street has reached the age of 40, the three-day work week will probably have been long established. Furthermore, it is probable that the enormous advances in biochemistry and in knowledge of body rhythms will permit him to stay awake in good functioning order for twenty-one out of every twenty-four hours. In all probability he will have vastly greater longevity and vitality than today's 40-year-old.

*He will live in a society that may exercise considerable control over the weather. Members of the community will have easy, cheap, virtually foolproof contraceptive methods. As the crowded descendants of the twentieth century population explosion they will probably be looking to exotic places for resources and living space.**

**The Futurist,* published by the World Future Society, P.O. Box 30369 (Bethesda), Washington, D.C. 20014.

As within the technological environment, the advances or successes seen in the biophysical environment—extended life spans, medical methods of prolonging life, and so on have actually accelerated the critical, high priority problems related to overpopulation.

"Moral problems lie at the heart of the American dream."

Urban violence is an outgrowth of biophysical successes if one assumes it is caused by the overcrowding produced by overpopulation and a concurrent problem of physical supply and demand of resources.

*The moral problems lie at the heart of the American dream: our nation's greatness is defined in large measure by what we can provide for the least-advantaged among us . . . the same desperate young who kill one another are also frightening the rest of us off the streets. As long as violence is an urban disease, no city dweller is immune from its contagion.**

*Franklin E. Zimring, "A Tale of Two Cities," *Wall Street Journal,* December 20, 1974.

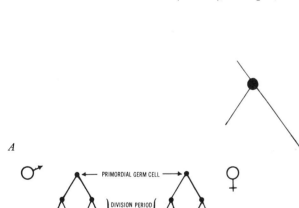

B

Program, consisting of sets.   Realization, consisting of diagrams.

A

C

Architecture must be co-ordinated hierarchically at all levels, from the local to the international

Similar graphic symbols of problem solutions relating to dissimilar levels of human experience. Set (A) exemplifies the origin of spermatazoa and ovum; set (B) demonstrates Christopher Alexander's momentous discovery that "a city is not a tree" and set (C) is Constantine Doxiadis' attempt to hide an age-old platitude behind a spurious scientific façade.

34

As Franklin E. Zimring, Professor of Law at the University of Chicago, stated in his *Wall Street Journal* article—urban violence has become a trend in American civilization only because the outcome does not present a direct threat to public political order and most of those who are killed are ghetto dwellers.

The paradox of urban violence

The apathy is growing because, as Zimring points out, "most of the urban body count in the United States involves the faceless young black male 'non-citizens' who live and die without conspicuous outpourings of social concern. . . . Americans have had ample time to get used to high homicide rates and, as Winston Churchill said, "Eels get used to skinning."

So on the one hand while social and moral consciousness is a growing trend, the paradox of urban violence is also a growing trend. Another paradox is that while most of the existing twentieth-century environment was created by men, over 50 percent of the world's population is women.

"Women live like bats or owls."

"Women live like bats or owls, labour like beasts, and die like worms," observed Margaret Cavendish, a seventeenth-century woman poet, but the American woman has made dramatic changes in recent years. The changes in women's lives and their relationships to planning policies were examined in a study funded by HUD's Office of Policy Development and Research:

She is more likely to work, either out of choice or necessity. She has fewer children and a longer life. She is more likely to live alone, both in her youth and in old age, and more likely to raise children alone. Yet the belief persists that she derives her whole sense of identity from her husband's job, her home, and her children.

*Because of this misconception, women are burdened by a system that fosters separation of work and home, a lack of diversity in housing, inadequate child care, and lack of transportation.**

City planners in the future may use land-use plans to integrate home, work, and recreation and new neighborhoods may be designed for mixed uses, diversity, and adult activities.

Definitions may be changed and redefined to reflect the new family models women have adopted. Child care should be zoned into all districts, and densities of dwelling units should be integrated.

Sex-role revolution

Through the sex-role revolution men may be relieved of their particular burden of environmental disease. Ulcers and heart attacks due to the excessive pressure of assuming sole responsiblity and leadership may now decline as women take on equal accountability in politics and business and men can unself-consciously develop sensibilities to children, culture, home, and less aggressive roles. The major contribution of the sex role revolution is to shift society's sexist definitions of personality characteristics toward acceptance of a more well-rounded, androgynous personality that unites the best characteristics of each sex.

The androgynous personality

The acceptance and the representation of the gentle and considerate with the strong will be the first step toward the establishment of the new belief systems. The design of cities will no longer be the

The reproductive process.
Nature as process, causality, and compatability: life as the evolution of a single egg into a complex organism. *Villee, C. A.: BIOLOGY, 6th edition. Philadelphia, W. B. Saunders Company, 1972.*

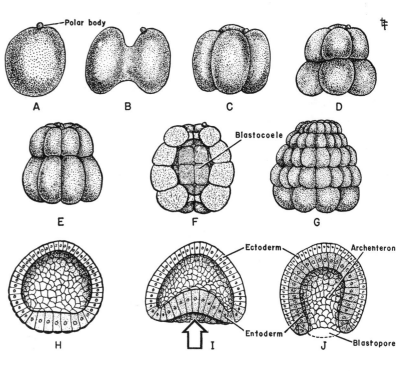

''man-made'' environment or the ''woman-made'' environment, as neither of these is an accurate perspective. For the first time since the primitive settlements, the birth and rebirth of cities may become the more fertile creations of a bisexual conception. Just as the androgynous personality is said to incorporate the best of the stereotyped male and female characteristics, the planned environment, too, should be based on a recognition of the *total* person who ultimately inhabits and uses it.

In the early 1960s, the first few architects, landscape architects and planners began to call themselves ''environmentalists'' and the almost-unheard-of word ''ecology'' came into everyday use. But even in 1966 when ECODESIGN (our professional firm) was founded as an interdisciplinary ecology-oriented planning firm, the phones would still ring with requests for services of economists or market studies. It was still many years before the term ''Eco'' was recognized for its real meaning rather than as an abbreviation for economics.

Rediscovering the physical structure of the ecosystem

Ironically, even as late as 1967, Ian L. McHarg was still arguing in professional journals for an ecological method for landscape architecture as ''an indispensable basis for regional planning.'' The irony is that such a valid approach to planning the physical environment even went out of usage to the extent that it had to be *reinvented*. That a new ''theory'' proclaimed that a study of geology and the use of ecological inventory should be used to analyze existing and proposed land use management shows how far from the earth structure we had strayed in the designs of our settlements since the days when cities grew from intersections in rivers and developed around resources of water, soil, metals, and transportation routes.

As the most obvious example of the use of this method, McHarg cites life and death.

Life is the evolution of a single egg into the complexity of the organism. Death is the retrogression of a complex organism into a few simple elements. If this model is true, it allows us to examine a city neighborhood, community institution, family, city plan, architectural or landscape design in these terms. This model suggests that any system moving towards simplicity, uniformity, instability with a low number of species and high entropy is retrogressing; any system moving in that direction is moving towards ill health.

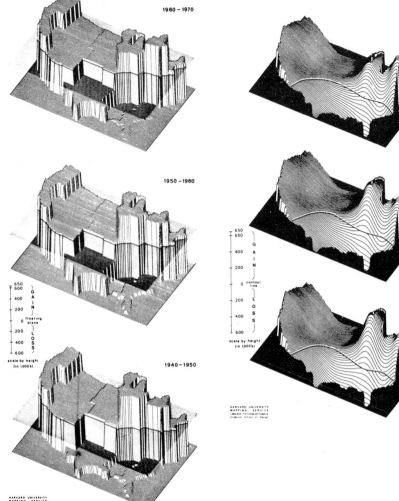

Conversely: complexity, diversity, stability, and steady states (with a high number of species and low entropy) are indicators of health and systems moving in this direction are evolving. As a simple application let us map, in tones on transparencies, statistics of all physical disease, all mental disease, and all social disease. If we also map income, age of population, density, ethnicity, and quality of the physical environment we have on the one hand discerned the environment of health, the environment of pathology, and we have accumulated the data which allow interpretation of the social and physical environmental components of health and pathology. Moreover, we have the other criteria of the model which permit examination from different directions. If this model is true and the method good, it may be the greatest contribution of the ecological method to diagnosis and prescription for the city.

	Retrogression		*Evolution*
ill-health	*simplicity*	*health*	*complexity*
	uniformity		*diversity*
	independence		*interdependence (symbiosis)*
	instability		*stability (steady state)*
	low number of species		*high number of species*
	high entropy		*low entropy**

The biophysical environment includes the bodily processes of all living things. Man, after many years of ignoring nature, is just beginning to reexamine the *beneficial* interactions of man with these processes of microorganisms and considering what is the human "fair share" of the world's resources—

Computers have eased the task of mapping income, age of population, density, ethnicity, and other characteristics of the physical environment. Net black migration, 1940 to 1970 by the nine geographical regions.

*Ian L. McHarg, "An Ecological Method for Landscape Architecture," *Landscape Architecture*, January 1967.

that is, *Do we consume unnatural quantities of resources in the carrying-out of our bodily functions? Yes!*

A family of four flushing uses 100 gallons of water per day.

The flush toilet is responsible for about half of the average household's consumption of water. A family of four, using standard plumbing, uses 100 gallons of water a day merely for flushing toilets. This water is used to carry wastes to the place of disposal. The consequences of this use are serious:

☐
Enormous amounts of pure drinking water are wasted.

☐
Lakes, rivers, oceans, and ground waters are polluted by wastes.

☐
Valuable, recoverable nutrients are lost.

☐
So-called advanced waste treatment plants must be constructed to attempt to purify the water. These are expensive, unreliable, and energy intensive.

☐
Sludge, the product of this "purification," simply creates a new disposal problem since it is a mixture of organic matter, chemicals, heavy metals, and poisons that cannot be safely disposed of anywhere. As "sanitary" landfill it pollutes water tables. Dumping it in the ocean causes pollution, no matter how far off shore the barges go. Burning it pollutes the air.

This vast economic and environmental problem is the cost of using fresh water to flush toilets. It is not necessary. *Man is the only animal whose wastes are not absorbed back into the ecological systems as useful by-products.*

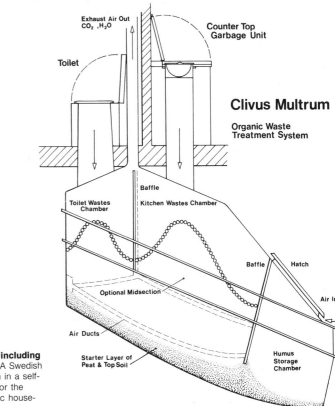

Clivus Multrum

Organic Waste Treatment System

Clivus Multrum ("including compost room"). A Swedish composting system in a self-contained system for the treatment of organic household wastes.

A system that is intended to eliminate the very notion of waste, generate a useful product from erstwhile pollutants, and directed toward a new era of rational use of technology is the Clivus Multrum Organic Waste Treatment System.

The Multrum consists of an impervious container set at such an angle that the organic wastes slide in a glacierlike fashion down the sloping bottom at a rate slow enough to ensure that they will be thoroughly decomposed by the time they reach the storage chamber. Tubes connect the container to the kitchen chute and toilet. A draft, which is maintained by natural convection, ensures that the process is essentially aerobic (one in which oxygen-breathing organisms do the work) and that the bathroom and kitchen are kept free of odors at all times. As carbon dioxide and water vapor are the main waste products of the aerobic bacteria, the vent gases are not noxious. The humus that finally reaches the storage chamber represents only 5 to 10 percent of the volume originally put in. This is because 90 to 95 percent is given off as waste gas, which goes up the vent. The end product is safe for use in gardens because of the long retention time in the container (two to four years) during which the disease-producing organisms are destroyed by the normal soil bacteria. After this time, *the process, being continuous, will generate three to ten gallons of humuslike soil fertilizer per person per year.*

Tuning in Earth Rhythms

The biological clock of our existence ticks on. Do we use that time efficiently? Or are there universal life-energy rhythms given off by the earth that we are not yet attuned to? Or, perhaps at earlier stages our bodies *were* more attuned to rhythms of daily and seasonal cycles, while now they are dictated by corporate schedules and by the constant artificial environments of electric lighting and air conditioning.

How do these natural cycles relate to each other and to the needs of the individual process? A tool intended to address itself to this issue and to examining future options is Syncon or Synergistic Convergence. More simply put, this is the coming together of individuals for the betterment of all.

This coming together occurs inside a predesigned time span and environment, intended to highlight our present fragmented society. Inner sections of the wheel—Social Needs, Technology, Environment, Production, Government, and Other Regions—represent functional areas of any culture. The other sections represent areas of new potentials—Biology, Physics, Information, Extraterrestrial, Arts, Political-

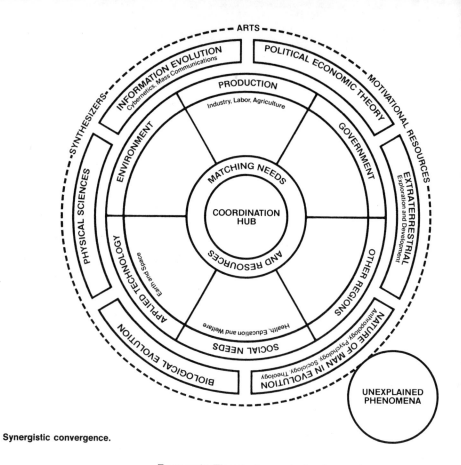

Synergistic convergence.

Economic Theory (a symbolically empty room to remind us that no postindustrial communications-age system has been invented or recognized). Unexplained Phenomena (Telepathy, Psychokinesis, etc.), included in the new potentials, is by its nature not in the same order as the others.

Thinking:
The Technological
Environment

It has been said that the technology existing today alone is capable of solving the whole spectrum of human and urban problems. On the other hand, some futurists have called for the development of new technological solutions to ensure the long-range control of our environment.

Some have argued that new technology is cheaper in the long run, others that the costs of change and technology transfer are expensive in the short run and still others say that technology alone is inadequate and not the answer. There is much truth in the statement that it is the insensitivity of technological solutions to what are essentially psychosocial and biophysical problems that has helped to generate the recent global techno-economic crises—the world energy situation being the most blatant example.

It may very well be true that existing technology is adequate if it is utilized correctly. But the problem to date has been that the people, the users, rarely have had the luxury of absorbing the social and environmental impacts of technological changes before the technology itself has become obsolete.

To find out whether we can make full use of existing and future technology, the people must:
☐
First, determine what the new technology actually is;
☐
Second, examine the interaction of technology with social, environmental, and economic constraints; and
☐
Then, analyze what must be done to remove or minimize the constraints so that technology can achieve its full potential for proper implementation within the ecosystem.

There are, of course, many technologies relating to the city that can be used in large-scale planning and offer opportunities to recycle whole environments into viable entities once again.

Marshall McLuhan has seen technology as moving us toward a breakdown in barriers between cultures—a "global village" in which audio-visual technology replaces personal interaction. But determining the basic direction must remain with man, not his machine. It is essential to understand enough about any technology, be it computers, or atomic energy, so that we do not relegate any responsibility to them. It is not "fate" that bears responsibility for our beliefs and how we can act on them—and neither is it the computer.

The next section illustrates some rather practical and realistic technological developments that have been tested and are applicable to urban use. These examples are in three major areas:
1
Planning Process and Data Collection
Computer Graphics
Computer Analysis
Earth Resources Technology Satellite (LANDSAT)
2
New Components
Industrialized Building Systems
Personal Rapid Transit (PRT)
3
Energy Systems and Conservation
Energy Conservation
Energy Sources

Planning Process and Data Collection

In the early 1960s, a movement was beginning in planning and urban design toward the development of new methods for solving the problems of the environment. Traditional ways of designing and planning the physical environment had become obsolete because of societal changes and uncertainties of our age. The inadequacy of the old methods has now been accepted by most practitioners in favor of more responsive methods that can recognize problems long ignored and handle the arithmetic progressions of data increases. The practioners of the traditional environmentally oriented professions of architecture, engineering, and planning have now been joined by psychologists, systems analysts, sociologists, and computer scientists in team approaches to problem solving utilizing *methodology transfer* from each other's professions.

Computer Graphics
The application of automated technology to the design process has accelerated in the past five years. The state of the art of computer-aided design has become the subject of much debate among architects, planners, and engineers as to its true value. Because of the availability of urban data (census files, for example), the complexity of urban design, the pending change to the metric system, and the rapidly decreasing costs of computer technology, there is an increasing incentive to use computer technology.

For instance, computer-generated simulation models are commonly utilized for large-scale housing projects and facilities investigations into alternative building patterns and density studies. The goal is to find the optimal balance between costs and benefits of different design schemes and to do so as quickly as possible so as to better grasp the most realistic financing requirements and physical resources.

The computer model can set up a number of empirical relevant variables and then it generates, optimizes, and evaluates various possible configurations and densities.

Automated hill shading of Mt. de Morcles, Switzerland. Computed from elevation data using a 100-meter grid and information from ridge lines.

Geometric figure to test shading routines.

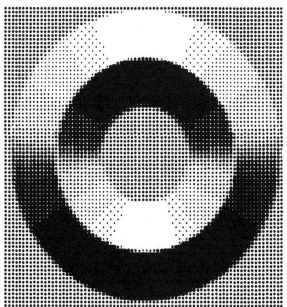

Other applications are:

Animated demographic surfaces. Using computer technology, it is possible to generate and plot demographic data (or other types of statistical variables) as continuous surfaces. This has been accomplished using socioeconomic factors or with actual topographic reliefs of the study areas, which is generated automatically from landform maps by using a digitizer.

Urban Planning Models (Urban Information Systems) can express the benefits and costs of the various urban activities and interactions. Sub-models can handle traffic flow, air pollution, access, services, land prices, and many other urban variables.

Computer Animation. Change over time is a factor in urban planning that is often particularly meaningful to represent graphically. Quite dramatically, the computer can juxtapose differences in population, say for the years 1975 and 2000. However, the change through time in the relationships of variables is the key to understanding the workings of time on urban areas.

SYMVU generates a three-dimensional view of a statistical "surface." Having once defined a surface, the user may produce many different views—displaying graphically, spatially variable data.

41

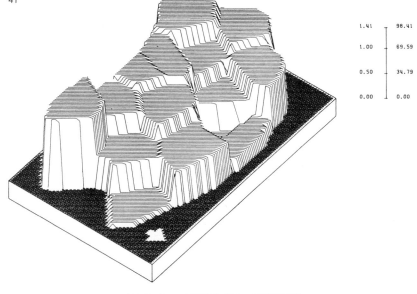

FIGURE A: MANTEGNA BAY - CONFORMANT

AZIMUTH = 231   ALTITUDE = 45
*WIDTH = 6.00   *HEIGHT = 2.00

* BEFORE FORESHORTENING 09/25/70

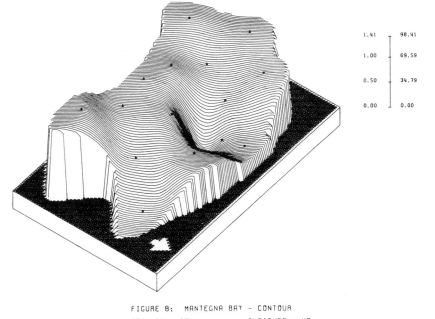

FIGURE B: MANTEGNA BAY - CONTOUR

AZIMUTH = 231   ALTITUDE = 45
*WIDTH = 6.00   *HEIGHT = 2.00

* BEFORE FORESHORTENING 09/25/70

SYMAP produces maps depicting spatially arrayed quantitative or qualitative information. Data is assigned to a set of value ranges or categories which are represented on the maps by a scale of tones from black to white, created by combinations of standard printer symbols.

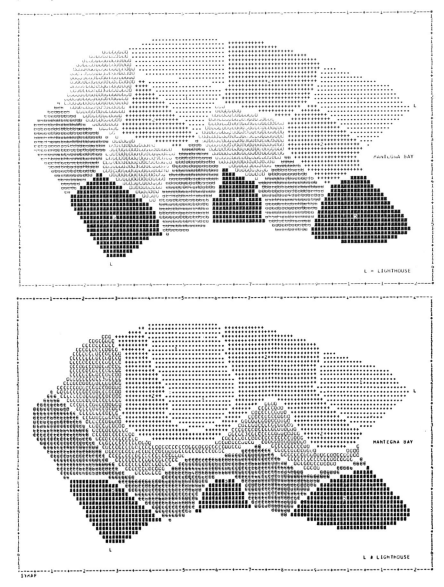

Population density by major regions in the Eastern Hemisphere (1971). The computer can readily display world distributions of population, energy consumption, etc. and continually update a world Data Bank.

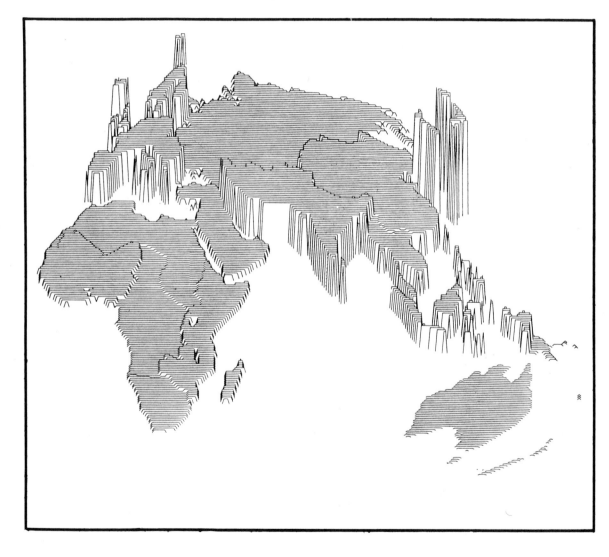

Computer Analysis

New information systems are raising the consciousness as well as the credibility of planners because of the increased ability to correlate data from a greater variety of sources.

Information from such noncompatible urban sources as police departments, the national census, city planning commissions, city engineers, and environmental protection agencies can all be merged and reduced to the smallest unit common to all.

One of the major problems in urban research has been the difficulty of integrating information from differing and often conflicting sources. This new information technique can begin to resolve this problem and create solutions to problems never before imagined.

Unfortunately, because of the lingering lack of familiarity of the public with the computer or the immediate inconvenience of dealing with facts scientifically, this technology is not being used to its potential. In January 1975, at a meeting of the American Geographic Society, complaints were aired because many government decision makers were not taking advantage of computer mapping services, or they were ignoring the output. "Administrators make political decisions and sometimes they don't like the facts to get in the way."

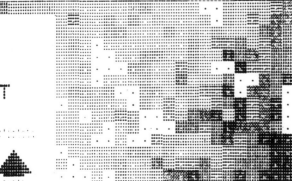

BOSTON REGION: SOUTHWEST SECTOR

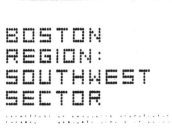

GRID produces a graphic representation of the urban and regional values. An example of a use of GRID is the mapping of natural resource data recorded from aerial photographs using a grid overlay to define each data collection zone.

Maps transformation and analysis of network characteristics. These distorted maps graphically depict changing toll rates for long-distance telephone calls from St. Louis, Missouri to the rest of the U.S. More useful, is map distortion to produce *cartograms*, in which the area is made proportional to some quantity characterizing a region such as population.

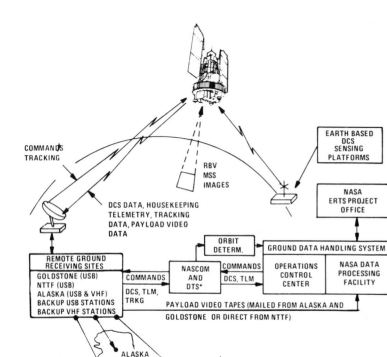

COMMANDS TRACKING

RBV
MSS
IMAGES

EARTH BASED
DCS
SENSING
PLATFORMS

FEEDBACK
DATA
REQUIRE-
MENTS

DCS DATA, HOUSEKEEPING
TELEMETRY, TRACKING
DATA, PAYLOAD VIDEO
DATA

NASA
ERTS PROJECT
OFFICE

ORBIT
DETERM.

GROUND DATA HANDLING SYSTEM

REMOTE GROUND
RECEIVING SITES
GOLDSTONE (USB)
NTTF (USB)
ALASKA (USB & VHF)
BACKUP USB STATIONS
BACKUP VHF STATIONS

NASCOM
AND
DTS*

COMMANDS

COMMANDS

DCS, TLM

OPERATIONS
CONTROL
CENTER

NASA DATA
PROCESSING
FACILITY

USER
EVALUATION

DCS, TLM,
TRKG

PAYLOAD VIDEO TAPES (MAILED FROM ALASKA AND
GOLDSTONE OR DIRECT FROM NTTF)

ALASKA

NTTF
(AT GSFC)

GOLDSTONE
(CALIF.)

* DIGITAL TRANSMISSION SYSTEM

LANDSAT system consists of satellite-based sensors that obtain data from the earth's surface reflections. These data are digitally recorded and transmitted to ground station computer tapes and delivered to the NASA LANDSAT Center. There the data are further processed into 1:250,000 scale images of each band, color composites of three of the four bands, and computer compatible tapes.

LANDSAT, or Earth Resources Technology Satellite

One of the key missions of the NASA Skylab program since its launch in 1972 was to develop the technology of studying earth's resources from a satellite in orbit 275 miles above the earth. This satellite program was known as the Earth Resources Technology Satellite (ERTS), and is now called LANDSAT, and it accomplishes the task of large-scale data acquisition and processing covering the entire globe. Data is collected every eighteen days (and has been collected since early 1972) in a digital format and it is then processed, resulting in images, map overlays, and other professionally useful data formats.

Multilens cameras are utilized for this remote sensing, each equipped with special filters and film supply, so that each looks at a particular range of the spectrum. The filter/film combinations examine different narrow sections of the visible light and infrared spectrum. Because everything has its own degree of reflectivity ("spectral signature") it is possible to identify otherwise hidden resources and man-made elements. This type of magnification can be better than 90 percent accurate down to the scale of an acre and a half. This new data offers users a high accuracy of categorization, it can be corrected for scale and earth rotation and its output is in large-scale computer-generated color map overlays.

With a Multi-spectral Data Analysis System (M-DAS) an investigation can easily distinguish crop types, forest types, surface water, water sediment, contamination, and chlorophyl concentration, geological formations, bare or disturbed areas such as surface

Major lineations of the U.S.
The power of the LANDSAT
data is its broad view directly
from above. The view is one
hundred miles wide as it
rapidly travels North to South
and when these tracks are
laid side by side, major faults
not previously mapped
become apparent.

mining, road building, erosion, urban areas, new
development, and other features.

The most opportune usage will be in the less developed sections of the world—the large areas of the
globe which have not yet been data banked by
traditional aerial photography and other methods.

Oil and mineral companies are checking LANDSAT
data for potential wells and mines in remote areas
they may have overlooked. Utilities are analyzing
the information in order to decipher the suitable
sites for nuclear power plants that avoid faults in
the earth's crust. Agriculturists can now predict
harvests and urbanists have an infinite range of
uses for which LANDSAT cuts the expenses of
working in remote areas and heightens the accuracy
of large-scale planning efforts.

MAJOR LINEATIONS

New Components

The humanizing of the engineering process is the greatest indication of a better future. One has only to look at the revolt against congestion and freeway construction and one sees that new "personalized rapid transit" (people movers) will come to the forefront of our technological options for problem solving. The high interest rates, materials shortages, and increasing labor costs have caused engineers and architects to seek industrialized building systems and other new techniques to create new living environments faster. Pollutants of the air and water, noise, clutter, and the concepts of limitless growth have been frustrating to the point where engineers have been devising new systems to alleviate dangerous pollution levels on gargantuan new scales. Conventional engineering and technology does not suffice, and in order to develop something new, it has become necessary to cast off old ideas and techniques. It has become necessary to develop technological concepts that meet the needs of individuals and communities, and of both the public and private sectors. Professional architects, engineers, and planners are the necessary catalysts in developing the new concepts and in explaining them to the decision makers and their communities for implementation.

Industrialized Building Systems

Industrialized building systems are defined as the total integration of all subsystems and components in building construction into an overall process that fully utilizes industrialized production, transportation, and assembly techniques.

This integration is achieved through the exploitation of the underlying organizational principles. Once this is understood, industrialized housing systems may be classified in a variety of ways, of which the most obvious type is the box, otherwise known as a monolithic unit.

☐

Monolithic units are generally factory-produced and preassembled volumetric elements with a high degree of finish and a minimum amount of required site erection time (utility connections). They may be further categorized as a function of their relative degree of self-containment.

Lightweight units or mobile-home types are totally self-contained housing units that can retain their mobility or be permanently installed and grouped or stacked with the addition of a demountable frame. In most cases mobile homes are completely preassembled and finished, and require only site utility connections for occupancy.

Heavyweight or volumetric components are roomsize (or smaller) volumes of concrete, steel sandwich, wood or fiber-reinforced plastic, which can be grouped horizontally and/or stacked vertically (if bearing) and dry connected to form singlefamily or multifamily attached or detached housing. In some cases, these volumes may be incorporated in traditional structural/mechanical space grids to provide high-rise multifamily housing. Stacked bearing units often avoid the necessity of producing six-sided volumes by wall and slab sharing, and, in some cases, bonus room units are acquired by checkerboard stacking. Other types of systems employ discontinuous room units to provide for mechanical chases, sound insulation, and structural fireproofing.

Basically, monolithic units are restricted by travel radius from the plant (action radius), and they are also extremely costly to handle. They are usually considered "closed" systems because it is not possible to mass the volumes in very many different ways; thus, monolithic systems restrict the flexibility of urban designs dependent upon them.

☐

Biostructures. Some commentators on the environment see the housing building blocks of today as problematic in their lack of flexibility while the more practical see the problems as a lack of housing—whether flexible or inflexible. It may be true that traditional design philosophies of architecture are based on a "set system of visual order" and on "attributes of duration" that have little relevance for the dynamic architecture that may some day be needed, but this dynamic disposable architecture is another example of technology taking a lead without man's full thought as to the desirability of the direction or the consequences.

Henry Van Lier maintains that the future environment should be composed of a "synergetic network of structures," which means that the "traditional link with containers will be replaced by an operations link, thus establishing a completely new kind of architectural order."

**Monolithic units (boxes)—
industrialized building
systems for housing.**
Generally factory-produced
and pre-assembled volumetric
elements with a high degree
of finish. This apartment
tower in Beersheba, Israel,
cantilevers room units
from a central core.

This new order could include terrestrial, subterrestrial, marine, submarine, and even extraterrestrial structures. They will probably be modular microstructures that promote cellular growth, contain disposable architecture and other means that overcome the static nature of today's structures.

The technology certainly exists to design new buildings that respond to a changing dynamic process, but what is the "changing dynamic process?" Clip-on, plug-in architecture, throw-away buildings, inflatable ministructures, modules that are plugged into three-dimensional grids, bridge structures, multiuse container spaces capable of independent movement, hydrogenetic biotecture and people-moving urban transportation systems have all been theoretically designed and, in some cases, actually developed. Biostructures, built on the principles of growth and change, may be more relevant to emerging lifestyles than are bricks and mortar. They may also be the hypnotic fascination with the "gadget-fix," which could obscure the immediate priorities for housing that represents basic needs of shelter, clean water, and waste disposal for the many as opposed to the refinements of "flexibility" for the few.

48

Personal Rapid Transit (PRT)

PRT is the technical term for the new advanced urban transit system more commonly known as a "people mover."

Herbert S. Levinson has said that "some half century ago, no city was without its electric railway; by the year 2000 no city center will be without its "people mover."*

PRT may be defined as a small passenger vehicle (carrying either individuals or a group traveling together utilizing either a rubber-tired, suspended, or air-cushioned vehicle), which operates under a central computer control system on a guideway at relatively low speeds for short-haul collection and distribution in major activity centers.

The idea of locating a PRT system in the existing city fabric is a relatively new one. In the past, urban freeways have been insensitively placed in our cities by many politicians, planners, and engineers with varying degrees of aptitude and for differing interests. This new form of movement system readily accommodates the new needs of today—i.e., low noise levels, nonpolluting, personal modules, rapid service—more sympathetically than traditional freeways.

PRT systems have two major assets: 1) the system can be designed to be as least visible as possible; 2) it can be an integral structuring element for the growth of the whole city.

In transportation, the technology is available, but the commitment to large-scale urban applications has not yet been made.

*People Movers: Planning & Potentials, Herbert S. Levinson, Yale University, Jan. 17, 1972.

A people mover undergoing a test on its guideway. In transportation, the technology is available, but the commitment to large-scale urban application has not yet been made.

Headway between people movers is close and efficient. UMTA is testing a PRT system in Morgantown, West Virginia, the only real demonstration project to date.

Airtrans people mover in use at an airport. The system can also be utilized for freight and service movement in off-hours while a city sleeps.

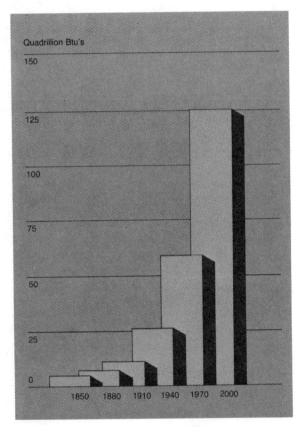

Quadrillion Btu's

150

125

100

75

50

25

0

1850 1880 1910 1940 1970 2000

America's energy-hungry lifestyle. Total U.S. energy consumption.

Energy Systems and Conservation

Compact versus Dispersed Development. Is energy consumption fated to keep going up and up? Even with zero population growth the nation's existing life-style and energy dependence make an increase seemingly inevitable. Suburban living and the dispersed "country living," touted as being made possible by advances in transportation and communications, are perhaps the greatest offenders of our various lifestyles.

Automobiles, which are the only convenient means of transportation in the suburban situation, require far more energy on a per capita basis than railroads and other forms of mass transportation. On a per capita basis, more energy is needed to heat and cool a single-family dwelling than an apartment house.

Towns and cities on the other hand are increasingly more congested and unattractive with the inhabitants more exposed to environmental hazards all the time. Whole regions are increasingly ghettoized and the commercial strips between urbanized areas are less and less humane. Deterioration, banality in architecture, the encroachment of asphalt, the ever-receding natural environment and the low expectation of society is the trend for the future, but need not be its ultimate destiny. We have less than one generation to stop the war against our environment and to begin a planned intervention.

The management of all ecosystems includes recycling resources. For example, in the natural eco-system, mineral resources are utilized and then returned to the soil. This kind of recycling is not 100 percent efficient and in fact, man is the only

living element not part of the recycling system. We can, however, improve its efficiency by getting man to not only contribute the debris of industrialization but to understand the law of limiting factors— a basic ecological principle that states that "an organism has certain basic requirements for essential materials and environmental factors."[*] For example, the natural ecosystem rarely has the population explosions that are characteristic of man-made communities. In nature when one species increases suddenly, others will consume it and the natural balance remains. The consequences of man's population explosions require massive readjustment, relocation, or reorientation planning or else they, too, will be controlled by starvation and/or wars of need for control of resources.

After finally becoming aware of the need for ecosystem management, man is forming a better understanding of resource use and he has begun to develop the new energy sources and new pollution control products that are necessary for intelligent ecosystem management. This section illustrates a few of these products, but this utilization of technology has just begun to be explored after the environmental demonstration and legal acts of the 1960s. Now the energy crisis of the 1970s has begun to weigh the priorities more toward the development of new energy sources that will relieve a resource dependency that is totally contrary to American tradition and temperament. Pollution controls must remain a strong and simultaneous part of our new technology programs.

[*]"Exploitation, Evolution, & Ecology," David M. Gates, *Technology Review,* December 1968, p. 41.

51

A total ecological home.
This dwelling emphasizes
use of sun, wind, rain, and
wastes. 1) Solar roof captures
sunlight to heat water; 2) rain
water is collected for home
use; wind powers windmill;
3) water is purified and
stored; 4) decomposition of
wastes produces methane
gas for stove in house; 5)
water from treatment systems
flows to fish pond and 6)
vegetable garden; 7) animals
provide nourishment for
people in house, thus
completing the recycling of
wastes. Copyright 1972
Clifford Harper Epic
Productions.

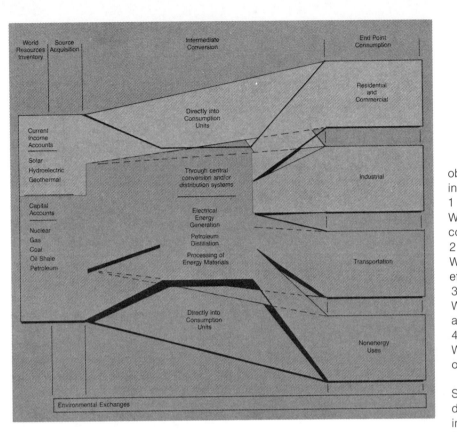

Within the figure:

World Resources Inventory | Source Acquisition

Intermediate Conversion

End Point Consumption

Residential and Commercial

Directly into Consumption Units

Current Income Accounts

Solar
Hydroelectric
Geothermal

Through central conversion and/or distribution systems

Industrial

Capital Accounts

Nuclear
Gas
Coal
Oil Shale
Petroleum

Electrical Energy Generation

Petroleum Distillation

Processing of Energy Materials

Transportation

Directly into Consumption Units

Nonenergy Uses

Environmental Exchanges

The basic energy system:
Energy conservation defined.

Energy Conservation

"Project Independence," President Gerald Ford's energy conservation concept, has indicated in its charter that there will be a rapid depletion of current reserves. (The United States possesses 115 billion barrels of undiscovered oil, plus roughly 40 billion barrels of proved reserves.) By 1985, we will have increased our use by 50 percent over current levels. Federal Energy Research and Development Administration (ERDA) officials have said that the United States must prepare for a "massive synthetic fuels industry" to fill the gap that will occur in 1985.

Before seeking newer and better energy sources, the most obvious intermediate step is to begin to conserve the energy we are currently wasting. The simple obvious ways are being used by nearly everyone today in one way or another, but more efficient, less obvious possibilities are at hand. Our overall objectives in the conservation of energy should include the following:

1
We must conserve energy by reducing overall consumption.
2
We must conserve energy resources through efficient usage.
3
We must make practical use of recyclable energy and new sources—solar, wind, tidal, etc. energy.
4
We must make practical use of intermittent sources of energy.

Some simple energy conservation design guidelines developed by the General Services Administration include:

1
Cover exterior walls and/or roof with earth and planting to reduce heat transmission and solar gain.
2
Shade walls and paved areas adjacent to building to reduce temperature.
3
Collect rain water for use in buildings.
4
Select sites with high air quality to enhance natural ventilation.
5
Select sites that have topographical features and adjacent structures that provide windbreaks.
6
Select sites that allow optimum building orientation and configuration to minimize yearly energy consumption.

7
Select sites that allow occupants to use public transportation systems.
8
Select building configurations that give minimum north wall exposure to reduce heat losses.
9
Construct exterior walls, roof, and floors with high thermal mass, for example, 100 pounds per cubic foot.
10
Consider the length and width aspects for rectangular buildings as well as other geometric shapes in relationship to building height and interior and exterior floor areas to optimize energy conservation.
11
Do not heat parking garages.
12
Consider the amount of energy required for protection of materials and their transport on a life-cycle energy basis.
13
In zones where conditions are suitable for natural ventilation for a major part of the year, install windows that open.
14
Use corridors as heat transfer buffers and locate against exterior walls.
15
Consider landscaped open planning which allows excess heat from interior spaces to transfer to perimeter spaces which have a heat loss.
16
Locate equipment rooms on the roof to reduce unwanted heat gain and heat loss through the surface. They can also allow more direct duct and pipe runs reducing power requirements.

17
Use open planning that allows more effective use of lighting fixtures. The reduced area of partitioned walls decreases the light absorption.
18
Provide controls to shut down all air systems at night and on weekends except when used for economizer cycle cooling.
19
To enhance the possibility of using waste heat from other systems, design air handling systems to circulate sufficient amounts of air for cooling loads to be met by a 60° F air supply temperature and heating loads to be met by a 90° F air temperature.
20
Design HVAC systems so that they do not heat and cool air simultaneously.
21
Adopt as large a temperature differential as possible for chilled water systems and hot water heating systems.
22
Consider the use of thermal storage in combination with unit heat pumps and a hydronic loop so that excess heat during the day can be captured and stored for use at night.
23
Consider the use of solar energy collectors for heating in winter and absorption cooling in summer.
24
Consider the use of a total energy system integrated with all other systems.
25
Use high efficiency transformers, which are good candidates for life-cycle costing.
26
To reduce the quantity of hot and cold water used, consider the use of a single system to meet hand washing needs.

27
Consider the use of solar water heaters using flat plate collectors with heat pump boosters in the winter.
28
Heat building to no more than 68° F in winter when occupied and 60° F when unoccupied.
29
Cool building to no less than 78° F when occupied and no cooling when the building is unoccupied.
30
Light a building when occupied only.
31
In selective lighting, consider only the amount of illumination required for the specific task, taking into consideration the duration and character and user performance required as per design criteria.
32
Turn off lights that are not needed.
33
Schedule cleaning and maintenance for normal working hours or when daylight is available and sufficient for task.
34
Draw drapes over windows or close thermal shutters when daylight is not available and when building is unoccupied.

New energy sources.
Concrete legs for a North Sea
platform rise 310 feet above
construction site in Norway.

Energy Sources

The high costs of energy compiled with shortages
and increasing labor costs have caused engineers to
seek new sources for power. Estimates by the National Academy of Sciences on remaining oil resources reemphasize the difficulty of achieving
petroleum energy independence and point to the
need for attention in the areas of unconventional
energy sources. The energy crisis aside, but simultaneous to it, the United States has entered a new
era, and no one doubts that the old order has begun to be abandoned. In the November 18, 1974,
issue of *Time* magazine it was stated that "the
United States must increase domestic energy supplies while decreasing consumption." There is no
doubt that energy conservation is possible, with
some sacrifice, but the US government has not
applied itself to a firm course of action.

The private sector and some foreign governments,
however, are proceeding rapidly with exploration of
new energy sources. In Israel, where some of the
most advanced solar energy systems have already
been developed, the Israeli Atomic Energy Commission (AEC) scientists have completed construction
of a high-power laser beam to study the possibility
of producing cheap energy through controlled
nuclear fusion. This laser would be used to create
laboratory conditions similar to those at the center
of the sun or the core of a hydrogen bomb explosion.

So far, no one has been able to emulate the sun,
but the Nahal Soreq neodymium glass laser is designed to break the impasse. Every few minutes,
a short pulse of laser light (about 0.1 billionth of
a second long) is shot into a spherical target (a few
tenths of a millimeter across) of hydrogen-containing

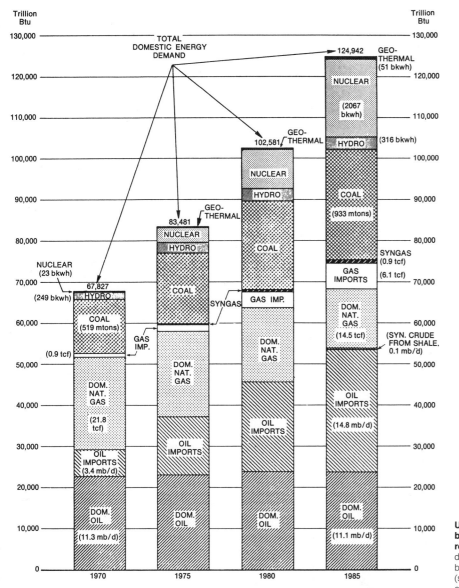

Trillion Btu (left and right axes: 130,000 / 120,000 / 110,000 / 100,000 / 90,000 / 80,000 / 70,000 / 60,000 / 50,000 / 40,000 / 30,000 / 20,000 / 10,000 / 0)

TOTAL DOMESTIC ENERGY DEMAND

1970 — 67,827
- NUCLEAR (23 bkwh)
- HYDRO (249 bkwh)
- COAL (519 mtons)
- GAS IMP. (0.9 tcf)
- DOM. NAT. GAS (21.8 tcf)
- OIL IMPORTS (3.4 mb/d)
- DOM. OIL (11.3 mb/d)

1975 — 83,481
- NUCLEAR
- HYDRO
- GEO-THERMAL
- COAL
- GAS IMP.
- SYNGAS
- DOM. NAT. GAS
- OIL IMPORTS
- DOM. OIL

1980 — 102,581
- GEO-THERMAL
- NUCLEAR
- HYDRO
- COAL
- GAS IMP.
- SYNGAS
- DOM. NAT. GAS
- OIL IMPORTS
- DOM. OIL

1985 — 124,942
- GEO-THERMAL (51 bkwh)
- NUCLEAR (2067 bkwh)
- HYDRO (316 bkwh)
- COAL (933 mtons)
- SYNGAS (0.9 tcf)
- GAS IMPORTS (6.1 tcf)
- DOM. NAT. GAS (14.5 tcf)
- OIL IMPORTS (14.8 mb/d)
- (SYN. CRUDE FROM SHALE. 0.1 mb/d)
- DOM. OIL (11.1 mb/d)

U.S. energy balance, 1972, by types and origins of resources. Categories are domestic oil (millions of barrels per day), oil imports (same units), synthetic crude oil from domestic shale (same units), domestic natural gas (trillions of cubic feet), natural gas imports (same units), syngas (natural gas produced by coal gasification, same units), domestic coal (millions of tons), hydroelectric power (billions of kilowatt-hours), nuclear power (same units), and geothermal power (same units).

material. As a result, for a slight fraction of a second, the extreme temperature and pressure conditions needed for nuclear fission are able to be studied.

In our western states "private enterprise" is rediscovering our vast resources of coal and coal shale. Celebrities, such as Robert Redford and other wealthy environmentalists, are building costly solar heated homes and collecting energy from windmills. The question of energy sources is not so much what, but how they can be made safe, convenient, and economical for the average user.

Steam Generators/Pollution Control. Today, steam generator plants utilize sub-bituminous coal as the primary fuel such as in the plan illustrated. The volume of coal consumed carries with it a considerable transportation problem with about 3500 tons per hour or two 100-car trains unloading about 35 cars per hour with an on-site turnaround of four hours for each train. The components of such a steam generating plant include: superheater, reheater, and economizer, fuel-firing system, turbine generators, water supply-conditioning, and quality control.

It is now conceivable that large cities can burn their solid waste for its energy content. Hennepin County (Minneapolis), Minnesota, is leading a group of public and private institutions in a feasibility study for collecting and burning solid waste to generate energy—steam and/or electricity. This feasibility study will identify and resolve institutional, economic, and financial problems involving legislation, licensing and contractual agreements. It will also explore technical questions such as whether to incorporate the total energy concept of recovering waste heat from electricity generation and whether to use an automated waste-collection system.

Still other plans are proposed to convert garbage from urban centers into low-energy gas for electricity generation. The Stanford University Energy Report says that although this would supply only a small part of our needs, it is sound economically and ecologically because it disposes of solid waste efficiently.

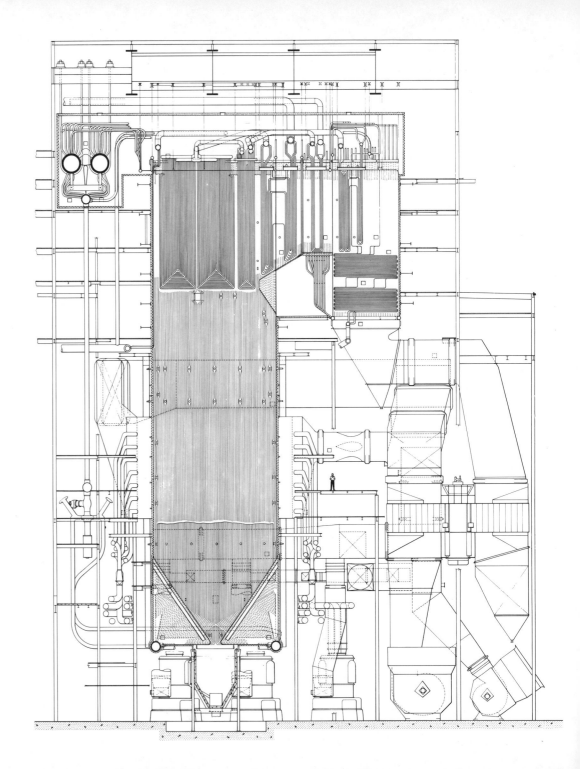

Steam generator side elevation.

Side section of central generating complex.

Transport of coal to steam generator plant in Nigeria.
Coal Aerial Conveyor built by the Nigerian Power & Electricity Authority.

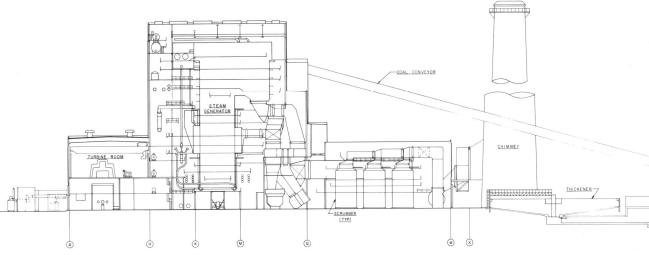

Nuclear Power. Nuclear power generation has overshadowed the impressive growth of fossil-fueled power generators in the last few years. With increasing energy demand and the diminishing fossil fuel supplies, there is even the likelihood that the day might arrive when we will need nuclear power plants about every 100 miles apart. There are investigations underway to study both the practicality and the safety of these plants. The "thermal pollution" problem is said to be inherent in the present-day reactors and many environmentalists say that it may cause an upset in the marine ecosystems in lakes and rivers contiguous to the plants, which normally are stable at lower temperatures.

Proponents of nuclear energy have suggested the positive diversion of such otherwise negative aspects as waste heat toward promoting growth of some marine life such as lobster or fish farming, or central municipal heating/cooling systems. Opponents to such power plants have emphasized the radioactive emissions and accidents that can occur. Yet by the year 2000, America will need almost four times as much electricity as in 1975, in order to simply maintain our current lifestyles. Therefore, we need other ways of generating power in addition to fossil fuels. Currently, there are thirty-nine nuclear power plants operating in the United States and enough new ones on the drawing boards so that in ten years, 30 percent of our kilowatts could be generated by nuclear power.

Recently a group of thirty-two distinguished scientists, eleven of whom are Nobel Prize winners, issued a public statement advocating nuclear power as a key to the solution of the energy crisis.

Nuclear system. The nuclear steam supply system consists of the pressurized water reactor, steam generators, primary loop piping and pumps, plus instrumentation and controls. All major components are located within the reactor containment building.

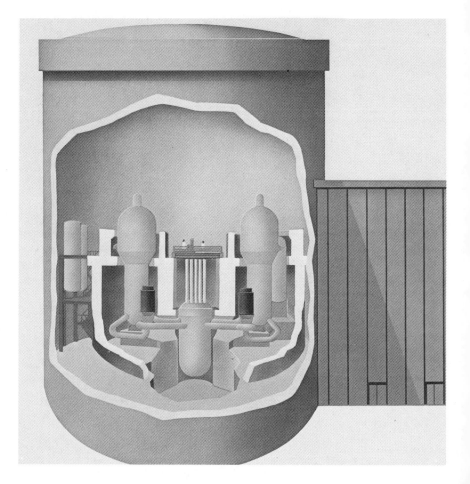

59

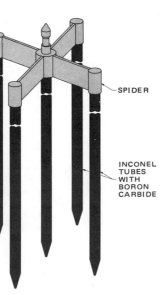

SPIDER

INCONEL TUBES WITH BORON CARBIDE

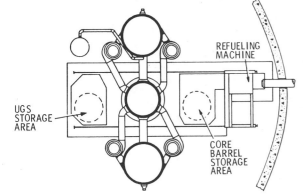

REFUELING MACHINE

UGS STORAGE AREA

CORE BARREL STORAGE AREA

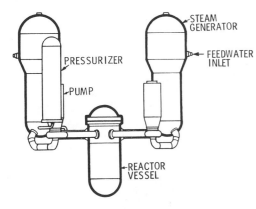

STEAM GENERATOR

PRESSURIZER

FEEDWATER INLET

PUMP

REACTOR VESSEL

Reactivity control. Control of core power distribution and reactivity is achieved by a combination of fuel loading patterns, chemical shim, and selected patterns of insertion and withdrawal of Control Element Assemblies.

Reactor vessel design. The internals, fabricated entirely from stainless steel, consist of two major subassemblies—the upper guide structure and the core support assembly. The upper guide structure protects the Control Element Assemblies from the effects of coolant cross-flow and directs the coolant to the outlet nozzles.

Reactor coolant loop. Removes heat from the reactor core and transfers it to the secondary steam. A 1300 MWe system includes two steam generators connected to the reactor in parallel by identical heat transfer loops. Each loop has two circulating pumps and connecting piping.

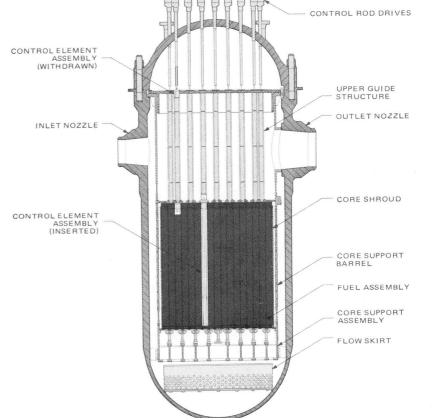

CONTROL ROD DRIVES

CONTROL ELEMENT ASSEMBLY (WITHDRAWN)

INLET NOZZLE

CONTROL ELEMENT ASSEMBLY (INSERTED)

UPPER GUIDE STRUCTURE

OUTLET NOZZLE

CORE SHROUD

CORE SUPPORT BARREL

FUEL ASSEMBLY

CORE SUPPORT ASSEMBLY

FLOW SKIRT

Solar energy via satellite.
An orbiting satellite collecting solar energy in space, where sunlight is most intense, converts it to electricity, then converts the electricity into microwaves for transmission to selected power stations on earth. At these earth stations (containing 36 square mile antennas), the microwaves would be reconverted to electricity and integrated into a normal regional power grid.

Solar Power. Although the sun is the indirect source of all fossil fuels, the concept of harnessing solar energy for specific use by man on a mass scale was not recognized fully until the recent energy crisis. The potential for such an energy source is greater than one can truly comprehend. For instance, the energy in the sunlight falling on the surface of Lake Erie in a single day is greater than the entire United States' present annual energy consumption. The National Science Foundation and the National Aeronautics and Space Administration reported in 1972 that by the year 2200, the sun could provide 35 percent of heating and cooling in buildings, 30 percent of the nation's needs for gaseous fuels, and 20 percent of its total electricity. To date, relatively little has actually been accomplished in solar energy systems, and only a few experimental solar house-heating systems have been built. But there has been substantial production of solar hot water heaters recently.

Solar power plants mounted on satellites in an earth orbit have been proposed by Dr. Peter E. Glaser with the obvious advantage of not being affected by cloud cover. The suggested system would utilize photovoltaic cells to produce electricity as direct current, which would then be converted to radio energy at microwave frequency (3000 MH$_2$) for transmission to the earth's surface where conversion to AC power would occur.

Such a system may soon become competitive in cost with more conventional energy sources. This likelihood is based on the probability that the costs of energy derived from conventional sources such as fossil fuels and nuclear energy may rise faster in the near future than the costs of building large-scale solar energy power systems.

The use of solar energy should have a minimal environmental effect, since such systems would operate from an energy source that produces no pollution and is external to the earth's atmosphere.

Although it is a clear notion, solar energy has current problems in that the technology and the hardware are lagging behind the conceptual projections. Economical storage cells capable of storing and serving this energy source in a massive and efficient manner are not yet developed, and would require additional lag time for product development, production, and mode transferral. It is patently clear that solar power will not be utilized unless it is economically advantageous in comparison with available alternatives. There are not any large-scale or significant solar energy systems in operation in the United States at this time.

Geothermal Power. Limited exploitation of geothermal resources (heat from the interior of the earth) has occurred since the early part of this century. Geothermal power is obtained by extracting heat from the earth; it is a major source of cheap, non-polluting power. In fact, just north of San Francisco, at the geysers (Mayacmas, Clear Lake), steam

(10,000 Mw of electric power) comes out of the ground and quite cheaply satisfies about a third of San Francisco's demand for energy.

The Geothermal Act of 1970 provides for the lease of public lands for the development and utilization of geothermal steam and other associated resources.

The potential of geothermal energy is in several forms:

☐
Hydrothermal reservoirs containing steam or hot waters
☐
Impermeable hot, dry rock
☐
Deep high-pressure aquifers
☐
Near surface intrusions of rock such as lava

Hydrothermal energy is characterized by low-temperature, low-pressure steam, which consequently requires the use of low-pressure turbines with efficiencies of only about 15 percent.

Much geothermal energy, however, is stored in hot, dry rocks and is retrieved by splitting the rocks and inserting water into the fracture. The San Diego Gas and Electric Company is building a $3 million pilot plant in the energy-rich Imperial Valley of southern California and the Department of Interior plans to lease fifty-nine million acres of geothermal land in fourteen western states as an energy resource.

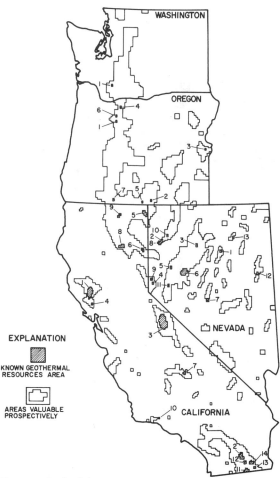

EXPLANATION

KNOWN GEOTHERMAL RESOURCES AREA

AREAS VALUABLE PROSPECTIVELY

Known and potential geothermal areas in western U.S.

Drilling rig encounters geothermal steam at the Geysers. Conventional oil drilling rigs, especially adapted for team application, are used in tapping the steam deposits almost two miles below the surface.

Geothermal drilling.

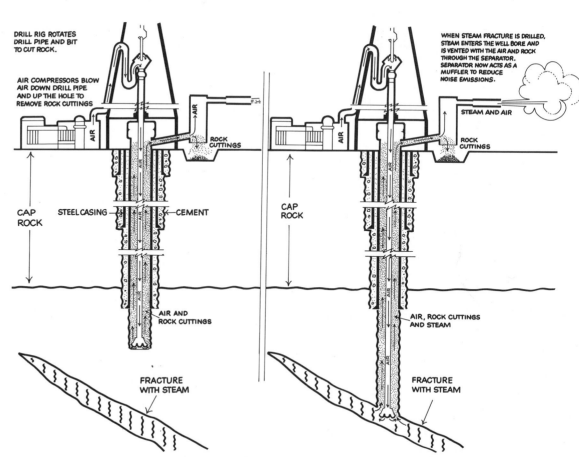

DRILL RIG ROTATES DRILL PIPE AND BIT TO CUT ROCK.

AIR COMPRESSORS BLOW AIR DOWN DRILL PIPE AND UP THE HOLE TO REMOVE ROCK CUTTINGS

AIR

ROCK CUTTINGS

CAP ROCK

STEEL CASING — CEMENT

AIR AND ROCK CUTTINGS

FRACTURE WITH STEAM

WHEN STEAM FRACTURE IS DRILLED, STEAM ENTERS THE WELL BORE AND IS VENTED WITH THE AIR AND ROCK THROUGH THE SEPARATOR. SEPARATOR NOW ACTS AS A MUFFLER TO REDUCE NOISE EMISSIONS.

STEAM AND AIR

AIR

ROCK CUTTINGS

CAP ROCK

AIR, ROCK CUTTINGS AND STEAM

FRACTURE WITH STEAM

Wind Power

Wind Power. The energy in winds and air currents can be utilized to help us meet our energy needs. Wind energy has several distinct advantages including:

☐
It is a free, clean, and nondepleting energy source.

☐
It could supply a significant amount of electrical energy, and is cost-competitive with fossil-fuel systems.

☐
It is technically feasible and has been used for hundreds of years as a source of mechanical power.

The oldest use of wind power was to drive large sailing vessels. However, in the early nineteenth century, great sailing ships were replaced with more dependable oil and coal burning vessels.

The first windmill appeared in the tenth century. In 1850, the use of windmills was great, but a few short years later in 1870, the amount of power produced by windmills had been halved. The steam engine, driven by fossil fuels, had rendered windmills practically obsolete.

Carousel windmill in eighteenth-century Hudson, N.Y. The windmill first appeared in the tenth century, and its design continues to evolve.

Wind power. New style windmills could produce inexpensive electric power for homes. Studies indicate that this vertical-axis wind turbine could supplement conventional sources of power at comparable cost, provided the annual mean winds are ten miles per hour or higher.

The tidal turbine runs on the energy of the ocean tides.

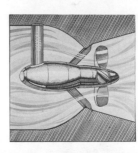

If man harnessed all the world's tides, the resulting electric power would meet about half his present power needs. Incoming tide waters of the Rance River in Brittany, France. Here a tidal power plant already is in operation, but the prospects for tidal power are slight.

The most obvious negative aspect of wind power is the nature of the wind's energy; the crucial question is what to do when the wind stops blowing. There are several answers to that leading question:

☐ Power can be stored in batteries by power plants producing direct current power.

☐ Use a flywheel for energy storage.

☐ Use a wind generator to furnish an electrolyzer, which would break water down into hydrogen and oxygen and then compress the hydrogen and store it for use as a high-grade fuel later.

NASA has suggested the selection of particular areas in the United States "where they have the right kind of wind velocity, and the right kind of wind durability, and put your windmills up and feed their power into a grid. . . . On a day when you have no wind, which will probably not happen for all windmills anyway, you use conventional fossil fuel power if you need to." *

*Ernst Cohn, Manager of Solar Chemical Power Systems, NASA.

Water/Tidal Power. The rise and fall of the tides, where the range is great (perhaps as much as fifty feet), is a great source of energy. It has been estimated that if man harnessed all of the tidal power in the world, it might furnish 1 percent of our total present-day needs. One apparent problem is the fact that the power is too dispersed along the beaches throughout the world, and only in unique places can it be harnessed.

The Russians have developed a Tidal Power System at Kislaya Guba in the Soviet Union. Some fifty other sites have been identified in the world, including the Bay of Fundy in Canada. In fact, the concept of harnessing tidal power in the Bay of Fundy has been discussed for over fifty years. It is interesting to note that engineers have estimated that tidal power has greater potential as an energy source than all the world's lakes, rivers, and streams by a factor of ten times! However, the costs are phenomenal because of the large-scale nature of dams that would be required. Hydroelectric dams show an economic advantage over other energy sources only when coupled with another use, such as flood control.

Wood Energy. It is interesting to note today that in the mid-seventeenth century, each household in New England required a half an acre of woods in order to survive, and the reason for dispersion and development in the 1600s was to gain energy sources. By the mid-1880s, the United States was burning ten times as much wood as any other country in the world, and by 1880 we changed energy sources from wood to coal. In less than twenty years, coal was our main source of fuel and forty years later in 1920, we switched again—but this time to oil. About thirty years ago, we began using natural gas, hydroelectric power sources, and now nuclear power.*

According to a Stanford University Report, the eucalyptus tree could be the source of 15 to 20 percent of US energy needs by the year 2020. The researchers of the Stanford University Report did not attempt to convert environmental costs such as reclamation of strip mining or the storage of expanded nuclear fuels into dollar figures for comparison. Instead, these were dealt with as factors to be alternatives weighted by decision makers. There should be such a fact sheet, as well as an analysis that compares the stages of the fuel development visually and environmentally. For example, would you rather live next to an oil field full of rigs, or a forest growing eucalyptus trees for fuel, as suggested in the Stanford Report?

The graph shown here compares the cost of available heat units (BTUs) in a gallon of fuel oil, which yields roughly 138,000 BTUs and an average cord of dry hardwood, which yields about 20,900,000

*Richard Wilson, "Nuclear Fusion: Our Best Energy Bet for the Future," *Harvard Magazine,* November 1973, Cambridge, Massachusetts.

An alternative to drilling rigs—a eucalyptus tree? "It grows much faster than any other tree, and its energy is very high density." Studies say it could be a source of 15–20 percent of U.S. energy needs for 2020 A.D.

Wood versus oil. A cost comparison of available heat units.

BTUs. The line represents a break-even point between the costs of the two fuels. Any price relationship falling below the line indicates an economic advantage in using wood, while one falling above the line shifts the advantage to oil.

The comparison, in which the relative efficiency of the heating units is assumed to be equal, does not take into account either the efficiency of the heating plants, or the convenience of handling the fuels. Fireplaces are notoriously inefficient, thus a closed stove is assumed.

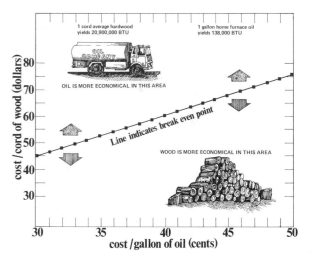

Timetable for the Technological Environment*

To best sum up this section, "Thinking—The Technological Environment," this timetable, with experts' estimates, shows the year by which time there is a 50 percent chance the event will have occurred.

1971
Energy sources become the great pawn of international politics—the beginning of the great energy crisis.

1978
Environmentally motivated higher price for energy.

Acceptance of the idea that all consumers share responsibility for pollution and its cost.

1980
Safe, large-scale disposal of radioactive wastes.

Abolition of "growth for growth's sake" concept; recycling cities accepted everywhere.

1981
Effective, harmless control of accidental oil spills.

1983
"Fail-safe" nuclear power generation

Development of waste heat utilization (desalting, heating, sewage treatment, etc.).

Total control of thermal pollution in water.

1985
Fast breeder reactors in use.

New car systems and modules developed (batteries, fuel cells, steam, etc.)

Offshore siting of large power plants is commonplace.

1986
Removal of noxious matter from fossil fuels before combustion.

1988
Establishment of worldwide environmental quality standards (air and water).

1990
Taxes to alleviate pollution problems (effluent taxes, tax incentives for dispersal of people from large cities.)

Establishment of worldwide environmental surveillance and warning agency.

Suppression of sound along highways and airways.

1991
Large-scale use of industrialized housing systems internationally

1992
Personal Rapid Transit Systems in common use.

1995
Coordinated international planning of energy consumption.

2000
Planned decrease of per capita energy demand and consumption finally implemented.

Effective population control enforced worldwide.

2005
Conservation of fossil fuels for other future needs.

2010
Man will largely destroy his ability to survive in great numbers and in great cities.

2020
Utilization of heat sinks other than atmosphere and surface waters.

After 2020
Polar siting of large power plants.

Earth-based solar energy devices for bulk power generation.

Elimination of all generators using fossil fuel.

Utilization of gravitational energy (antigravity).

*Adapted from "Energy and the Environment" by Vaclav Smil, in *The Futurist,* Feb. 1974, p. 11.

3

Why Recycled Cities?

What do we do when, after form has dutifully followed function, function decides to move to the suburbs? Too often, our response has been to demolish the abandoned form—and leave a hole that may eventually be filled by a new building; meanwhile, we'll have a place to park our cars.

But it is now clear that the abandoned form may have an integral life of its own worth respecting . . . it may contribute an emitable personality to its neighborhood.

—Stanley Abercrombie

Only by recycling our cities can we retain the historic and social values of American civilization. In order to plan for recycling, whole communities must first look at the imprints of history on the architecture, examine the patterns of growth of the city, and understand their own demands and needs for the future. The needs of a city must be evaluated in terms of an existing functional context and must be juxtaposed against the existing fabric of the city.

The philosophy that "old is bad, new is good" is indigenous to America. This feeling imbues all aspects of American life and is best exemplified (although not exclusively) on Madison Avenue and on Wall Street. It is one of our mutually shared, yet not fully recognized, great national tragedies.

Throughout the world, in every other nation ranging from the less developed countries to the most industrialized nations, people have always revered and respected their heritage as manifested in architecture and in their urban centers. It is the architectural monuments and the cities that most obviously display a nation's glories and triumphs as well as its failures and losses.

These urban centers permit even the most bucolic peasant to relate to his more sophisticated forebears and all that they have created and destroyed before him. Old is good sometimes; new is good sometimes.

Why recycled cities? Because many of the earliest cities were set in the best geographic locations, because we can no longer afford the throw-away environment, because building construction is land destruction, because . . .

Appropriateness of
Early Urban Settlements:
Lifestyle Location

The earliest settlements were located for purely pragmatic reasons in the most defensible and convenient positions. These locations were usually on the water as boats were the best and fastest means of transportation. Water was the quickest means of communication and sometimes a means of irrigation. So even in the very beginning real estate agents must have used the phrase, *"the three most important things to look for in a property are location, location, location."* Towns located on the seacoast or a river's edge provided the community with the self-sufficiency it needed in days of old. Today, there is still a surge to the coasts and waterfront property is at a premium. The oceans, lakes, and rivers provide water for physical and recreational needs as well as a spiritual sense of unboundedness.

In the United States the early towns flourished as commercial ports and the towns that developed around rivers became industrial centers where the water then acted as a power source or a place to dispose of unwanted materials and wastes. With the shift in industry from labor intensive to mechanization and with the dramatic move of mills in New England from the North to the South the great water-oriented cities have experienced unemployment, emigration, and deterioration. Some of these cities lie in the best urban sites available in the entire country and they already have the infrastructure of utilities, roadways, sewerage systems, and architectural monuments. Additionally, there are the most desirable amenities of:

☐
The oceans, lakes, rivers, and mountains for recreational use.

☐
The convenience and economies of existing transportation and service networks and closeness of home to work.

Newburyport, Mass. The waterfront and harbor 100 years ago.

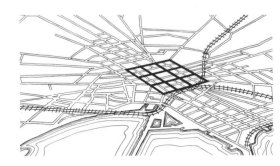

New Haven: the earliest planned community in the American colonies. Established in 1638, New Haven consisted of nine squares, the central one a common square or green, which has been preserved to the present day.

□
An existing image and personality of a specific city in the form of extant architecture, institutions, monuments, urban space, and other elements.
□
General quality of life benefits due to the sense of a place and a potential inherent in the physical environment and location as compared to the plastic shopping center cities of strip development.

Early industrial development. The coming of the railroad creates a spiderweb pattern of streets, added to the original squares, which have been cut through with new streets to provide more frontage for expanding commerce.

For example, such early settlements as New Bedford, Providence, Newport, Portland, and Newburyport were once among the largest cities in the United States and founded, because of the appropriateness of their coastal harbor locations, for major ports. Now they are underused and underpopulated, but prime candidates for recycling because they still occupy what is geographically some of the most interesting coastline in the world and still retain their functional potentials. Shipping by water is still economical and our new concerns for energy conservation could accentuate this. Newport still retains the same beauty and beaches that once made her "America's First Vacationland." All these cities contain a heritage, a history and a sense of place that could never be duplicated artificially in a new town development. But such places must face their downtown blight and the tendency to sprawl away from it. As a city's essential use changes, there is no reason why new meaning cannot be instilled to preserve a continuum of use, urban space, and architectural character. This kind of change—say from a shipping center to a city emphasizing recreation and leisure-with-work—would symbolize the historic process of evolution in a city by recognizing its new validity as a "lifestyle location."

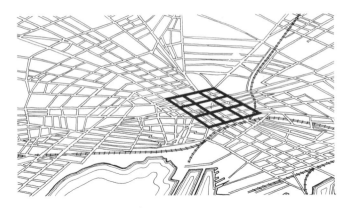

The automobile age: the expansion of suburbia, with its new centers of population and services, creates a pattern typical of American cities of about 200,000 population.

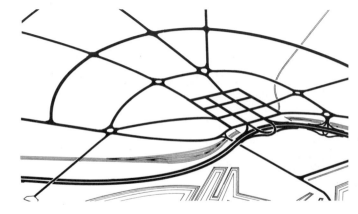

Service-industry development. The over-all plan of the city, which began as a mercantile grid, has now become a radio-concentric pattern in character, insofar as the harbor and topographical features permit.

Devouring Our Heritage

The whole notion of recycling cities and the preservation of architecture is a much larger issue than simply that of preserving city streets or buildings as works of art. We are and have been devouring our heritage, and we will need to replace it. There has always existed a cycle of perpetual motion from construction to destruction to construction and at each step we are using more and more of our resources and wasting energy.

There are calls from environmentalists to return to the preindustrial past and, along with the communes, we now find people of all ages retreating to lovely homes in the hinterlands and an environmentally pure existence—to a Pre-Raphaelite life.

Their understanding is that everything is morally corrupt, that all food is unpure, that there are no virgins left, and that over all there is a continuing and progressive impoverished quality of life throughout the world. The tendency has always been to save only the artifacts of the affluent few whether it be the creations of kings and popes in the past or of the Fortune 500 companies' corporate headquarters today. Botanist Barry Commoner, author of *Science and Survival,* has said,

It seems to me that the enemies are those who would duck the issue, and by that I mean the question of asking the basic question—what are the resources to improve human welfare? Are they to be used as raw material for a productive process which is governed by the immediate and often private gain? In other words, are we producing for the sake of a productive process, or are we producing for people? What has happened is that we have designed our buildings, our factories and the way we run our farms for the sake of extracting maximum immediate profits. It so happens that this *does not coincide with what's best for the environment or for human welfare, and I think that's what has to be changed.*

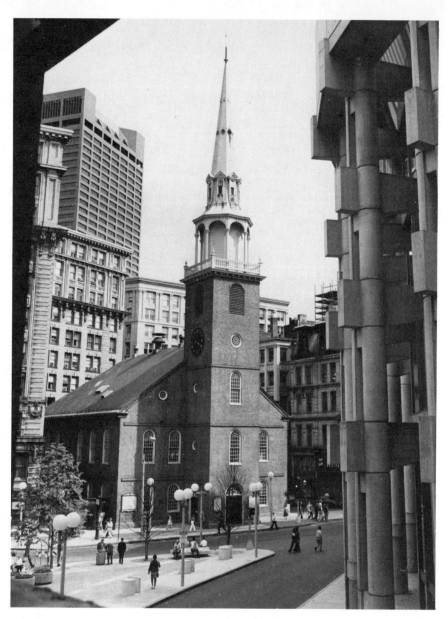

Devouring our heritage? Old South Meetinghouse erected in Boston in 1729, preserved, yet each year it is more encroached upon by new projects, which get bigger and bigger.

Cities as Personifications

"Chicago, Chicago—Hog Butcher for the World" (Sandburg)

Cities do personify their citizens, but why do Americans love to tour the capitals of Europe? Why has the American tourist become so visible all over the world? Where does he go when he visits abroad? The answers are obvious.

Americans tour London, Paris, and Rome to see the architectural monuments of the past. These cities are personifications of their respective nation's temperament—Paris is a painter on the Seine, London is a man in a bowler hat, Rome is an opera singer. The cities of Europe have a certain consistency that "holds them together," and Americans, like other people, feel comfortable in the setting. These cities were built in times when the technology was limited and heights to which buildings could be built were restricted by the nature of the materials. This technological handicap combined with the facts of theocracy or autocracy (which usually meant commissioning of projects, even whole cities, by a single client such as Pope Sixtus or Napoleon) meant that the structures that were built were consistent in all aspects from overall form and material to floor plans and moulding details.

This is true to a limited extent in the older sections of the United States. Witness Back Bay in Boston, which is all brick; all buildings are four or five stories in height, all have similar facade treatment, window fenestration, and rhythm. Tourists from all over the world enjoy Back Bay because it is consistent and in scale with human beings. In fact, many visitors to Boston, New Orleans, or San Francisco reflect on the similarities between these cities and many European cities they have visited.

The reasons are simply that there are more of these older reusable buildings in Boston and San Francisco. Also, more than most American cities, these two cities have retained the old, and thus their heritage, while others, such as New York City, have been under continuous pressure to grow and change.

But our cities are what we are, they are personifications.

The singular American concept of new frontiers has done a great deal to contribute to our inherent flexibility as a people, but it has also caused us to move on and use more land, more resources, and to create more newness. When a location has been befouled, we move on, when we can't move on, we tear the place apart and start anew. These places are our American cities.

The energy crisis of 1974 has caused most people to reassess this blatant waste of resources and infrastructure. The three "Rs"—"recycling," "reuse," and "rehabilitation," and other words beginning with a "re" have played an increasingly important role in the lip service of current fashionable talk. Only if our consuming and mobile national character changes—or even if old characteristics such as "Yankee thrift" and "American ingenuity" re-emerge—will our cities change, too.

Saving Places for People

It's one thing to save a single building, but it's something else again to preserve a place. To begin with, it's more complicated. Everything that has to be done to save an individual building gets multiplied in saving an area: the spaces as well as buildings that give an area its character must be identified, interdependent uses must be worked out for them; the political strategies are more intricate because there are more parties involved. And while one building may conceivably be out of use while it is being restored, an entire area can't be taken out of service.

It is a knotty problem, partly because a place, as opposed to a single building, is apt to loom large in the public mind. Saving one takes clairvoyance (to read the public mind), political acumen (because the decisions often end up in the political arena), a grasp of guerilla tactics (for the in-fighting that comes with preservation projects) and a touch of paranoia (because the threats to a place can be far more subtle than the threats to a building.)*

*"Saving Places for People," C. Page, *Progressive Architecture*, November 1972, p. 70.

Saving places for people rather than cars. Auto repairs at the altar of the Church of St. Michele at Ferrara, Italy.

Building Construction Is Land Destruction

Acting as ecosurgeons

It goes without saying that the act of building construction is also, by definition, an act of land destruction and that man-made built environments must destroy natural values. Every schoolchild today realizes that land, air, and water resources are becoming more scarce and that every time we take a little more of them, we get a little less air to breathe in return. This is indeed the basis under which we can all work. We should, in fact, attempt to improve the ecological situation by acting as "ecosurgeons" in some cases, by removing the beginnings of real estate development cancer and by attempting to put back more than we have taken in our projects.

But the incidence of ecosurgery is rare. We can cite only one case: in Portland, Oregon, a major new highway was excised shortly after construction, because the planners realized it was a mistake to build a highway cutting off the riverfront from the city.

There is much talk, of course; there are sales pitches from the "young Turks" of the real estate world all claiming their projects are ecologically aware and have sensitively placed green belts and hide their parking behind a berm. But anything they build on virgin land is taking more from the environment than it is giving, and they only have the cosmetic appearance of what they preach.

The AIA has suggested the filling in of the leapfrogged lands within existing suburban areas as a means to relieve the pressures of development in the outer fringes of metropolitan areas. Thus the exurban, undeveloped lands would be less likely to

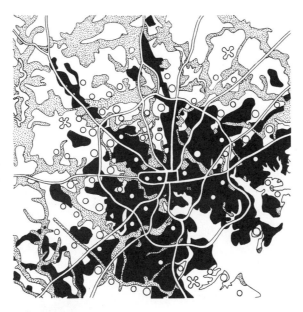

▇ URBANIZED AREA
▨ PARK AREA   ○ SITES OF 3000 UNITS
⚭ NEW TOWN   ○ SITES OF 500 UNITS

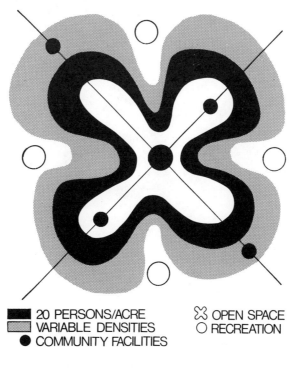

▇ 20 PERSONS/ACRE   ⚭ OPEN SPACE
▨ VARIABLE DENSITIES   ○ RECREATION
● COMMUNITY FACILITIES

be affected by urban growth and another technique could be utilized to recycle existing urban lands. The "growth unit" concept was developed by the AIA as an alternative to urban sprawl—it provides a well designed neighborhood monad containing 500 to 3,000 dwelling units and "a full range of physical facilities and human services that ensure an urban life of quality." In contrast with current urban growth patterns, the growth unit guarantees that essential services and amenities are available to residents from the beginning of the development and in the correct proportions throughout the city. This type of concept may well be the basic building block of future urban development.

Site availability analysis indicates those "leapfrogged" vacant sites in and around metropolitan areas.

Growth unit alternatives to urban sprawl providing "a full range of physical facilities and human services that ensure an urban life of quality."

The Popping of the New Town Bubble

The popping of the new town bubble. Inflatable City. Montage by F. St. Florian, 1967.

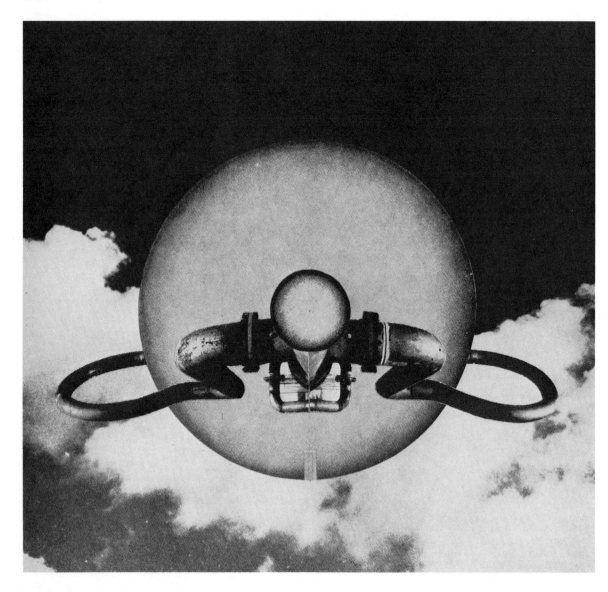

The new towns experiment of Great Britain began enthusiastically with the postwar New Town Act of 1946. They were extolled in the 1950s and 1960s, but are now reviewing themselves with a jaundiced eye. Do they provide a satisfactory way of life? Are they economically possible? The findings have tended to pop the new town bubble and indicate that renewed cities rather than new towns offer the best prospects for the United States.

Character. While the real old cities remain vital, most new towns have not been able to capture the "essence" of a city. They have not become "the complete community with industry, commerce, services, and housing all carefully blended together with a balanced labor force to keep everything in operation." They became instead dormitory suburbs that failed to attract newcomers and to grow, and which are limited in class and age mix. They destroyed, as well as created, when new land was taken for construction. Century-old rural village ways of life were diminished while new town residents claimed "there's nothing to do and no place to go."

Money. Again, the large, long-term investment is already in the existing cities and since new towns require such tremendous capital investments, which are no longer available (such as the HUD programs), they are not financially feasible in the United States. Even with the strong powers wielded by the national government in England, the growing pains of delays, shortcomings, and mistakes were substantial and costly.

Labor. Old cities still hold the balance of labor. They possess an existing labor force, which can be evaluated rather than merely projected, and a cus-

tom labor force that can be depended on. The English experience has been that new towns have often not been able to achieve or maintain a labor force balance that is compatible with the needs of industry. Meanwhile the old cities in the United States have tried to retain both industry and labor force and counteract industries' flight from their downtowns by attracting them to industrial parks at their perimeters.

"The fact that new towns are synthetic communities with little social texture may underlie much of the reason for the 'new town blues'. . . . A more basic change which government policy has adopted may bring somewhat better results for future developments. This is to make future new towns much larger and, wherever possible, attach them to already existing substantial communities."*

*George E. Berkeley, "Britain's New Town Blues," *National Civic Review*. Vol. 62, No. 9, October 1973.

Air-ocean environment developed in an artificial earth crater and grown until it reaches a programmed capacity. Then it becomes independent, controlled by light. Photomontage by R. J. Abraham.

The End of the Throwaway Culture

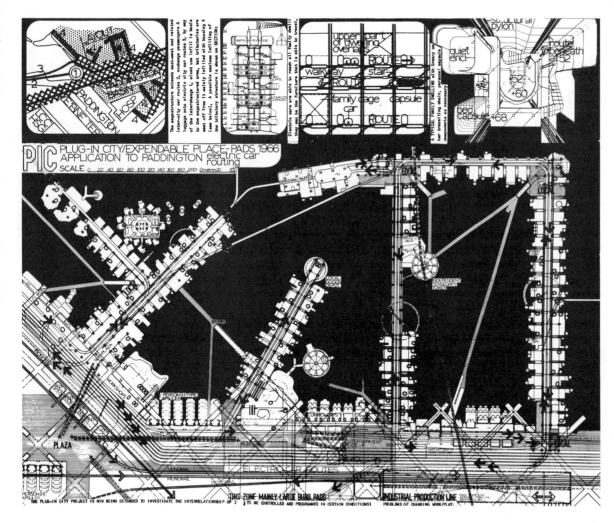

PLUG-IN CITY/EXPENDABLE PLACE-PADS 1966
APPLICATION TO PADDINGTON electric car routing

The end of the throwaway culture. Plug-in city/ expandable place-pads, 1966.

The folly of built-in obsolescence in the early 1960s, with the concept of "disposables" and "throwaways," spawned a whole movement in architecture and planning. The concept embodied the approach that building units functionally and physically related could be planned so that they could unhook their links to the city and move to new locations. The new technology creating greater mobility and faster communication networks was translated architecturally into hypothetical building forms. The most famous proponent of this approach was an English group, "Archigram"; their work was published and discussed widely, especially in the United States.

The lack of consideration for the "quality of life" in such environments coupled with the awakening to the fact that it makes little sense to make disposable soda pop bottles, let alone to create impermanent environments, stopped this movement from progressing beyond paper designs.

The Europeans have always been enamored with the American disposables; perhaps this is not surprising, since Americans have always admired the European sense of permanence. The thought of the American throwaway culture being applied to whole cities or even single buildings is abhorrent. As it happens, the American throwaway or disposable (euphemisms for wasteful) culture has ended as a concept in all its ugly ramifications and facets by hard times and resource shortages. Everything from bottles and newspapers to churches and railroad stations is now being recycled; so why not whole cities? The whole of the industrialized world will soon realize that it cannot afford to waste the investment of materials and machinery contained in

Feed-in adaptable travelators, marketplaces, high performance steel bathroom, variable rooms, 60° grid carried within spaceframe trays.

existing urban infrastructure and physically embodied in their heritage. Perhaps this pocketbook rationale is the greatest argument for recycling cities.

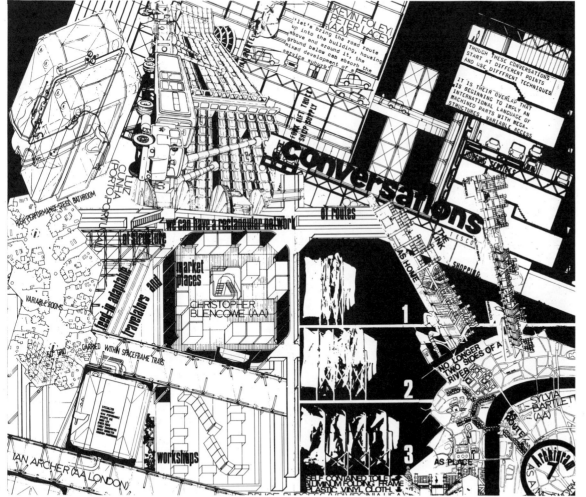

Communities Have Rejected Urban Renewal Like the Body Rejects Heart Transplants

In 1954, the city of New Haven inaugurated the first urban renewal program in the nation with the statement by Mayor Richard C. Lee that, ''The basic goals of the program would be concerned with giving back to the central city the vitality that traditionally belonged there.''

In fact, twenty years later New Haven is a virtual museum of handsome civic architecture with isolated examples of the so-called master architects sprinkled throughout the metropolitan area. Buildings by Louis I. Kahn, Paul Rudolph, Eero Saarinen, Marcel Breuer, Phillip Johnson, Skidmore Owings and Merrill, and others of the ''oldies but goodies'' schools of thought are all represented in New Haven. Yet, little of it creates the ''vitality that traditionally belonged there,'' and the people know it and have reacted to it over the years. The white city dwellers have moved to the suburbs, the major industries have either left the city altogether or are a dying breed, the black center city residents have rioted and many urban renewal sites remain vacant. While the city and its people reject urban renewal, the early proponents of the program are momentarily quasi-heroes in other settings—such as Edward Logue was in New York City with the ill-fated Urban Development Corporation.

During the heyday of urban renewal programs, there was money and impetus, but no comprehensive ideas. Today the ideas for city works, urban form, and recycling exist as reactions to users' needs and demands; it is all clear now, but there is little money available for urban design.

Ecosurgery at its best!
Court Street in New Haven—a successful demonstration/rehabilitation. This street was successfully transformed from a skid row into a desirable street, rather than being demolished.

Suburbanization
Has Not Been Successful

First the immediate countryside became suburbanized, then suburban areas became towns (Newton, Westport) as the towns became cities (Cambridge, Brooklyn) and the cities became regional centers (Boston, New York City) and the whole became the metropolis. The cities were the connections in a network, the joints that held the suburbs in the system. The new exurbs have been failing because they are not placed in the system in a way that relates to and maintains equilibrium with the cities.

But most important, can we justify taking more of our greatest natural resource—our land? As the saying goes, ''They ain't making any more of it.'' Can we continue to cover our land with sprawling and speckled urbanization? So much land has been consumed in this manner that it's secondhand use has compelling implications:

Given an economic life of 40 to 50 years for a single family dwelling, an average of 2 to 2½% per year of all urban land now in low density residential use will become available for recycling every year during the coming decades. *Even assuming that as much as 50% of this land could be recycled at its original density, that 20% were dedicated to new in-town parks, and that as little as 30% were re-developed with low-rise apartments or townhouses at densities of 12 to 15 dwelling units per acre, the* entire estimated growth of the urban population could be accommodated in the land being so re-cycled without need of further outward expansion.*

We must begin a process of giving the land back to nature, not taking more of it. We must revive the old sites and spare the new ones, stop subsidizing outward expansion, discourage demands for easy residential development on fresh land, and refuse to commit to urban use open lands of high agricultural and environmental value.

Land: They ain't making any more of it. Homogeneous suburbanization has not been successful, but recycling low density urban areas with mixed densities could halt wasteful sprawl as well as address the monotony of those areas.

*''Time We Started Recycling Our Older Inner Suburbs,'' *Los Angeles Times,* June 26, 1972

The Simplistic View of the American Power Structure

The way in which the power structure sees the environment is at the very least interesting to observe. We can see the US government's approach to programs that subconciously instigate urban sprawl.

The US Environmental Protection Agency, for instance, established guidelines for sewer grants that put sewer interceptors into suburban fringe areas, thus creating major incentives for real estate development there. The logic behind these $4 billion worth of award funds with which the government pays 75 percent of the costs of sewage treatment plants, interceptors, and other equipment, is to build in advance of a community's growth. The land-use effect of such politically motivated philosophies is obvious—more urban sprawl. Further irony is the fact that land use is not included as an impact in the sewer environmental impact statements for such projects.

This is an example of the bureaucratic fostering of urban sprawl that must change if there is to be any progress or any America left at all.

Now listen to the voice of the throwaway society: "Worn-out machines are replaced—worn-out communities should be." How utterly absurd a statement! Are cities merely machinery with built-in obsolescence like Detroit's hulking iron horses? Where does one put the worn-out carcasses of worn-out cities? Actually, the logic of such an argument would make ghost towns for mini-Disneylands to exploit and these ghost towns would litter the country like the broken-down and abandoned cars that currently litter the streets of our urban roadways.

New towns are *not* "begging to be built."

"New cities are begging to be built." The spirit of this advertisement is indigenous to Americans. Outward expansion, prematurely discarding something old by moving on to something new, avoiding the issue of responsibility for what we leave behind, whether it is paper litter or the litter of our used up cities.

"Our cities can work better today and tomorrow." Westinghouse acknowledges the basic economies of revising the existing cities because of their expensive infrastructure, but sees the rebirth of cities as dependent on the insertion of more hardware—this time "made by Westinghouse."

New cities are begging to be built.

Worn-out machines are replaced. Worn-out communities should be, but often are not.

Every nation has its ghettos. Neglected schools and inefficient factories. Inadequate roads, dams, bridges, and public utilities.

One of the urgent needs of our time is to create a physical environment that will enrich human life, not impoverish it.

Replacing what already exists, however, is only part of the story. Equally important is building to keep pace with growth and change.

FMC is concerned with both.

Our company provides equipment to the construction industry essential to many operations.

When there are rivers or harbors to be dredged, our clamshells and draglines can shorten the time.

When there is a need to improve environments with underground utilities, or foundations, footings, and pipelines to be laid, our hydraulic hoes make trench-cutting efficient and economical.

When pilings are needed to support massive structures, our diesel pile hammers can drive them.

When structures begin to rise, our cranes can lift loads up to 300 feet in one operation.

And when a city is built, FMC equipment can mow its lawns, maintain its parks, water its gardens, treat its wastewater, provide it flood control, give it fire protection, even sweep its streets.

The people at FMC have a strong conviction: no city should have to go begging.

FMC Corporation, 111 East Wacker Drive, Chicago 60601.

FMC

Our cities can work better today ...and tomorrow.

Modern ways to transport people.
Cities are having a rebirth, largely because developers are taking a new look at the tremendous investments in urban property. And modern mass transit ideas are helping make this rebirth happen. The automated, computer-controlled vehicles that have helped move people safely and conveniently through airports, are now being applied to the needs of downtown areas, colleges, industrial complexes and recreation centers. Westinghouse is helping make it happen.

Buildings designed to use less energy.
New buildings are saving energy these days by using existing heat . . . from the lighting systems . . . . to cut heating loads. Circulating water or air picks up the lighting heat and redistributes it throughout the building. In summer, the same system carries the heat out of the building to cut air conditioning needs. Total energy savings can amount to 10% or 15%.

Better lighting for better safety.
New Westinghouse Ceramalux™ high-pressure sodium lamps for residential streets deliver twice the light of ordinary mercury vapor lamps for 10% less power, helps discourage street crime. Ceramalux systems are being installed now in New York City, Washington, D.C., and dozens of other cities.

Westinghouse Electric Corporation Pittsburgh, Pa. 15222

Ⓦ Westinghouse   helps make it happen

Idea:
The Land Ferry

Although Arco hoped to promote the concept of public transportation, their first publicized proposal by a layperson is one that further encourages the flow of cars into the city and caters to the American go-nowhere-without-it addiction to their automobiles. . . .

Amy Farrell explains,"It brings you and your car downtown so you can use it during the day."

"I got the idea for the Land Ferry watching ferryboats. I thought a ferryboat on land could solve a lot of problems.

"It would be easy. We could use those trailers that carry new cars.

"In the morning you drive your car onto the Land Ferry. While it drives downtown you can sit and drink coffee and read the morning paper.

"Another advantage of the Land Ferry is you could put it into operation practically tomorrow morning."

Amy feels her idea would reduce pollution, rush hour congestion, and gas consumption. But there are other ways to go. Other ideas. You have them and we would like you to send them to us.

That's why it is not the intention of Atlantic Richfield to endorse any one idea. Public Transportation to meet everyone's needs, needs everyone's ideas.

Please note that all ideas submitted become public property without compensation and any restriction on use or disclosure. This allows the ideas to be used freely to promote the concept of Public Transportation. Our thinking is that since the subject is Public Transportation the ideas should belong to the public.

Send your ideas directly to: IDEAS
P.O. Box 30169, Los Angeles, Calif. 90030

Where's your idea on Public Transportation?

ARCO ◆

Petroleum Products of
AtlanticRichfieldCompany

Six Ideas on Public Transportation.

Stephen B. Barasch
Dallas, TX

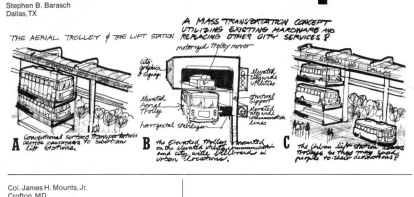

THE AERIAL TROLLEY & THE LIFT STATION

A MASS TRANSPORTATION CONCEPT UTILIZING EXISTING HARDWARE AND REPLACING OTHER CITY SERVICES?

motorized trolley mover

city graphics & signage

elevated citywide utilities

elevated Aerial Trolley

structural support

horizontal stabilizer

elevated citywide communication lines

A Conventional surface transportation carries passengers to suburban lift stations.

B The Elevated Trolley mounted on the elevated utility communication and city wide billboard in urban locations.

C The Urban lift station lowers trolleys so they may speed people to their destinations.

Col. James H. Mounts, Jr.
Crofton, MD

29 Sept. '74

Dear Sir;
My idea for mass transit is to finance all local transit systems through national transit bonds. These bonds would be backed by the U.S. Gov. general credit but be sold by Federal banks & local banks as a public service. The interest would be sufficient to have a good return but also would be tax deductible from federal income tax.

Sincerely,
James A. Mounts Jr.
Col. JAGC
U.S. Army

Ronald M. Uher
Crystal Lake, IL

A UNIT THAT COULD TRAVEL ON OR OFF TRACKS - OFF TRACKS BY BATTARY OR 2 SMALL GAS ENGINES FOR SHORT DISTANCES, ON TRACKS, IN CONSTANT MOVEMENT POWERED AVENUES

FIBERGLASS & ALUMINUM CONST.

OVERHEAD OFF TRACK THIRD RAIL

FLEXIBLE BUMPER

FLEX. BUMP.

TRICYCLE GEAR LOWERED FOR STREET TRAVEL

RAISED FOR RAIL TRAVEL

4 PEOPLE TO A UNIT

Michael R. Albino
San Diego, CA

10/6/74

Dear Sir;

Considering it would be an economical disaster of national perpotions to abandon our freeways, and knowing the freeway passes through or near more communities, towns and cities then does railroads, the nucleous of any concept of mass transportation must depend on them.

I submit the following as a stimulus for thought.

The lane bordering the dividing island of a freeway must be reserved exclusively for buses (and possible freight lines). Interstate busses would by law pick up and discharge local passengers along the highway route. This would necessitate the construction of bus stops in the island part of the freeway. A foot bridge above or below the freeway would permit excess to local mini buses serving the town.

The reason I chose the Island lane for buses is for future development. When a plan based on the above concept is built trand working, a special overhead electric cable would be installed. Gradually electric motor buses would begin replacing the gas engine and the bus would run in the manner of the electric trolly car of years past.

Sincerly

Michael R. Albino

Dr. Pierce Scranton, M.D.
Pittsburgh, PA

My idea would achieve three goals: ① Decrease pollution, ② Save fuel, ③ Stimulate the economy. It is as follows:
Corporations exceeding a certain size — say, with greater than 1000 employees at one plant would shut down their parking lots and provide free corporate bus transportation to-and-from work — via peripheral pick-up and drop-off centers in the local neighborhoods. Corporations could write-off the expense of purchasing these buses through special tax breaks - making it profitable for them to do this. Employees would not have the option to drive their own cars, as corporate parking lots would be closed. Instead of one thousand cars bringing in one thousand employees, 25 buses would arrive. Massive decrease in pollutants, stimulation of slumping auto (now bus) producers, corporations smell like a rose!

Pierce Scranton M.D.

Herbert Goldberg
Bronx, NY

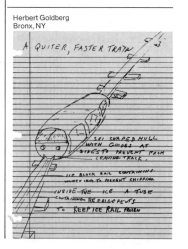

A QUIETER, FASTER TRAIN

SKI SHAPED HULL WITH GUIDES AT SIDES TO PREVENT FROM LEAVING TRACK

ICE BLOCK RAIL CONTAINING UNDER CHIP TO PREVENT CHIPPING

INSIDE THE ICE A TUBE CONTAINING REFRIGERENTS TO KEEP ICE RAIL FROZEN

But an interesting learning process took place and each successive proposal has dealt more directly with the real problems of public transportation in cities—not only with the hardware aspect, but with software programming and use concepts.

Our present value system:
Are new priorities in order?
Drawing by Forrest Wilson.

Recycling
Cities

4

Establishing a Dialogue

We are acquainted with a mere pellicle
of the globe on which we live. Most
have not delved six feet beneath the
surface, nor leaped as many above it.
We know not where we are. Besides,
we are sound asleep nearly half our
time. Yet we esteem ourselves wise,
and have an established order on the
surface.

—Henry David Thoreau

As citizens of single countries and inhabitants of individual cities, we attempt to establish a proper order of things in our environment. The development of effective programs for the environment, including urban and rural change, requires an approach to planning, design, and implementation that can integrate all the diverse human and natural forces that influence and shape today's complex life.

There are contradictions in our approach; we are surrounded by a tendency toward specialization everywhere in society. At the same time, we are and should be approaching more and more closely an era of "total environment" in that all aspects interrelate and affect each other and isolationism is impossible.

Still, the "totality" of such an environment patently is not amenable to treatment by generalists alone, and the need for the specialist is clear.

But then again, we are only too aware of what has happened when specialists alone were in charge of environmental changes in matters such as highway engineering, industrial plants, and real estate development. Although there are no simple answers to the dilemmas we now face, we submit that an urban design approach (with an ecological awareness as the ambient background) may draw us closer to the quintessence of true "community"—this is the role of the generalist/urban designer.

"Urban design is where business, government, development, planning, and design converge"*

Urban design as a profession is an attempt to replace specialization with a general comprehension that is achieved through combining a few in-depth studies with an increased awareness of the many related areas that contribute to a more correct

**Architectural Forum,* November 1973.

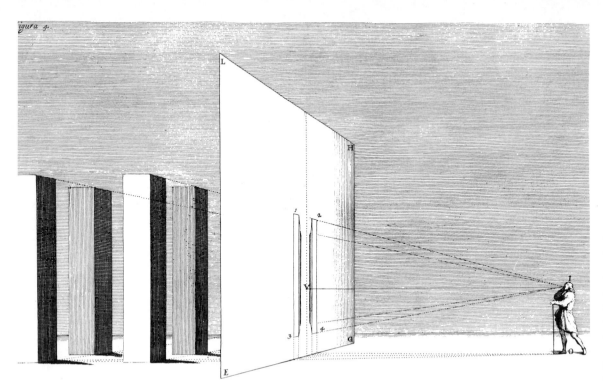

igura 4.

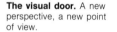

The visual door. A new perspective, a new point of view.

View of the city: Medieval hierarchy versus Renaissance perspectives

approach. The problems resulting from the rapid urbanization throughout the world have made it urgent to train individuals to deal with large scale design problems. Although the intent is not to make an architect into a geographer or an economist, or a planner into a psychologist, the necessary interdisciplinary approach can only be productive if the urban designer has sufficient cognizance of these fields to know what they can contribute toward the design synthesis and if he knows how to pose the right questions. Therefore, one can state that the urban designer is the requisite generalist.

We have tried to state our views with respect to the importance of this evolving field that did not even exist as a recognized course of study until recently (Harvard's Graduate School of Design established the first Urban Design Program in 1953), for it is the urban designer who can best begin to recycle cities by bringing together in a multidisciplinary approach the type of experience and resources required to lead a recycling team.

The Visual Door

Prior to the Renaissance, people viewed everything from an *external* point of view. That is to say that perspective drawing had not yet been invented and pictures of cities were usually drawn without perspective and emphasized the hierarchical order of life at the times—views were external. Churches were usually exaggerated in size and the rest of the city was pictured inconsequentially. Once the humanitarianism of the Renaissance developed the technique of perspective drawing, an *internal,* or rather personal, view of the city was possible. Perspective drawing, physically and philosophically, opened the way for people to look at things from many different points of view. Of course, the most important issue then became the question of "Who was viewing the subject?" and "What position was the view taken from?" The possibilities of multiviews of a specific subject and views as seen through the eyes of different social classes opened the "visual door" for a dialogue to begin. New interpretations and new understandings raised the consciousness of everyone for many centuries to come. Now that urban problems have become so complex we find that simple perspective study is not enough.

The city is no longer a stagnant single-point perspective of physical buildings, but rather it is a real-life drama with its many characters changing and evolving and carrying on a continuing, increasingly cacophonous, dialogue.

To understand the city, one must "tune in" on this dialogue at many frequencies and hear the different voices. Yet, it is extremely difficult to discern in this drama what the real problems and possible solutions for the city today are, as the voices are many and single focused.

The ability to feel many roles and situations

Each media type, each corporation, each government agency, each person views the city's problems in their own personal terms and from their own areas of expertise. No one takes the time to understand the other's point of view and interfacing with their problems. Perhaps now is the time to change the perspective of the city again, and to get an *internal* view of things. We would propose a Stanislavski method of planning or a "Synectics"* approach to establishing a dialogue with the city. The theater was revolutionized by the Stanislavski acting method,

*(See: William J. J. Gordon, *Synectics*. New York: Harper and Row, 1961).

which evolved from the concept that the true understanding necessary for great contemporary acting must come from the actor's internal understanding of the situation, not from the mimicry of external physical expressions. The environmental design profession awaits a similar revolution in concept. Synectics attempts to develop creativity in businessmen by instruction in the process of personification: "If I were (person or object), I would feel _____ and do ____;" and the process of comparison: "A _____ is like or as a ____." A new planning concept, too, would begin with the ability to feel many roles and situations. Such a dialogue may bring us closer to an internal understanding of the urban environment by a Socratic-like method of questioning and answering at many different levels.

Establishing a Dialogue: "If I Were (The Environment) (The City) (Its People), How Would I Feel?

The Environment: Frankly, I have quite mixed feelings about the city. On the one hand, recycling the existing cities can avoid the destruction of more of my virgin lands by sprawling suburbanized development and can help conserve my energy resources. On the other hand, the existing cities are the violaters who are responsible for the abandoned cars, air pollution, nuisance noise, poor sanitation, waste disposal, and clutter of lights, signs, and utilities, unmaintained streets, and the wasting of my energies.

The City: I do have problems, but I apparently still have something people need, want, and can't find elsewhere— so I'm far from obsolete. I still have much to offer—just unclog my circulation systems, reinforce my skeletal frames, repair the holes in my fabric . . . but do my people really know *what* they want from me?

Its People: We're having an identity crisis with our cities. Who and what are the cities now? What is it they have that makes it so hard to leave them altogether? How can we learn to understand them and help with their problems, restore their usefulness and pride and train them to provide for our changing needs and lifestyles?

Détente without dialogue doesn't work. How can the people begin to talk with their respective cities? One can't establish détente without dialogue and really we don't need or want a Henry Kissinger to do everything for us internationally *or* municipally. Simple tools can begin the dialogue and will actually permit people to begin to talk to their cities on their own terms. For instance, the media can be used to begin a dialogue.

To involve, inform, and understand the community

Input from an urban community is essential to urban designers because of the subjective nature of the profession. They can be guided by the people's expertise, but cannot hope to respond to the different needs and desires of individual communities or affected groups if communication does not exist. The greater the community participation in developing the criteria for evaluating a particular city's potential for recycling itself, the greater the likelihood that the final outcome will be viable and will respond to the people's feelings. Communication is, of course, a two-way process. Information on any development project—public or private—and the major directions that they may take should be revealed to the community so that their reactions can be used to direct the evaluation process. A combination of methods should be used to involve, inform, and understand the particular community. These include hearings and meetings, either public or with selected groups (but the selection method

A guide to issues—not a blueprint for design

must be considered). Also, radio, TV, and newspapers can be useful in disseminating information; questionnaires can be distributed by mail, in newspapers, or distributed to specific groups (for selected information); interviews with experts and other people with specialized knowledge and finally, workshops should be held when some methodology and evaluation has been worked out so that feedback and constructive suggestions can be obtained.

The specific combinations of methods for ensuring valuable citizen participation must be tailored for each project, depending upon the degree of interest within the community and its size and type of population (character, ethnicity, education, and so on). Each method has its advantages and disadvantages. Radio, TV, and newspapers can disseminate information but are not useful in getting citizen reaction (except in letters to the editor). Hearings and meetings usually involve formal presentations and, while reactions can be heard from a "regular" group of spokesmen, the full range of citizen feeling may not be represented, and the formal set-up may hinder the real working out of problems and might also deter those not given to public speaking from expressing their opinions. Questionnaires can be useful if they are properly set up, distributed, returned, compiled, and analyzed.

Citizen's Preference

In Newburyport, Massachusetts, on an Environmental Impact Statement study reviewing several different developers' schemes for the historic downtown center, ECODESIGN was able to reach 95 percent of the population directly. That was approximately the number of households that subscribed to the popular local newspaper and, in

Waterfront urban renewal: citizens' questionnaire

The Daily News Tuesday, November 27, 1973 7

Citizens preference questionnaire. Waterfront urban renewal.

this case, the daily newspaper became an important design tool—a call from which 10 to 15 percent of the community responded. Different media combinations can be used to reach people on all social levels and each city will have its own formula, depending on the media's view of its responsibilities and its real effectiveness. In Newburyport, the editor of the *Newburyport Daily News,* Bill Plante, understood the media's role and offered a full page, free of charge, to be used in soliciting opinions and attitudes. Our "Citizens Preference Questionnaire" was a unique type of "if you had your druthers" public opinion poll. The goal of the effort was receiving inner, personal feelings, emotions, and goals of a citizenry about their town; it was not to use statistics to establish what are commonly referred to as "facts."

This was an important departure from normal planning and environmental impact statement practices, and it is believed by HUD sources in Washington that this may be one of the few cases where virtually an entire city has had the opportunity to participate directly in the EIS and design process and to contribute to the creation of the new urban image for their city—in effect, designing it themselves.

The concept of the Citizen's Preference Questionnaire was that it would serve as a tool in gathering a broad-based range of opinions and concerns from which the professionals could determine the priorities of the factors that were dominant in the people's minds with regard to the development of the downtown and the image of the city.

The questions that were asked were general and phrased to encourage additional comments on subject areas not covered. It was made quite clear that this questionnaire was in no way used as, or intended to be, a census or vote-taking, but rather a "guide to issues, not a blueprint for design." The scenario envisioned in the questionnaire format was: "What do people care about?" "What land-use and design approaches seem to match with what people care about?" "Are these things that people care about (and the land uses, activities, and design that are needed to achieve them) good for, and workable in, Newburyport?"

The questionnaire that was printed in the *Daily News* was but one method of gathering public opinion data (radio contact, meetings, work sessions, and interviews were utilized as well), but it appeared to be the most likely method to reach all social, ethnic, occupational, and income groups in that city. This was especially important as the many previous *meetings dealing with the question of the downtown development had tended to attract "the same faces" and the people who were housebound or not given to speaking out in public were excluded from expressing opinions.*

Four hundred and seven questionnaires were collected by the newspaperboys (who were given a bonus to stimulate their enthusiasm, and therefore prompted more returns) over a period of three to four weeks. Once the tabulations were completed, a public meeting was held to share the analysis and decisions in the interpretation of the data.

**A work session
not a bitch session**

Because it was particularly important to receive additional input on the very subjective analytical process of developing the so-called Dominant Factors (preferences on issues of major public concern) from the Citizen Preference Questionnaire, public meetings were set up and run with this partic-

ular task in mind. The interested public was invited to what was to be a work session, as opposed to the "bitch session" that undirected public meetings often dissolve into.

The questionnaire tabulations and additional comments were read aloud along with ECODESIGN's summary analysis of questionnaire results based on our own professional opinion. Specific concerns of interpretation and observation were made by the Newburyport Redevelopment Authority, as well as by the public. This procedure of comments, feedback, and reaction was used in finding the Dominant Factors.

**Preferences on issues of
major concern**

Specific Design and Selection Criteria for selecting a design solution to the urban problems could then be evolved from the Dominant Factors expressing the desires and priorities of those Newburyport citizens who cared enough to become involved in the process.

The Dominant Factors stage thus served as a mixing pot for the physical conditions analysis and the existing data collection, questionnaires, interviews and meetings with government agencies, city consultants, proposed developers, and representative groups and clubs—and the formulation of specific Selection Criteria.

In order to succinctly illustrate this analysis stage, we charted these Dominant Factors with the positive or negative feelings of the community regarding these factors. These Dominant Factors were assigned symbols to express general approval or concern for the various items as expressed by the community.

Dominant Factors
General Selection Criteria

+ a positive reaction or value and a probable beneficial impact from that selection criterion

− a negative reaction, concern, and a possible negative impact to be avoided

Heritage and architectural quality		+
Water orientation	Physical linkage	+
	Visual access	+
Open space	For way to water	+
	For activities and landscape	+
Scale	Intimate feeling in relationship between building	+
	Intimate feeling between people and buildings	+
Pedestrian activity	Ease of circulation within CBD	+
	Access to water cut-off	−
	Ease of access to CBD/desire for bike and pedestrian paths	+
	Safety/security (day and night) through better lighting and good surveillance	+
Vehicular activity	Direct access and parking in CBD	+ / −
	Interference with pedestrians	−
	Interference with fire station	−
	Public transit access to CBD	+
"User" amenities	Greater variety and quality	+
	Public restrooms	+
	Drinking fountains (adult and child-size), shoppers' lockers, minibus, and promenade areas	+
	Protection from extremes of climate (by placement of structures)	+
Seasonality	Balance of land uses to avoid extreme seasonal fluctuations	+
	Specifically attract activities to avoid seasonality	+
Recreation opportunities (water related)	Active (fishing, biking, boating, swimming)	+
	Passive (walking, sitting, cogitating)	+
Housing	Moderate income	+
	Low income	−
	High income	−

Commercial activity	Fast foods and "chains"	−
	Clothing, hardware, food, and household needs	+
	Marketplace area	+
	Hostelry	+
Cultural activity	Performing arts	+
	Museum complex	+
	Cultural events (demonstrations/exhibits/concerts)	+
Transportation	Private auto parking on waterfront	−
	Local mass transit stop depot	+
	Downtown parking but inconspicuous or remote from core	+
	Minibus	+
	Water-based transport (ferries/shuttles)	+
Primary generator land use	Need hotel, inn, museum, pedestrian ways, gourmet store, clothing specialities, department store, hardware	+
Fabric land use	Shops: delicatessen, sporting goods, crafts, gourmet store, clothing specialties, department store, hardware	+
Support land use	Parking and service as required by zoning	+
Municipal finance	Tax revenues	+
	Capital costs	
	Maintenance costs	−
	Relocations	+ / −
	New resident type makes more demands on city services	−−
Social effects	CBD as a "mixing zone"	
	New resident type tends to spend more money	−
	Waterfront based river craft as links to other communities	+
	New job opportunities	+

Building orientations	Massing consistent with city's heritage of spaces and architecture	+
	Buildings perpendicular to Water Street, as with old wharf structures	+
	Buildings blocking views to waterfront	−
Role of redevelopment actors	Newburyport Redevelopment Authority	+
	Friends of the Newburyport Waterfront	−
	City political figures	−
	Taxpayers	+
	Outside consultants and developers	−
Action made	Quick implementation	+
	Contingency planning	+
	Get the job done	+

Technique for comparison of citizens' goals and developer selection criteria

The Dominant Factors stage of the EIS was also intended to compare the local Redevelopment Authority's general criteria for selecting proposals for downtown developers against those criteria expressed in the Citizen's Questionnaire. The Authority's design and selection criteria stated in their *Developers' Handbook* dealt only generally with: 1) how the renewal project should look, 2) how it should work, 3) what kind of activity goes on there, 4) who does what, and 5) when. *However,* 6) precisely how all this could be designed, 7) what would be the result of doing various schemes, 8) what issues took higher priority over others, and most importantly, 9) if there was any basic contradiction inherent in these priorities, were *not* clearly spelled out. In order to compare these general goals and criteria, a number of pertinent issues were structured into the questionnaire which could then be compared directly with the general criteria in the local Authority's *Developers' Handbook*. This allowed the EIS study to establish the acceptance of certain general criteria and then illustrate the need for more specific design and selection criteria by which to judge alternative schemes proposed.

Although the General Selection Criteria for the Newburyport downtown waterfront development issued to proposing developers by the Authority were generally acceptable to all, our findings were that these were not specific enough—they did not give enough real direction to the specific areas of concern. Everyone could easily agree on such general "God and country" goals as: "restoring and preserving the economic, functional, esthetic, symbolic values of the Central Business Area in its association with the Maritime history and the historic growth of the City of Newburyport." But the city was being fragmented and torn apart by their specific interpretations of how these general directives should be carried out. This problem was aggravated by a class conflict that was developing between the goals and objectives of the fast-growing new citizenry (who were drawn to the town's historic character) and the attitudes of the old-time Newburyporters (whose major concern was increasing revenue income).

The disruption of change and social stratification

Through the process described here, we eventually came to understand in fact that this social conflict was in many ways more directly responsible for the total breakdown in understanding and communications than any concrete disagreements over particular plans proposed for the downtown development. Each proposing developer was assumed to be more aligned with either the "new citizens' groups" or the "old timers," based on cocktail party invitations or local gossip, and this began to determine the public's support for one scheme as opposed to another, rather than the developers' actual plan proposal and its physical and economic repercussions for the city.

Also, we found that by acknowledging (instead of ignoring) the existence of personal prejudices and social conflicts, and by admitting their influence and then forcing concentration on specific design issues (which are not really associated with these prejudices)—the many factions of a city can be forced into a dialogue with each other on the real considerations about the downtown plan. Then the citizens can be shown that their different objectives can be resolved in a single, successful compromise scheme.

People on different frequencies—shoppers and merchants

Compromise as a Concept

Gardiner, Maine,* presents another example of how meaningful dialogue can be started between different fractions of a community. The consciousness of both shoppers and merchants was raised by taking on-the-spot surveys and then quoting the people interviewed—but juxtaposing the quotes of the shoppers and the merchants. By locating the exact quote on a downtown map on the spot where it was spoken or to which it referred, and by comparing the different attitudes of merchants and their customers, it became apparent that there was a communications breakdown between the merchant and his shoppers, or at least the merchant's image of himself, his goods, and his store was very different from the shopper's notion of them. This technique also reveals to the average person the sometimes contradictory or exclusive nature of their personal feelings.

Could part of the economic decline in the town be due to the merchants' antiquated merchandising? Did older merchants even know who their new customers were? Did the merchants and the shoppers even agree on how they saw and used Water Street (the main commercial spine)? Did the city government agree with the citizens? Were they protecting the interests of their downtown merchants in the face of the temptations of fast and easy outskirt shopping centers? *Illustrating specific differing opinions and points of view regarding the same issues caused many people to awaken themselves to the need for compromises in arriving at a solution to the downtown's problems.*

*This project received the 1975 *Design and Environment* award for excellence in Environmental Design. ECODESIGN was cited "for its important contribution to the nationwide urban landmark preservation movement."

GARDINER, MAINE
SHOPPERS
SURVEY
COMMENTS

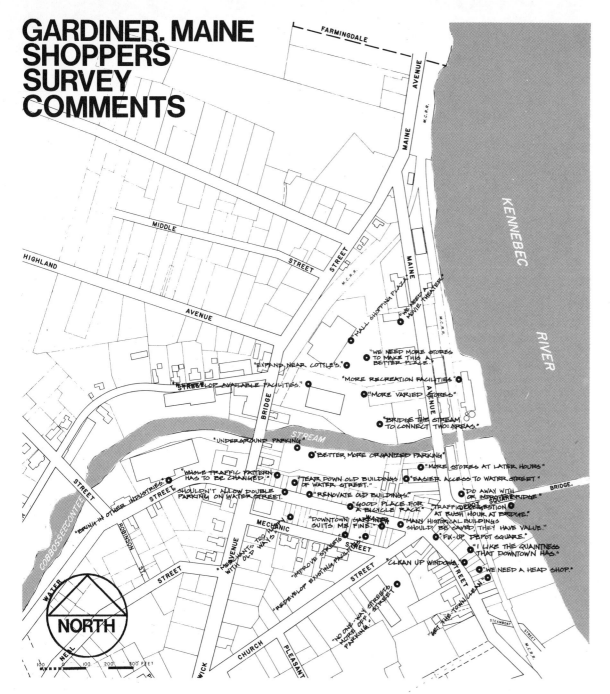

Shoppers Survey Comments.
Gardiner, Maine

GARDINER, MAINE MERCHANTS SURVEY COMMENTS

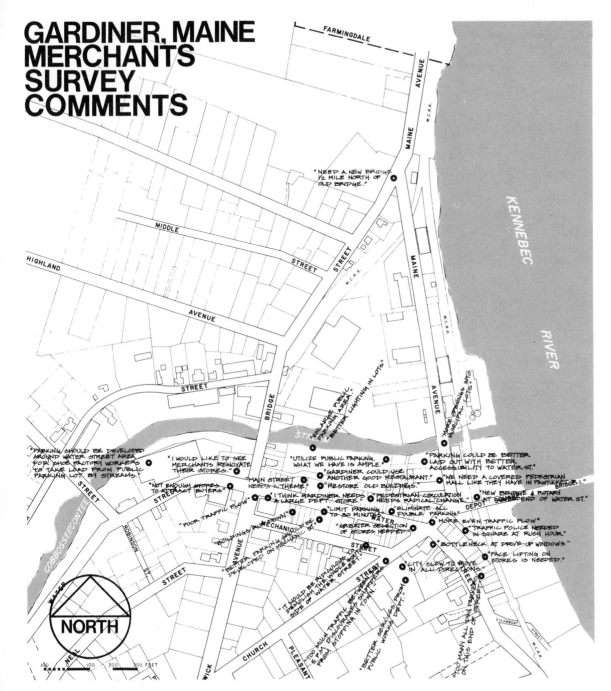

**Merchants Survey
Comments,** Gardiner, Maine.

Compromise then becomes an interesting new concept for both shoppers and merchants to utilize. The merchant, for instance, realizes that his image needs modernizing and his shop needs tidying up, and the shopper realizes that the merchant isn't so happy with the all-day parkers blocking the front of his shop. They begin compromise and through dialogue begin to reveal the design criteria for a plan made up of compromise.

The plan is constructed by urban designers as the professional element on a team that includes the townspeople—for who knows better what the city is and what it should be than the people who live there? It then becomes the professional's job to open the visual door, teach visual literacy, and then to help interpret needs into priorities, and priorities into meaningful concepts.

The Professional versus the Layman

If the townspeople *do* know best, why do they need the professionals? Because what they know best is how they feel, what their desires are for their city or town. *They are the professional's own expert consultants in the specialized field of feelings and emotions, goals and objectives,* but the professional is critically needed to help analyze, interpret, clarify, refine, arbitrate, and implement them.

Are all voices equal?

Are all the townspeople's voices equal? This can become another confrontation as each separate interest group will argue and will claim precedents and special preference based on greater numbers, growing influence, higher motives, and expert knowledge.

These special claims should be confronted directly, not avoided. They can be considered and used for exactly what they are. For example, Cambridge, Massachusetts contains perhaps one of the highest concentrations of experts and professionals, and is known worldwide in the fields of technology and environmental planning. In the Harvard Square area, planning, architecture, and engineering are the strongest nonuniversity professional businesses. Any planning for this area, therefore, has to confront the unique conditions of this special interest group— the planning professional as citizen.

In developing a methodology for assessing the "quality of life" in Harvard Square for the John F. Kennedy Memorial Library Environmental Impact Statement, it was necessary to establish the existing conditions of the amorphous, but important, EIS study area of Quality of Life. It was possible to assemble substantial data concerning the physical and functional components that make up the quality of life, such as: use and user needs, legal restrictions, physical amenities and characteristics, circulation, and service amenities. However, determining the attitudes and personal goals of the existing citizenry by which to judge quality of life was more problematic. In many cases these goals existed on such an exceptional level of intellectual awareness that it was necessary to examine the professional intuitions of the specialized, intensely involved populace who were, in fact, the major percentage of the citizens of the Harvard Square area.

Fears, expectations, and intuitions of people—the beginning of policy

In order to get the total picture into perspective and to determine the proportional intensity of issues, it was necessary to tap, on a more detailed level, those people who were either experts in related fields and/or who cared enough to be intensively involved as policy setters and spokespersons for various interest groups. In reality, then, all people are not equal voices to the extent that they do not care equally.

Therefore, in addition to the more scientific data collection, *there was a need to document the involved public's intuition and gut reaction, because this is the very beginning of policy development—the fears and expectations of people who care enough to get involved.*

For this reason, special data collection sheets were drawn up as a discussion guide for individual interviews with persons having specific knowledge and expertise in the area of urban design/quality of life. These data sheets were neither questionnaires nor polls, and were clearly explained and intended as: 1) a *check* on data collection procedures by

The following is a partial indication of elements that contribute to the existing character of Harvard Square and the project impact area. Please indicate your personal evaluation of a positive or negative contribution of each element, then assume what the Square could be like after project completion. Add verbal qualifications and priorities, as necessary. Priorities may be indicated +++, or ++, or = for no change.

Quality of life documentation, Harvard Square.

EXISTING Indicate + or − or =	"QUALITY OF LIFE" HARVARD SQUARE	AFTER Indicate + or − or =
	Physical Character	
	. Spatial qualities and defintion of area	
	. Size and layout of Square area	
	. Pedestrian scale (is it?)	
	. Pedestrian circulation (works?)	
	. Architectural treatment	
	. Landscape treatment	
	. Building materials	
	. Building colors	
	. Automobile traffic (does it contribute anything to character of Square?)	
	. Public transportation (Square as transportation exchange)	
	. Signage	
	.	
	Land Use Characteristics	
	. Meeting Place	
	. Unique retail and merchandizing	
	. Servicing of basic needs	
	. Quality of housing available	
	. Type and scale of business	
	. Types and scope of restaurants/bars	
	. Types and scope of hostelry	
	. University/town compatibility	
	. % of shoppers from out of city	
	.	
	Circulation	
	. Automobile traffic	
	. Modal mix	
	. Signals and signs	
	. Direction	
	. Public transportation	
	.	
	Natural and Historic Resources	
	. Recreational resources of river (assume access)	
	. Park system	
	. Sycamore/English Plane trees	
	. Air	
	. Noise	
	. Water	
	. Historic districts and sites	
	. Historic visitors' sites	
	. Existing museums and attractions	
	. Cultural resources of University	
	. Use of river banks	
	. Use of Common	
	.	
	Life Style and Values	
	. Activity Types and Levels	
	. Geographic origin of visitors	
	. Social stratification	
	. Nationality and ethnic mix	
	. Educational mix	
	. Age distribution	
	. Tourism to Harvard and historic sites	
	. Old resident types	
	. New resident types	
	. Street people activity	
	. Demographic trends	
	. Jobs available	

knowledgeable parties, 2) an aid in assigning *priorities* to the many community concerns, which were well documented by the media and the interest group memoranda, 3) a guide in determining the *range* and *intensity* of attitudes toward various alternatives and remedial actions that have been proposed.

Different types of information

Several different types of information were requested for sampling along these lines:

☐

Personal information including profession, sex, and organization membership, was requested not to infringe upon civil liberties, but to see how homogeneous or heterogeneous the impact and involvement was.

☐

What, to you, are the key issues relating to the _____ project?

☐

Which of the following statements most closely approximates your attitude with regard to the proposed project? Rank by number, if more than one applies. (The attitudinal paragraph statements to be checked were compiled from citizen reaction comments already expressed in news media.)

☐

Toward what kind or extent of development do you think the area is headed without the project? Give comparable development examples, if appropriate.

☐

Viable alternative uses for the proposed site might be (relate your attitude, preference, and "highest and best use")

Park/Recreation
_____

Housing   Income: high/medium/low

	Density: high/medium/low
Commercial	Density: high/medium/low
Institutional/University	Density: high/medium/low
Mixed Use	Density: high/medium/low
Other	

☐
In your opinion viable alternative sites for the project are _____ . Why?

☐
Which best indicates your identification with the Impact Study Area? I am:

____ Resident/Owner ____ years
____ Landowner/Landlord ____ years
____ Resident/Tenant ____ years
____ Resident/Student ____ years
____ Work in area ____ years
____ Area Merchant ____ years
____ Area Businessperson ____ years
____ University ____ years
____ Nonresident ____ years
____ Other ____ years

☐
What physical or program ideas do you have or have you heard that might minimize possible adverse impacts or maximize beneficial impacts (i.e, concepts to relieve pedestrian congestion, retain unique retail, improve physical environment, zoning controls, etc.)?

☐
The following remedial actions and proposals have been collected from news media and other data sources. Please indicate your attitudes and intuitions as positive (+) or negative (−).

Character of the area

☐
Finally, a very subjective appraisal of specific elements which the respondents felt contributed positively or negatively to making up the existing character of the area or the existing quality of life. To the same elements the respondents expressed their fears or anticipations after the completion of the proposed project.

Although this very extensive and specifically directed survey was successful in obtaining intelligent, knowledgable, and quantifiable information from the involved professionals in the area, the accumulation of subjective, emotional response was still the most telling, as can be seen in the "collage statements" assembled in response to likes and dislikes in Harvard Square, cited from all the questionnaires gathered by both ECODESIGN and community interest groups:

What do you like about Harvard Square? "The activity; universality; internationality; people; entertainment; human scale; vitality; compactness; access to mass transit; culture and educational opportunities; well-rounded environment; alive; cosmopolitan; small-town atmosphere; small, cozy coffee shops and restaurants; people walking; sidewalk peddlers; concerts; intellectual atmosphere; sophisticated specialty shops; history; architecture; ebullient human life; a micro-metropolis; an urban village; large variety of stores; facilities; bookstores; browsing unhurriedly; the human social traffic; one-of-a-kind shops; identity; not homogenized; unselfconsciousness; pedestrian scale; chance encounters with friends; stimulating and exciting place to live, eat and work; can bike; shops concerned with their customers; friendly; freedom; a perpetual carnival; intercultural; informal; goods reflect my tastes; and

The city is dead, finished as a living organism.
Panorama of a devastated city from the film "Earthquake," 1974.

An archaic, limping system

like a village; balanced diversity between: activity and quieter spots, strangers and old friends, luxurious stores and little holes in the wall, stuffy but well-kept campus buildings, scruffy but alive street people, very established things and all types of new growth and change, transients and old time residents.''

What do you dislike about Harvard Square? ''The filth; pedestrian congestion; traffic; smugness; expensive; jaywalking; street vendors; panhandling; increase of big franchise stores and restaurants; lack of enforcement of traffic laws; pickpockets; shoplifters; pushers; vulgar behavior; lack of security; parking; too few areas for 'loiterer'; dogs; lack of planning; hippies; ugliness; fast-food places; touristy look; smell; not enough trees and benches to sit on; Kennedy Library idea; tourists; lousy common; everything and nothing; and narrow sidewalks.''

Some Recurring Complaints

There are no easy answers to the problems of urban development raised in a dialogue with a city. Although many professionals consider the so-called urban problems to be totally negative, people from other countries sometimes aspire to the very things our own professionals find repugnant. The most obvious example, of course, is large-scale highway programs and vast urban renewal in all sections of cities. There has always been a tendency in the less developed countries to model their development after a US pattern. Many of the urban problems that we do understand, which are obvious to us and are also recurring, are identifiable and quantifiable. They continue to exist in this country, and also exist in foreign countries.

There is not as yet a single document that fully outlines both the positive and negative aspects of the urban development in the United States that would share our US experience with others and amongst ourselves. A document that speaks to these points in a truly interdisciplinary manner (synthesis) would be a major step both in communicating this urban knowledge to foreign friends and in gaining reactions. This would be most useful in terms of truly understanding our direction, much in the same objective way as Alexis de Tocqueville in his *Democracy in America* was able to give an arm's length objective analysis of where the United States was heading many years ago.

It is easy for citizens in any country, under any political system, to complain. and it is certainly psychologically relieving for them to complain—the state of the urban environment gives citizens the grandest opportunity for such psychological release. Yet, the actual fact is that the complaints are justifiable, there is administratively or economically little one can do to ameliorate the problems and the desire for change and improvement is usually shared by everyone—politicians, professionals, and citizens alike.

Complaints

General environmental complaints in urban America continue to be:

Abandoned automobiles. Traffic jams, noise, air pollution, esthetics, and all the other well-voiced negatives about cars have been expressed. The newest and most recent phenomenon is that of the abandoned vehicle in large urban centers. More and more frequently we see figures rising into the hundreds of thousands of vehicles left as rusting, stripped hulks on the thoroughfares of great cities.

Air pollution. Whether it is visible smog or invisible, complaints have generated Environmental Protection Agency air monitoring stations across the country to test for toxic elements (hydrocarbons).

Air traffic noise. Flight patterns and departure/arrival procedures have been altered in recent years over urbanized districts. However, although noise abatement procedures and laws are generally enforced, the net effect of air traffic noise has not decreased by a noticeable percentage.

Pigeon control. The few city dwellers who feed pigeons in parks are outweighed by the millions who find them distasteful—their rapidly increasing numbers, their excrement and filth, and the general nuisance they cause.

Rodent/poison control. Every urbanized area has a twofold serious problem with rats, mice, and other rodents and insects, but also with rodent poison control as a whole separate complaint. Tangential to that complaint is the lead paint poisoning of many young ghetto and middle-class children. The whole issue of control and education related to such unnecessary trauma is mentioned here.

Sanitation. The collection, processing, recycling, and disposal of domestic, commercial, and industrial wastes only really bothers people when there is a Sanitation Department strike. The rest of the time we have learned to live with dented ashcans lying on their sides with the adjacent gutter littered with used Kleenexes and dog manure.

Street and pothole repair—Endless repairs, endless problems—unnecessary street widenings made, necessary street widenings never undertaken.

Miscellaneous general complaints include:

Street lights. Not enough lumens, too few, too high, poor spacing, too tall and inhuman in scale, none at all.

Traffic lights. Not sequenced correctly, wrongly placed, ambiguous directions, need for.

Trees. Removal of dead trees, not groomed correctly, not enough, blocks views, too close to roadway, disease spreading ("Yellowing Palms" in Florida; "Dutch Elm" in New England).

Vacant lots/buildings. Vandalism, rubble, rubbish, rape.

Not to mention crime in general, poverty, and other complaints the reader has on his own private "gripe list."

Conflicting image and goals of its citizens in that some may think of the city as a sleek new place for industrial growth and redevelopment, and others may want to reinforce the 1860s Civil War period image and rehabilitate.

Transportation systems. In some cases a rapid transit system or a PRT system may be the best possible solution to many of the particular city's problems, but the U.S. Department of Transportation may have precluded that option by providing funds for improving bus service only and the citizens may not be "educated" to the benefits of any public transportation systems.

Economic Blight in Downtown Areas. All the best shops and department stores have already been relocated or are moving to the suburbs, and half the stores are empty and are becoming eyesores.

Social Stratification of Remaining Population. Quite obviously the people of upper and middle social classes are fleeing the inner city for good reason: city taxes are high and "undesirables" are moving in and not pulling their share of the load, thus the schools are getting dangerous, quality of education is suffering, and the cycle continues to escalate the exodus to the suburbs and exurbs.

The City is Dead, Finished as a Living Organism

It has been said that today the city is dead, finished as a living organism, and no longer economically viable in a culture whose demands are so complex that the services needed to support urban life are impossibly expensive. This is definitely a fact if we look at the costs of creating a new town. The act of creating a new city is through the destruction of a natural environment by asphalting over the earth like a tablecloth and then placing heavy loads of concrete, steel, and glass on it, so that it can generate death-spewing chemicals and pollutants on its inhabitants.

One can also argue that the costs of rehabilitating an archaic, limping, infrastructural system may exceed new systems, but alas, that argument has been dissipated by the energy crisis, inflation, labor costs, and more importantly, the subconscious drift toward an appreciation of our heritage.

The New Clergy are Urbanists

These classic confrontations, this sensitivity to ecology, this new age of consciousness-raising, this post-Nixon era has created a new clergy. Urbanists are the new clergy, speaking in their amplified roles of saviours of the old cities, and attempting, wherever an audience is ready to listen, to persuade planning boards, civic associations, professionals, community groups and the lay public of their message.

The successes are limited, but are piling up and gaining more attention. The people with limited technical background are becoming experts.

What of the city? The city is saved if it can be promoted correctly. One must turn to an analysis of the urban fabric, diagnose the urban functions, repair the urban frame, mend the urban fabric, unclog the urban systems and find some raison d'être for the combined effort that will bring together these components: "sectionalism; private and corporate greed; religion; tradition; class distinction; political factions; labor unions; foreign population; reformers; welfarers; civic, commercial, and social organizations; woman suffrage; native prejudice; indifference; and technical bias—all play their part in the life of the city. These must be blended into a harmonious whole." *

*Walter D. Moody, *What of the City?* Chicago, Illinois: A. C. McClurg and Co., 1919, 441 pp.

Whiz bang quick city.
Ecologists, farmers, planners, musicians, craftsmen, architects . . . coming together to build a temporary city in the woods, in one day.

WHIZ BANG QUICK CITY 2

A TEMPORARY COMMUNITY BUILT IN THE WOODS, IN ONE DAY, BY PEOPLE INTERESTED IN EXCHANGING NEW IDEAS AND REDESIGNING THEIR ENVIRONMENTS.

ECOLOGISTS FARMERS PLANNERS MUSICIANS CRAFTSMEN DO-IT-YOURSELFERS ARCHITECTS COMMUNE PEOPLE FILM MAKERS VIDEO PEOPLE ARTISTS

MAY 26th to JUNE 9th NEAR WOODSTOCK, N. Y.   LET US KNOW IF YOUR COMING   WBQC CITIZENS 33 UNION SQUARE WEST N.Y.C.   10001

5

The Process and the Prototypes

Our life is frittered away by detail . . .
SIMPLIFY, SIMPLIFY!

—Henry David Thoreau

Simplification is advice easier to give than to achieve because it requires total comprehension or it will lead inevitably to inaccuracies and oversights. The details must be present, be understood, and then simplified. Simplifying a complex process is quite different from starting off with a simplistic notion.

A complex intellectual principle is best appreciated in its most refined terms when it is relegated to a simple formula or a clear diagram. By the same token, diverse information is best understood when it is simplified to its basic system, which can then be analyzed for breaks in the process.

Another aspect of simplification is the essence of living in any society—and having a basic trust in that society. Trust, on the other hand, is based on the capacity to predict and to interpret the behavior of others. But in our rapidly changing society, the level of predictability in social behavior falls with the rising complexities of life and the ever-increasing lack of trust in corporations, in institutions, and in governments and legal procedures.

The Process: Planning with Environmental Assessment

We have tried to develop a new technique that would be a means of establishing trust and under-standing in the planning process through simplified concepts. It is a systematic technique, a process that has begun to evolve out of our execution of many complex revitalization reports, downtown plans, and environmental impact studies. It can be simplified to a flow diagram, but the important components are present and clarified by Tasks. Each task, which must be performed to complete the process, has a sequence, an action, a product,

and components, and considerations that make up the Task. The Tasks occur in overlapping order and actively integrate public participation into each stage of priority and criteria development.

106

THE PROCESS: DESIGNING WITH ENVIRONMENTAL ASSESSMENT

TASKS:

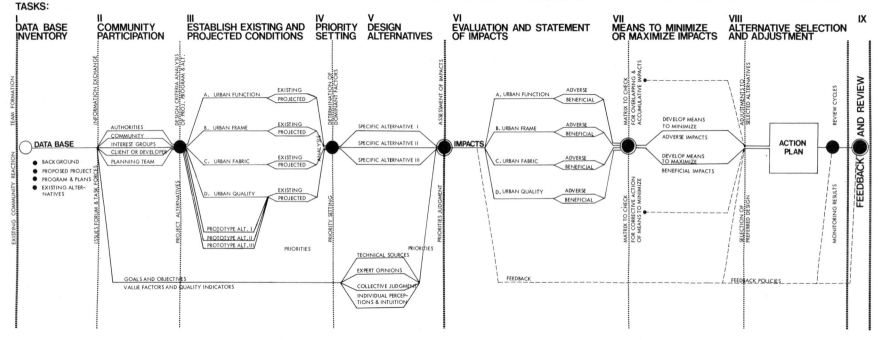

I DATA BASE INVENTORY

II COMMUNITY PARTICIPATION

III ESTABLISH EXISTING AND PROJECTED CONDITIONS

IV PRIORITY SETTING

V DESIGN ALTERNATIVES

VI EVALUATION AND STATEMENT OF IMPACTS

VII MEANS TO MINIMIZE OR MAXIMIZE IMPACTS

VIII ALTERNATIVE SELECTION AND ADJUSTMENT

IX

Urban design is, or should
be, the process of designing
with environmental
assessment.

Outline of Component Tasks

Task I
Data Base Inventory

General description of the project
—History, chronology, and statistical base
—Purpose and design criteria
—Proposed program and plans
Description of project areas
—Physical environment
—Socioeconomic environment

Task II
Community Participation and Reaction

Methods of citizen participation
Information from community
Information to community
Modes
—Hearings and meetings
—Radio/TV/newspaper
—Questionnaires
—Interview
—Workshops
—Others
The appropriate uses, advantages, and disadvantages
  of various methods and modes—groups reached
Community involvement necessary to discern
—Mutuality of goals & user needs
—Dominant factors
—Priorities of issue
—Alternatives proposed or favored

Task III
Establishing Existing Conditions and Analyzing Impacts of Projected Conditions

Urban Functions
—Existing conditions
—Projected conditions
Urban Frame
—Existing conditions
—Projected conditions
Urban Fabric
—Existing conditions
—Projected conditions

Urban Quality of Life
—Existing conditions
—Projected conditions

Task IV
The Establishing of Priorities Through Value Factors in Order to Evaluate Alternatives

Establishing quality indicators for conditions described
  above
—Urban design quality indicators (sources of value factors)
—Socioeconomic environment quality indicators (sources
  of value factors)

Task V
Design Alternatives
Schemes/Projects Alternatives

Presenting, comparing, and evaluating alternative schemes
Project physical program and plan

Task VI
Stating Impacts & Developing Means to Minimize Adverse or Maximize Beneficial Effects

Impact areas include:
—Response to goals & objectives
—Responsibility, cooperation, and communication
—Project physical program & plans
—Project operation program & use
—Urban function, frame, and fabric
—Urban quality of life components
Overlapping impacts
Adverse impacts & means to minimize
Beneficial impacts & means to maximize

Task VII
Adjustments and Alternatives to Establish a Final Action Plan

Task VIII
Review and Feedback

Management of assessment and review process
—Assessment—review cycles with agencies & community
  constituents
—Monitoring interim results—testing by both professional
  analysis and user review
Feedback into design & funding decisions & stages
Feedback into local environmental inventories, plans, values
—Creation of local environmental base data for future use

Within each simplified Task category the complexity of considerations increases. Just within Task III—Urban Function, Urban Frame, Urban Fabric, and Urban Quality of Life—there are myriad possibilities in describing the components and concerns of a city. Besides, what is an urban frame? Like a living body, the city includes a skeleton or a frame and several separate circulation systems. The city, too, includes a nervous system, which causes various parts to function and behave in particular ways. There is also the flesh or the fabric of a city, and there is the spirit—a quality of life about it that makes it special and individual.

With each part there are particular concerns. We recently outlined these elements for the US Department of Housing and Urban Development. This general Urban and Rural Design Checklist, which was developed as an aid in assessing and classifying conditions of urban areas, has also been keyed and numbered for use in cataloging an Urban Studies Library. For example:

B	urban frame	a	collection
408	infrastructure solid waste	01	1st book in this category
		ECS	country or state

Table 1
A Checklist of Considerations in Assessing
Urban Function, Urban Frame, and Urban Fabric

A   **Urban Functions**

A100   **Image goals**

A101   Goals & objectives
A102   General criteria
A103   Problems & potentials/trends & tendencies
A104   Project organization & methodology
A105   Character of environment: physical & spiritual
A106   Government & laws
A107   Regional context
A108   International relations

A200   **Social functions**

A201   Character of community
A202   Demographic background & change
A203   Regional & local projections
A204   Lifestyle/user needs
A205   Social stratification/grouping
A206   Values, problems, and potentials
A207   Worker/Resident/Visitor interface
A208   Displacement, relocation, and migration patterns

A300   **Economic functions**

A301   Regional & local projections
A302   City tax base
A303   Cost to city
A304   Feasibility
A305   Marketability
A306   Employment
A307   Education
A308   Housing
A309   Business—large, small, mail order
A310   Commercial—retail, wholesale
A311   Tourism—commercial, recreational
A312   Agriculture—social factors, food resources
A313   Industry—industrial planning

A400   **Natural and site functions**

A401   Local ecology
A402   Local geology
A403   Topography
A403a   —Slope gradients & contours
A403b   —Special land forms and outcroppings
A403c   —Suitability for development
A404   Soils
A404a   —Composition & depth
A404b   —Characteristics—permeability, loadbearing, cohesiveness
A405   Vegetation
A405a   —Trees/Shrubs
A405b   —Ground cover
A405c   —Climate adaptability & density
A406   Wildlife
A406a   —Marine/Land
A406b   —Native types
A406c   —Effect of development
A407   Hydrology
A407a   —Availability
A407b   —Quality
A407c   —Surface & subsurface
A407d   —Movement, storage, and erosion
A408   Microclimates
A408a   —Sun angles and orientation
A408b   —Wind effects and directions
A408c   —Shade/Shadow
A408d   —Snow/Ice/Frost action
A408e   —Rainfall/Temperature/Humidity
A409   Natural hazards
A409a   —Flood/Fire
A409b   —Hurricane/Storm
A409c   —Tornado
A409d   —Earthquake
A410   Resources
A410a   —Energy
A410b   —Air
A410c   —Water
A410d   —Land/Parks
A410e   —Minerals/Vegetations
A411   Pollution control
A412   Conservation & preservation of natural resources
A413   Maximization of natural resources

A500   **Cultural resources**

A501   History of area
A502   Heritage and legend
A503   Archeological sites
A504   Aesthetics and literature
A505   Museums, historic buildings, universities
A506   Local taste factors
A507   Behavior modes and personal space
A508   Preservation and maximization of cultural resources

A600   **Standards and design for health, safety and security**

A601   Fire safety codes
A602   Building codes—structural, heating, ventilating, air conditioning, electrical, gas, plumbing
A603   Sanitation standards—water, sewage, waste treatment, solid wastes
A604   Transportation standards—highway and traffic engineering, railway, airport
A605   Health and safety standards
A606   Educational standards
A607   Labor standards
A608   Power standards
A609   Environmental standards
A610   Industrial process and equipment standards— welding, pressure vessel, piping

A700   **Citizen reaction**

A701   Defining goals & objectives
A702   Pros versus cons
A703   Public awareness
A704   User needs
      Information networks:
      —Public officials
      —Civic associations
      —Public interest groups
      —Neighborhood groups
      —Newspaper/Magazine/Newsletters
      —Radio/TV/Movie
      —Individuals with specific expertise
      —Other
A705   Interpreting design & selection criteria
A706   Comparison of goals & objectives
A707   Risks & responsibilities

B   **Urban Frame**

B100   **Massing**

B101   Form generators

B102 Gateways & barriers
B103 Centers & nodes
B104 Connectors, lines and interchanges
B105 Density, proportion, scale, and rhythm
B106 Zoning, building heights, floor area ratios
B107 Spatial sequence, views, vistas
B108 Adjacency conditions: hard, soft
B109 Transitional zones & flexibility—directions, signage, and visual pollution
B110 Building prototypes & groupings
B111 Historic massing
B112 Urban frame analysis

B200 Land use

For:
B201 —Residential
B202 —Recreational
B203 —Institutional
B204 —Commercial
B205 —Industrial
B206 —Agricultural
B207 —Mixed Uses
B208 Location, quantity, development units, amenities
B209 Fabric & focus elements
B210 Historic district and sites
B211 Open space system
B212 Land values & availability of types
B213 Economic feasibility
B214 Existing generators
B215 Development patterns & growth
B216 Interaction of above & mixed use proportions

B300 Circulation

B301 Traffic projectors
B302 Modal split and demand
B303 Access patterns, origin and destination patterns
B304 Public transportation—PRT, air networks & capacities
B305 Schedules, signage, and signals
B306 Automobile—primary & secondary networks & capacities
B307 Parking requirements, signage and signals
B308 Pedestrian & bicycle—networks & capacities
B309 Physical facilities—existing and changes
B310 Terminal facilities and stations

B312 Physical form of network—partial, linear, loop, radial
B313 Interface and interaction of above
B314 Regional interface & interaction

B400 Infrastructure

B401 Programs, future demands and goals, alternatives Access to and quality of service facilities for:
B402 —Water—supply, treatment, storage, distribution
B403 —Sewer—collection, treatment, disposal
B404 —Storm/Flood—drainage systems, installation, maintenance
B405 —Electric & gas—production, generation & distribution
B406 —Lighting—streets & highways
B407 —Telephone—facilities and other communications systems
B408 —Solid waste—collection, transport and disposal
B409 —Pollution controls: air, noise, water
B410 —Street amenities: public toilets, benches, bike racks, fountains

B500 Public facilities and services

B501 Programs, future demands & goals, alternatives Access to and quality of facilities for:
B502 —Fire—fire prevention
B503 —Police/Crime prevention
B504 —Emergency/Safety
B505 —Schools/Education
B506 —Health
B507 —Public transportation

C Urban Fabric

C100 Building programs

C101 Goals & capacities
C102 Building use & mixed use
C103 Adjacency diagrams of functions
C104 Square footage/acreage
C105 Number of floors, units, or rooms
C106 Substructures/Foundations
C107 Open space/Site coverage
C108 Architect's plans and procedure

C109 Construction techniques & materials: labor availability
C110 Owner's management policies and phasing
C111 Public facilities & services compatability
C112 Preservation & maximization of resources
C113 Urban function: urban frame fit

C200 Building Treatment

C201 Comparative studies of building types & design
C202 Materials & structure
C203 Texture & color
C204 Proportions & scale
C205 Visibility requirements
C206 Compatibility with existing
C207 Landscaping & siting
C208 Signage & visual pollution controls
C209 Alternatives

C300 Building land use prototypes

C301 Housing
C301a —Site plan type—cluster, P.U.D., site & service, etc.
C301b Unit & building types, plot & plot use
C301c —Programming space for user needs, amenities, schedules & family composition
C301d —Relationship to circulation & utilities systems
C301e —Building system types and selection
C301f —Building design, engineering & phasing
C302 Education and health
C302a —Programming space with educational & health system goals, needs and schedule
C302b —Prototype development for various levels
C302c —Building systems types and selection
C302d —Building design, engineering and phasing of schools, colleges, training centers, hospitals, clinics and other health care and education facilities
C303 Institutional facilities and public uses
C303a —Programming, building design, engineering and phasing
C303b —Governmental administrative areas
C303c —Cultural, symbolic, or civic centers
C303d —Libraries
C303e —Postal buildings
C303f —Fire/Police stations
C303g —Court houses

C304   Retail and commercial facilities
C304a   —Community commercial centers
C304b   —Local convenience services
C304c   —Shopping malls, marketing places and bazaars
C304d   —Regional malls, marketplaces and bazaars
C304e   —Central business centers
C304f   —Office and administrative areas
C304g   —Transient residential accommodations
C304h   —Entertainment
C305   Recreation and entertainment facilities
C305a   —Open space systems—parks and recreation
C305b   —Playgrounds
C305c   —Gymnasiums
C305d   —Tracks
C305e   —Zoos
C305f   —Pools, rinks, courts
C305g   —Arenas and athletic complexes
C305h   —Stadiums
C306   Religion and community organization facilities
C306a   —Religious and community buildings for town
    center and neighborhoods
C307   Industrial facilities
C307a   —Distribution centers
C307b   —Storage facilities
C307c   —Light manufacturing, service industry,
    cottage industry
C307d   —Heavy industries
C308   Agriculture
C308a   —Existing and reversed use
C308b   —Distribution centers
C308c   —Storage facilities
C308d   —Location
C308e   —Water availability
C308f   —Productive capacity
C308g   —Livestock
C308h   —Forestry

D   Urban Quality of Life

D100   The Synthesis, or how the parts come together

**D200   The Composition or mix of all the elements
of consideration above**

D201   Proportion of percentage of elements
D202   Priorities or emphasis of elements

**D300   The Interaction of all the elements
of consideration above**

D301   Degree of mutuality of goals and objectives
D302   Coordination, cooperation
D303   Overlapping of elements
D304   Critical mass
D305   Conflicts and compatability

D400   The Character or image of the total place

D401   Physical and spiritual imageability
D402   Richness and variety to simplicity and clarity
D403   Chaos and insecurity to blandness and boredom

D500   The Well-being of the individual

D501   Physical and psychological
D502   Self-realization
D503   Options for privacy or sociability

D600   The Well-being of social groupings

D601   Physical and psychological
D602   Activity groupings, amenities
D603   Validity of groupings
D604   Purpose and fulfillment
D605   Legal, governmental and social constraints

Developing a Methodology

In theology no one religion holds the key to all knowledge—so it is with planning theories. Planning theories proliferate because planning methodologies tend to evolve in response to specific and unique sets of problems. This is as it should be.

The best planning theory is, in fact, the hybrid

As each urban area and each set of problems is different, a methodology should not be a dogmatic imposition of a monolithic and inflexible thought process. The best planning theory is, in fact, the hybrid—a responsive adaptation of the best characteristics of many proven methods.

A thorough understanding of existing methods and of their strengths and inadequacies is necessary when planning with incremental adaptation, optimization, structural analysis, or other accepted methods. Necessary too, however, is the creative ability of a team to make adjustments or, when necessary, to devise totally new procedures through which to evolve a plan, or better yet, a method of growth and change for an urban area.

The choice of the appropriate set of planning techniques or methods is conditioned upon the prevailing local conditions and needs and upon the available base of statistical data and other information. For example, techniques applicable to highly industrialized countries (where the data base is broad and historically comprehensive) are usually inappropriate to countries or areas that have a less well-developed information system. When needs for basic amenities, such as roads, water, and housing, are pressing and information is lacking, planning must aim at achieving results rapidly without waiting for extensive data.

In the absence of an extensive data base, it is possible to rely on international standards and rules of thumb, comparative or cross-national analysis, and direct analysis augmented by carefully selected sample surveys to produce results with the speed and sensitivity required. Conversely, to spend an inordinate amount of time in less-developed areas or countries assembling the extensive data base normally available to planners in highly developed areas will only delay the realization of results. Due to the unpredictable nature and difficulties of standardizing data gathering and analysis, there are often lengthy delays and, all too frequently, indefinite, misleading, or inconclusive information results when the area being studied is undergoing a rapid transition or change.

To quote from the conclusions and recommendations of the United Nations Group of Experts on Metropolitan Planning and Development:

Statistical and other information concerning the economic, social and physical structure of a metropolitan area and its probable evolution is clearly essential for comprehensive planning. It was appreciated that the relatively less developed areas, in particular, need to develop their statistical and research services and, consequently, augment the supply of trained personnel for this purpose. However, the lack of such adequate services should not preclude a program of immediate action with regard to metropolitan planning and development. It should be possible at the outset to prepare some preliminary plans, at least in schematic form, outlining the more urgent objectives, it being understood

that these would be periodically reviewed and revised as the statistical and research services improve and more precise data and information became available. *

A comprehensive scale technique for action planning

Although the notions of "Action Planning" and "Intermediate Approach to Planning" have been discussed at length on the academic level and in fragementary subject areas, a comprehensive scale technique has not yet been developed. In developing the methodology to guide the speedy preparation of a wide range of immediate action plans (from regional master planning for seven urban areas in Nigeria to downtown action plans for American cities and towns) we have evolved at ECODESIGN a planning process, a method of working, that is flexible in adjusting to varying levels of information and in accommodating a variety of planning strategies. Yet, as a process, it imposes the required planning order and becomes a structure to control the more intuitive planning strategies.

A structure to control the more intuitive planning strategies

This process has been explained in its simplified outline form and diagramed (pp. 106–125) throughout this chapter. However, when applying the procedure to more complex problems we have expanded upon the basic process and incorporated various new and required techniques through a "Methodology Compatibility" inventory analysis.

*Planning of Metropolitan Areas and New Towns, 1969.

Inventory of Techniques

In the section, "Technique: Design Methods," from his book, *Site Planning,* Kevin Lynch gives a thorough inventory of current planning methods. For purposes of explaining the inherent flexibility and versatility of the planning procedure that has been evolved through ECODESIGN's work in urban and rural design, we will expand on this inventory and summarize it, while taking some additional editorial liberties in commenting on each technique's appropriateness and failings for a specific context. This inventory of planning techniques follows:

Incremental Adaptation

Incremental adaptation of solutions previously used (stereotypes) is perhaps the most pervasive and often used technique. It is most useful "when changes in the external situation are slow relative to the pace of environmental decision—when objectives, behavior, technology, motivations, physical settings are all stable. In addition, the available stereotypes must have some reasonable relation to the problem." This is clearly not a methodology appropriate to newly urbanizing or rapidly growing areas.

Optimizing the essential function (linear programming)

Planning must always move constantly between the general and the specific. This method proceeds from the general structure to the specific details of a problem. One abstracts the essential function of an environment, "then imagining a form that will satisfy this general function as well as possible, one then adapts this form to satisy other functions and constraints." This is also called Linear Programming. In the case of essential human needs such as water, roads, or infrastructure, this programming concept provides an important and direct impetus, but one that must be carefully guided.

Optimizing general functions

The "optimizing of functions" is a more valid and secure method when it is used as part of a more comprehensive and general design strategy. In early planning stages it points the way and gives programming and design criteria. "This technique is surely correct in pointing to the importance of purpose or function . . . getting right at the heart of a complex problem wherever there is an obvious dominant function" or functions to be corrected or optimized.

The structure of the problem

This is the most physical of planning approaches and is perhaps at its strongest in the absence of statistical data. It deals primarily with "possibilities inherent in a physical setting," but other aspects of the planning can be dealt with in a physical or spatial manner, such as "political power structure, behavior settings." The strongest advantages in this methodology lie in the reduced time element, the fact that "suggestions for design solutions seem to rise immediately out of the problem," and that the data input need not be in statistical form.

Disaggregation

Disaggregation attempts to confront multiplicity (as opposed to coping with complexities) by zeroing in on a critical problem. Here it is assumed that "multiplicity can be managed if it is divided into many parts." These smaller area units or modules,

however, must be of a size "large enough to deal with the important issues of the plan." The closest analogy is perhaps the English system of town-plan Layouts. Its failure is most marked in developing countries (and previous British colonies) because its success is dependent upon a total planning system. The unit must be a piece fitting into a strong existing master plan for a city and based on nationally accepted behavior criteria for development and intended lifestyle.

Design by behavior settings

This is perhaps one of the most current and innovative techniques. Basically, an area is "divided into relatively independent, stable patterns of customary behavior together with their appropriate physical settings, which are units in time as well as space. These are more logical divisions than purely spatial ones since they follow the grain of the way a place is used." The major failing of this technique would be "single-focus neglect of larger relations"— such as the inter-relations of activity patterns, movement patterns, regional influences, etc. On the other hand, it does open the door to more intuitive techniques in the absence of a standard data base.

Breakdown by criteria

To prepare "ideal plans for each of a number of major purposes (access, diversity, cost maintenance, etc.) "is a similar tactic to optimizing a single function, but it is less superficial in that "correspondences are sought and reinforced and conflicts are avoided (note that to this point, the technique closely approximates the Environmental Impact Statement Process) or compromised on some intuitive basis of weighing to give solutions

that correspond to many criteria at once." The EIS Process, which examines conflicts to be resolved or avoided, is discussed separately in the following section as it is a basic derivation of the methodology that is explained in this chapter.

Design decision branching

This very complete planning method "involves the development of forms appropriate to separate criteria, though only when the criteria are so finely divided that they are no longer verbal generalities, but are operational statements about what characteristic of form is needed in a particular circumstance. . . . Then a tree-like path of design is constructed in which each design decision (verbal or graphic statement) considers the conflicting requirements of only two subdesigns, the more important conflicts being resolved as early as possible. The final result is a solution that reflects the whole branching chain of suboptimizations and compromises."

Although Multiplicity is explicitly dealt with here, in practice the method is inoperative in terms of time and inability to make system-wide reconsiderations in a new light or to change directions midstream. This method is derived from *Notes on Synthesis of Form* by Christopher Alexander. Because of its comprehensiveness, our adapted methodology attempts to amplify and incorporate this aspect.

Focus on means

"Rather than concentrating on objectives or on problems, design may proceed from the opposite end. In such a case it will begin by assembling or imagining possible means (solutions) to see what they are good for.''

This general category also includes other direct, intuitive, but, as yet, non-scientific, unprovable, and thus inconclusive means, such as: 1) community participation, 2) shift in context, time, location, or size, 3) synectics approach, 4) Stanislavski or Socratic methods, 5) analogies, personifications, and other gaming simulation, brainstorming, and team approaches. These are valid paths to invention that need to be solidly integrated into a planning process. This integration, in fact, the fast-tracking of these means into the total process, has been a major intent described in this book and in particular, this chapter.

Another group of techniques that would appropriately be categorized as a ''Focus on Means'' include 6) Experimental prototypes which can either be a physical simulation or a small-scale trial action. These are most useful for small-scale problem solutions and the learning emphasis is on the monitoring and feed-back.

Sieve mapping

Sieve mapping is a simple, straightforward method for aggregating and analyzing complex information patterns in a spatial context. The basic notion is that by simultaneously viewing transparent overlying maps, one is able to see a consensus of separate pieces of information projected onto one final map. This method produces a composite piece of information that is subjective only inasmuch as professional interpretation on particular overlays is necessary.

In the typical sieve mapping-site suitability analysis, a site suitability matrix is developed by overlaying mapping of the following types of survey information: *Soils* (Soil types, erosion, permeability, bearing capacity, shrink-swell or erosion susceptibility); *Geology* (Texture and depth to bedrock, ledge, outcropping, deposits, landforms, orientation of foliation, regional faulting and fractures); *Hydrology* (Streams, flows, flood plains, swales, surficial run-off, subsurface flow, soil yield potential, upland flats, percolation and depth to watertable); *Vegetation* (Hardwoods, softwoods, interspersion, spare-dense, wildlife, visual enclosure, timber resources, open field, forest-edge condition); *Topographic* (Percentage of slope, recommended maximums for industrial, residential, or road development); *Climate* (Warm/cool slopes, air flow, solar orientation)

All these are overlayed as sieve process maps of site features to determine the site suitability in terms of available acreage, frontage, road access, utilities, and acquisition costs. In this way unsuitable areas and most suitable areas for development of particular projects are identified prior to the design of schematic plan alternatives.

This method produces a most important product in the absence of, or in augmenting, a data base in that it aggregates existing physical information into a meaningful and factual form.

Computer-aided design

The use of the computer in storing and sorting data for programming, for displaying this data either verbally or graphically has proved to be a valuable planning tool, which has been discussed in Chapter 2. However, the computer is only useful when there is a large and complete data base with which to work.

When the data is available, the computer can be used by a creative programmer to display the information graphically through special mapping techniques, animated demographic surfaces, planning models, etc., shown on pages 40 through 43. Laborious calculations can be made—such as projected populations and other demographic or financial data, traffic and parking demands—even perspectives can be drawn. However, because all of these functions depend on availability of data base, equipment, and trained personnel, computer-aided techniques cannot be widely utilized in planning in developing areas, nor even in many parts of the United States.

Roots of the Process

The background: environmental impact statement— E.P.A., 1970.

Each of the methods discussed under the Inventory of Techniques have one fault in common: they are not total planning and design processes. They are piecemeal strategies and, as planning methodologies, are prone to error and omissions. Elimination of such omissions, however, was one of the major goals of the ''Environmental Impact Statement Process'' introduced in 1970.

As the result of the critical and previously unprotected environmental and growth policy situations developing in the United States, the National Environmental Policy Act was developed and, in spite of its inherent bureaucratic handicaps, it represents the concept of the most comprehensive, if controversial, new planning procedure to be devised in any country in the past decade. It is innovative because it incorporates several important techniques into a process—the most important of these techniques being the testing of a "what if" series of alternatives against shifts in context.

As the first planning procedure to evolve from a legal act of Congress, the process, of necessity, had to be constantly tested and loopholes closed. By the same token, this very legal raison d'être began, precedent by precedent, to develop an EIS Process that tended to be less human-oriented and more technical-oriented. The legal threat of subjectivity was forcing the emphasis less on planning for human needs and more on quantifiable levels of acceptance of the more scientifically measurable impacts of air, noise, water pollution, traffic, and displacement. The quantifiable impacts that could be measured and then compared to established legal or safe levels of acceptance or non-acceptance (thus avoiding any threat of subjectivity) meshed too easily and inflexibly with the legal structure from which the EIS Guidelines had been generated.

The other major criticism of the EIS Process was that it is wasteful in time, professional energies, and, therefore, money because it was designed to follow, rather than to precede, a proposed plan of development or action.

The process: planning with environmental assessment— ECODESIGN, 1975

Because several of the most important Environmental Impact Statements in the United States

relating to whole urban areas and downtown Master Plans have been undertaken by ECODESIGN, we were asked by Andrew F. Euston, Jr., Urban Design Program Officer, U.S. Department of Housing and Urban Development, to develop an urban design EIS methodology that was responsive to both professional and community critiques of the existing governmental EIS guidelines.

Our report to the U.S. Department of Housing and Urban Development stated that:

The Urban and Rural Planning Process is, or should be, the process of designing with Environmental Assessment. The purpose of the current Environmental Impact Statement process is to identify the impacts of a particular project on the environment and to develop means to minimize adverse impacts and to maximize the beneficial ones. Within these goals, the difference between the Regional and Urban Design Process and the Environmental Impact Statement process is one of timing—the phasing and the additional objective that, if the process is followed in the course of design, the costly, time-consuming needs of Environmental Impact Statement writing after design will be minimized.

Both a Flexible Structure on Which to Plan and a Control Mechanism

The planning methodology developed at ECODESIGN has proved to be a means of establishing broader guidelines for the Environmental Impact Statement process through simplified concepts and a clarified procedure. Although it is a systematic process that evolved out of many complex revitalization reports, downtown plans, and environmental impact

studies, it has been simplified to a Work Flow Diagram, a sequenced Outline of Specific Component Tasks, and a Checklist of Urban and Rural Design Considerations.

Plugging in relevant techniques

The methodology, however, is intended as an adjustable structure that would serve simultaneously as a methodology, a schedule of major milestones, and a format for work tasks enumeration. Most importantly, however, we have attempted to construct a process into which various techniques can be plugged and utilized as appropriate. It is a network through which information and creative planning input would pass. It includes a checklist and channels designed to avoid some of the pitfalls of oversight of the single-focused and isolated techniques described above and to "fast-track" some of the more comprehensive, but overly time-consuming, techniques of disaggregation of problems and sequential generation of alternatives.

The four "Impact Areas" (Urban Function, Urban Frame, Urban Fabric, and Urban Quality) also serve as a calibrator to guard against overemphasis such as of physical versus nonphysical and technical versus human-oriented techniques. The individual techniques described in the preceding inventory can thus find their useful positions within the Impact Areas, depending on the particular planning project needs. For example:
□
Urban Function—(Socioeconomic Functions)
Optimizing of particular functions
Breakdown by criteria
Cause/Effect matrices
Dominant factors grid

115

Shifting of context
Testing of "What if?" alternatives
□

Urban Frame—(Physical Land Use and Form)
Problem structure
Design language and diagrams
Form juxtapositions
Sieve mapping process
Spacial location (with and without computer aid)
□

Urban Fabric—(Area Units and Urban Texture)
Means orientation to specific problems
Suitability: compatibility matrices
Modular development units
Testing of prototypes
□

Urban Quality—(Behavioral Patterns and Preferences)
Matrix to check for corrective actions
Design by behavior settings
Time mapping—operations, schedules, cycles
Brainstorming and gaming techniques
User needs/Community participation techniques

Checks Against Oversights Are Built-in, Cyclical Events

These Impact Areas are set into the process as a work-flow chart so that problems of comprehensiveness, alternatives consideration, and feedback are made *imperative cyclical events;* for example, testing against and assessment of alternatives are recurring tasks that occur both as generic (or prototypical) alternatives and as specified detailed alternatives. The use of generic alternatives in an early stage (for example: Alt. I—Linear Form, Alt. II—Radial Form, Alt. III—Grid Form) becomes a means of fast-tracking and eliminating some time-

consuming aspects of the "tree-like path of design" described in Alexander's *Notes on Synthesis of Form.* The overall intent is that the procedure can be simplified and clarified so as to be understood by a broader professional and lay group while still incorporating the means of dealing with great complexity.

The four Impact Areas are also used as *convenient groupings for the checklist* and for the final *fine-tuning* procedures, as well as the overall evaluation and statement of impacts when adverse and beneficial impacts are identified and means to minimize the adverse impacts or maximize the beneficial are developed. At the impact statement stage the "Matrix to Check for Overlapping and Accumulative Impacts" or the "Matrix to Check for Corrective Action of Means to Minimize" (See page 230) would again be a built-in assurance of comprehensiveness and a guard against causal and accumulative effects and risk-taking.

The ultimate planning procedure must move constantly from the general to the specific, must constantly cycle new information input and feedback into the process; it must insist on the most scientific of proof available, but still allow for and, in fact, insist on the incorporation of intuitive judgments or solutions.

The Prototypes

Functional systems and their prototype components

The elements of consideration involved in contemplating policy programs or plans for the revitalization of cities are overwhelming in their numbers and complex combinations, but the tools for simplification are the systems and their prototypes. With those

tools, it is possible to simplify the component elements of the Urban Functions, Urban Frame, Urban Fabric, and even the Quality of Life to their basic ingredients. When reduced to their isolated and most typical essentials, they can be examined first as an independent system that has a purpose, a method of working (or of not working), and an apparatus. Once the system is made clear, it can be evaluated in terms of its functioning, malfunctioning, overloads, and bad connections—and the problem points can then be identified. Prototypes, on the other hand, are useful because they distill and define the essential concepts.

The basic systems that cause cities to function or not to function as they do range from the theoretical, such as the governmental system, to the physical, such as circulation systems and open space systems.

There are functional systems with both theoretical and physical impacts, such as educational systems, public transportation systems, and the security systems of fire and police.

The infrastructure of a city is dependent on both the management and the physical apparatus of water systems, sewerage and drainage systems, electrical utility systems, and road systems.

116

a. A complete cloverleaf
intersection with pedestrian
overpasses.

b. Diagram of a single kidney
tubule and its blood
vessels. *Villee, C. A.:
BIOLOGY, 6th edition.
Philadelphia, W. B. Saunders
Company, 1972.*

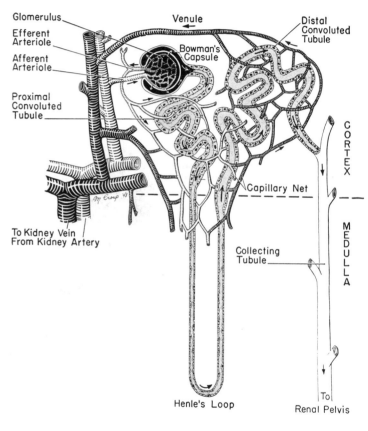

COMPARATIVE VEHICLE DIMENSIONS

SYSTEM	PLAN	ELEVATION	L	W	H
1 AUTOMOBILE			18'-7"	6'-8"	4'-8"
2 MINIBUS			24'-0"	8'-0"	10'-0"
3 BUS (EXPRESS)			45'-0"	8'-0"	11'-0"
4 RAIL RAPID TRANSIT			70'-0"	10'-0"	14'-0"
5 BOEING			15'-6"	6'-8"	8'-9"
6 DASHAVEYOR			18'-0"	6'-0"	7'-6"
7 FORD			N.A.	N.A.	N.A.
8 AIRTRANS			22'-0"	6'-0"	9'-0"
9 MONOCAB			9'-6"	5'-6"	7'-0"
10 STARRCAR			12'-6"	6'-8"	9'-0"
11 TTI			14'-8"	7'-6½"	8'-0"
12 WABCO			24'-3"	7'-6"	10'-8"
13 WESTINGHOUSE			30'-6"	8'-8"	10'-0"

(Plan scale: 0 20 40 60 FEET; Elevation scale: 0 10 20 30 FEET)

a. **Comparative vehicle type.** The typologies or categories of vehicle units within the transportation system.

Component types. Units necessary for a system to operate. All systems, theoretical, physical, or both, are made up of component parts. These parts can be examined independently and in relation to their respective systems for size, efficiency, effectiveness, and economy. They can be compared to comparable components of other systems or sub-systems. The various types of these components may be categorized in a series of physical units necessary to cover a range of conditions such as vehicle types within transportation systems.

b. **Differentiated eggs and sperm.** Vehicles in the sexual reproduction system of the green alga, Oedogonum. *Villee, C. A.: BIOLOGY, 6th edition. Philadelphia, W. B. Saunders Company, 1972.*

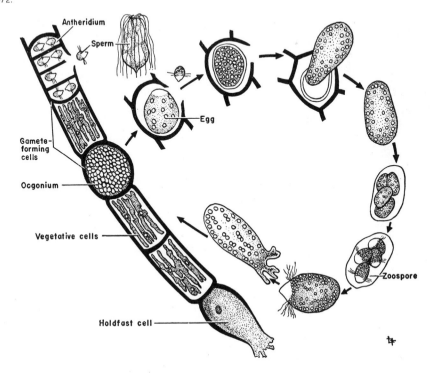

Labels: Antheridium; Sperm; Egg; Gamete-forming cells; Oogonium; Vegetative cells; Zoospore; Holdfast cell

118

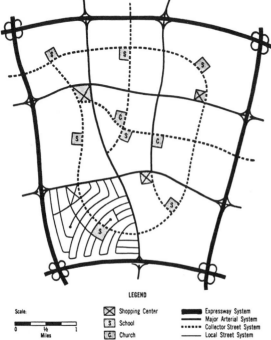

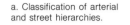
Scale:

0   ½   1
Miles

⊠ Shopping Center
Ⓢ School
Ⓒ Church

■ Expressway System
— Major Arterial System
···· Collector Street System
— Local Street System

a. Classification of arterial
and street hierarchies.

**Classification and
hierarchical order.** Data
overload can only be dealt
with by simplification of
information. For instance,
once components are reduced
to generic types, the number
of prototypes alone may still
be unmanageable. Then the
prototypes can be further
clarified by classifying them
in hierarchical orders that
might represent size or
function.

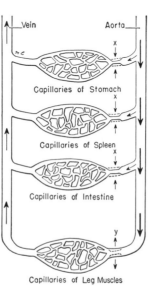

Vein   Aorta

Capillaries of Stomach

Capillaries of Spleen

Capillaries of Intestine

Capillaries of Leg Muscles

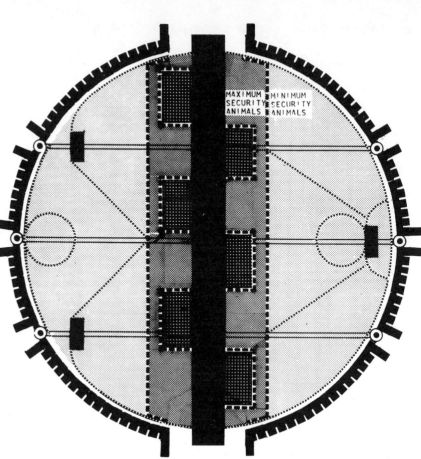

MAXIMUM
SECURITY
ANIMALS

MINIMUM
SECURITY
ANIMALS

a. Conceptual diagram.
Intensity of usage and
control.

b. Diagram of the reactions
of the circulatory system
during exercise. *Villee, C. A.:
BIOLOGY, 6th edition.
Philadelphia, W. B. Saunders
Company, 1972.*

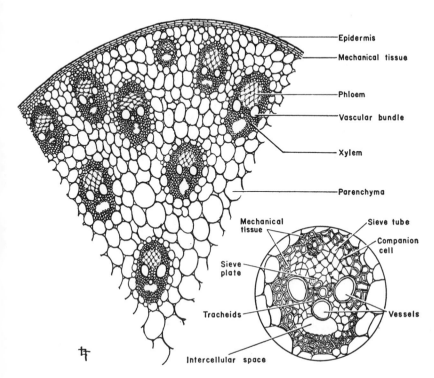

Epidermis

Mechanical tissue

Phloem

Vascular bundle

Xylem

Parenchyma

Mechanical tissue

Sieve tube

Companion cell

Sieve plate

Tracheids

Vessels

Intercellular space

■ NEIGHBORHOOD CENTER
● LOCAL SHOPPING
✛ CHURCH/SYNAGOGUE
▲ PRIMARY SCHOOL
◖ HIGH SCHOOL

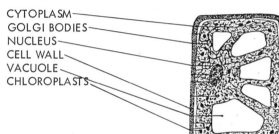

CYTOPLASM
GOLGI BODIES
NUCLEUS
CELL WALL
VACUOLE
CHLOROPLASTS

Conceptual diagram. Using the prototype as a tool and the diagram as an aid in problem solving, even elements such as park facilities or neighborhoods can be expressed simply as prototypes in conceptual diagrams. A prototype diagram can explain a concept or an intended order of things, the component type included, in the relationship of the components, the massing and density of development, and the intensity of usage and control.

b. The structures and functions of a seed plant. *Villee, C. A.: BIOLOGY, 6th edition. Philadelphia, W. B. Saunders Company, 1972.*

Prototypical diagrams.

a. Neighborhood cell. Relationship and function of components within a unit.

b. Diagram of a typical plant cell. *Vilee, C. A.: BIOLOGY, 6th Edition. Philadelphia, W. B. Saunders Company, 1972.*

KEY: PHYSICAL ANALYSIS

NODES / MAJOR		LANDMARKS / MAJOR		VIEWS / VISTAS		SHELTERED PLACE
NODES / MINOR		LANDMARKS / MINOR		GREENSPACE		
PATHS / MAJOR		DISTRICTS W / DESCRIPTION		OPEN SPACE		
PATHS / MINOR		BARRIER W / DESCRIPTION		TRANSITIONAL / SOFT ZONE		
		BRIDGES		DETERIORATING CONDITION		

KEY: CIRCULATION

VEHICULAR	SPECIFIC USE	PEDESTRIAN	RAILROAD	INTERCHANGES
MAJOR ARTERIALS	HEAVY (H)	HEAVY	LINE & STATIONS	NODE
MINOR ARTERIALS	MODERATE (M)	MODERATE	ON GRADE CROSSINGS	
COLLECTOR STREETS	LIGHT (L)	LIGHT	GRADE SEPARATED CROSSINGS	MODES
PARKING	ONE WAY			
	TWO WAY			

KEY: LAND USE / ACTIVITIES

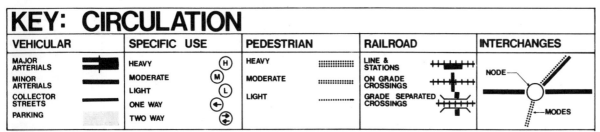

COMMERCIAL	RESIDENTIAL	INSTITUTIONAL / CIVIC	INDUSTRIAL	OPEN SPACE	SPECIFIC LAND USE		
					HEALTH	GOVERNMENT	EDUCATION
CORE OR HIGH DENSITY	HIGH DENSITY	FEDERAL / GOVERNMENT	HEAVY	PARKING	MATERNITY CLINIC (M)	MINISTRY (M)	PRIMARY
SUPPORT OR LOW DENSITY	MEDIUM DENSITY	EDUCATIONAL / RELIGIOUS	LIGHT OR COTTAGE	PUBLIC	GENERAL CLINIC (h)	DIVISION. HDQR. (D) / POST OFFICE (⊠)	SECONDARY (SS) / TRAINING (TS)
MARKET	LOW DENSITY			GREENSPACE	HOSPITAL (H)	LIBRARY (L)	UNIVERSITY (U)
OFFICE				AGRICULTURE		POLICE (P) / FIRE (F) / WATER (W)	RELIGIOUS (C)

A graphic vocabulary.

The Consistent Vocabulary

The need for consistency

Consistency is necessary so that apples can be compared to apples—consistency of approach, consistency in level of detail, in vocabulary of presentation and explanation, and of course, of judgment criteria. Consistency may be (as Oscar Wilde once described it), "the last refuge of the unimaginative" when applied to the design development stage or to the resulting products of synthesis. However, at the analytical stage it represents the *place and need for organization in even the most imaginative mind.* It is the only guarantee against oversights during the process of analyzing and of problem statement.

For example, to judge the effects of any type of urban development action it is necessary to compare conditions before and after that action. Because the aftereffects are not empirically known, it is necessary to determine and state clearly *the conditions of the existing Urban Frame and then to project the impacts of the proposed plan on the Urban Frame.* Because of the inability to scientifically verify the precise impacts, the projection must be based on laboratory-like "control groups" and must include a series of alternatives on which projections can be based. Just as laboratory experiments use "control groups" to simplify the number of causal relationships, so the analysis of existing conditions and the statement of proposed alternatives must simplify by means of diagrams and consistent verbal and graphic vocabulary.

Diagrams and graphic devices are used by urban designers not as "pretty pictures," but as important problem-solving tools with which they can examine and compare some of the important issues of their discipline—such as size, location, identity, intensity, relationship, and process.

In the course of urban design work at ECODESIGN, we have developed a method of graphic analysis and notation. This "graphic vocabulary" is a tool for problem solving that is used in a consistent way to document what we call the Existing Urban Frame of cities and when projecting future Urban Frames based on alternative proposals. Some of this graphic vocabulary is illustrated by the following set of keys.

The key for Physical Analysis deals with the nodes or Activity Generators (major and minor), the paths linking them, the isolated events, the definition of districts, the barriers to movement, development or view, the sequences of views, and the character of areas—hard, soft, and transitional.

The Circulation key documents the hierarchy of streets, the intensity and direction of use, the pedestrian activity, and the nature of intersections and of overlapping of modes.

The Land/Use Activity key is an attempt to translate the idea of an International System of Land Use color keys into black and white. This is important because Land Use indicators should be universally used and color is not often economical for mass publication of reports, proposals, and so on. The key we have developed has been worked within a variety of city situations, and we find that it is flexible and expressive of scale and the intensities of use, and that it utilizes patterns that are compatible and easily differentiated from each other.

Existing and Projected Urban Frames

An Urban Frame Diagram examines the strength and weakness of an environment and how a development or action might fit into that environment. The following series illustrates how our graphic vocabulary is used with this analytical tool to describe and compare an Existing Urban Frame to a Projected Urban Frame of an action to be undertaken.

Physical qualities and areas vulnerable to change become evident as well as cohesive districts or views to be retained and protected, potentials for improvements, or the strengthening of a preferred path or node. The Projected Frame may point up weaknesses in the Urban Frame that must be planned for if uncontrolled effects are to be avoided. These might be different types of pressures resulting from an overabundance of transitional land use or ownership or a sudden increase or change in types of activities carried on in a given district.

The beneficial aspects or problems that analysis of alternatives might illustrate include goal achievements or deficiencies, accessibility versus inaccessibility, land area availability, compatibility of adjacent uses, or barriers to growth. The same vocabulary is then used to demonstrate the existing conditions of an Urban Frame of alternative urban areas for siting the proposed development.

122

Urban frame diagrams. The same graphic vocabulary is used to diagram the consequences of a project on the urban frame. For each action there is an existing and projected diagram.

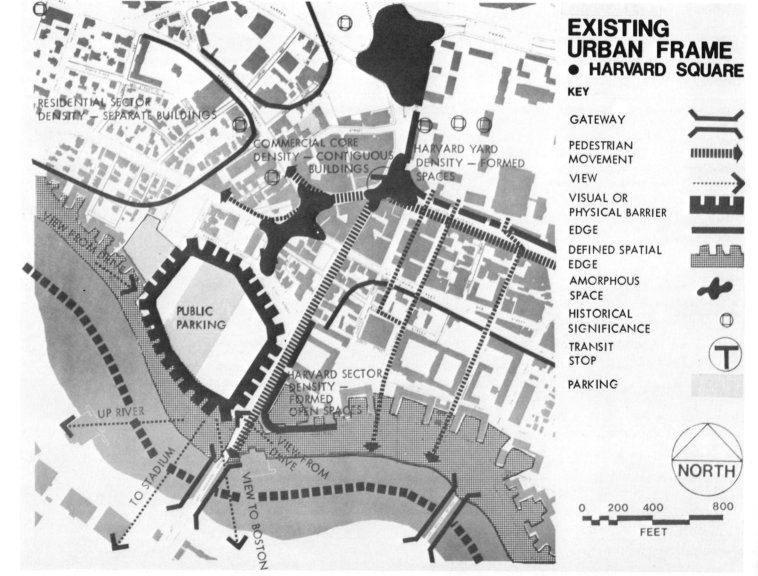

RESIDENTIAL SECTOR DENSITY – SEPARATE BUILDINGS

COMMERCIAL CORE DENSITY – CONTIGUOUS BUILDINGS

HARVARD YARD DENSITY – FORMED SPACES

VIEW FROM DRIVE

PUBLIC PARKING

UP RIVER

TO STADIUM

VIEW FROM DRIVE

VIEW TO BOSTON

HARVARD SECTOR DENSITY – FORMED OPEN SPACES

EXISTING URBAN FRAME
● HARVARD SQUARE

KEY

GATEWAY

PEDESTRIAN MOVEMENT

VIEW

VISUAL OR PHYSICAL BARRIER

EDGE

DEFINED SPATIAL EDGE

AMORPHOUS SPACE

HISTORICAL SIGNIFICANCE

TRANSIT STOP

PARKING

NORTH

0 200 400 800
FEET

123

a. Existing urban frame: Harvard Square

b. Projected urban frame: Harvard Square Excerpted from the preliminary John F. Kennedy Library Draft Environmental Impact Statement as prepared by ECODESIGN.

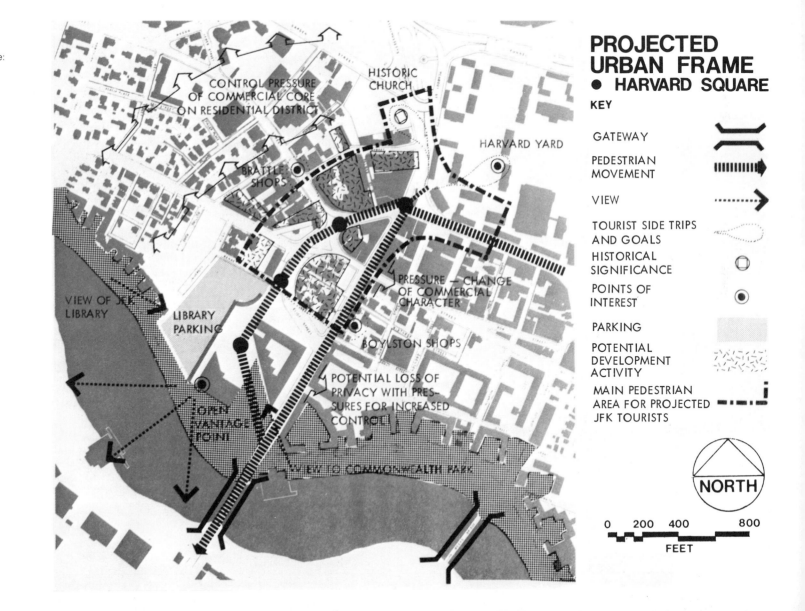

CONTROL PRESSURE OF COMMERCIAL CORE ON RESIDENTIAL DISTRICT

HISTORIC CHURCH

HARVARD YARD

BRATTLE SHOPS

VIEW OF JFK LIBRARY

LIBRARY PARKING

PRESSURE — CHANGE OF COMMERCIAL CHARACTER

BOYLSTON SHOPS

OPEN VANTAGE POINT

POTENTIAL LOSS OF PRIVACY WITH PRESSURES FOR INCREASED CONTROL

VIEW TO COMMONWEALTH PARK

PROJECTED URBAN FRAME
● **HARVARD SQUARE**

KEY

GATEWAY

PEDESTRIAN MOVEMENT

VIEW

TOURIST SIDE TRIPS AND GOALS

HISTORICAL SIGNIFICANCE

POINTS OF INTEREST

PARKING

POTENTIAL DEVELOPMENT ACTIVITY

MAIN PEDESTRIAN AREA FOR PROJECTED JFK TOURISTS

NORTH

0   200   400   800
FEET

124

**Benefits and deficiencies of
alternatives.** Existing urban
frame analysis of alternatives.

a. Charlestown Navy Yard—
Hoosac Pier

b. Watertown

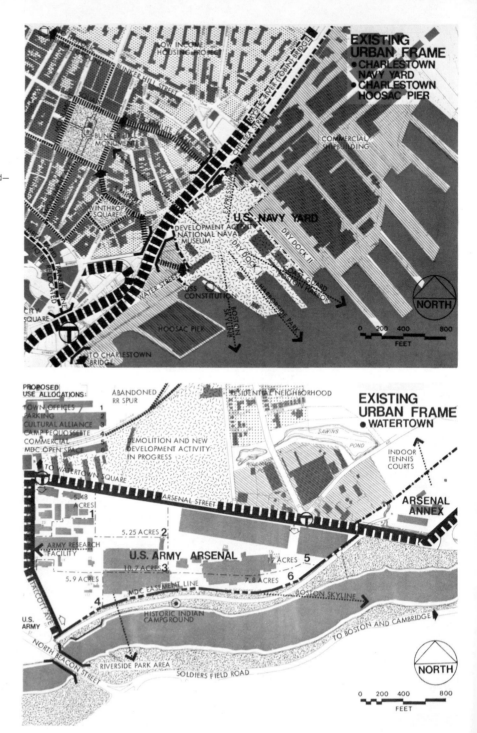

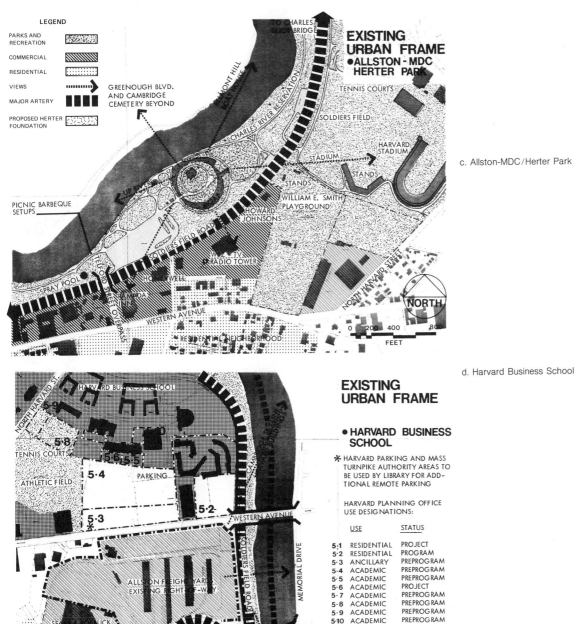

LEGEND

PARKS AND
RECREATION

COMMERCIAL

RESIDENTIAL

VIEWS

MAJOR ARTERY

PROPOSED HERTER
FOUNDATION

**EXISTING
URBAN FRAME**
● ALLSTON - MDC
HERTER PARK

GREENOUGH BLVD.
AND CAMBRIDGE
CEMETERY BEYOND

TENNIS COURTS

SOLDIERS FIELD

HARVARD
STADIUM

STADIUM

STANDS

WILLIAM E. SMITH
PLAYGROUND

HOWARD
JOHNSONS

T.V.
RADIO TOWER

PICNIC BARBEQUE
SETUPS

HONEYWELL

RAMADA

SPRAY POOL

WESTERN AVENUE

RESIDENTIAL NEIGHBORHOOD

CHARLES RIVER RESERVATION

SOLDIERS FIELD ROAD

TELFORD STREET OVERPASS

NORTH HARVARD STREET

BELMONT HILL

BOAT HOUSE

TO CHARLES
ELIOT BRIDGE

NORTH

0   200   400   800
FEET

c. Allston-MDC/Herter Park

d. Harvard Business School

**EXISTING
URBAN FRAME**

● HARVARD BUSINESS
SCHOOL

✱ HARVARD PARKING AND MASS
TURNPIKE AUTHORITY AREAS TO
BE USED BY LIBRARY FOR ADD-
ITIONAL REMOTE PARKING

HARVARD PLANNING OFFICE
USE DESIGNATIONS:

	USE	STATUS
5·1	RESIDENTIAL	PROJECT
5·2	RESIDENTIAL	PROGRAM
5·3	ANCILLARY	PREPROGRAM
5·4	ACADEMIC	PREPROGRAM
5·5	ACADEMIC	PREPROGRAM
5·6	ACADEMIC	PROJECT
5·7	ACADEMIC	PREPROGRAM
5·8	ACADEMIC	PREPROGRAM
5·9	ACADEMIC	PREPROGRAM
5·10	ACADEMIC	PREPROGRAM

NORTH

0   200   400   800
FEET

HARVARD BUSINESS SCHOOL

NORTH HARVARD ST.

TENNIS COURTS

ATHLETIC FIELD

5·9

5·8

5·6   5·5

5·4   PARKING

5·2

5·3

WESTERN AVENUE

CAMBRIDGE
BUILDINGS

SOLDIERS FIELD ROAD

ALLSTON FREIGHT YARD
EXISTING RIGHT-OF-WAY

MEMORIAL DRIVE

SEARS ROEBUCK
WAREHOUSE

RESIDENTIAL
NEIGHBORHOOD

SPUR ACCESS FROM
TURNPIKE

ALLSTON
INTERCHANGE
MASS. TURNPIKE

CAMBRIDGE STREET

RIVER STREET

BOSTON EXIT RAMP

COCA-COLA
PLANT

6

The Diagnosis

Dr. Stockmann:
The source is poisoned, man! Are you mad? We are making our living by retailing filth and corruption! The whole of our flourishing municipal life derives its sustenance from a lie!

Peter Stockmann:
All imagination—or something even worse. The man who can throw out such offensive insinuations about his native town must be an enemy to our community.

—Henrik Ibsen, *An Enemy of the People*

The key to diagnosing or analyzing a city is to think diagrammatically. Once a city is pulled apart and simplified into generalized systems and components, then and only then is it possible to comprehend the existing framework and to better grasp the potential for recycling the respective elements and even the whole.

This is the technique of analyzing urban dynamics. As shown in Chapter 5, The Process and the Prototypes, major forces and events can be represented by consistent graphic symbols—for example, deteriorating force, regenerating activity, focus element, synthesis, barriers—and the interaction of these forces can then be studied. To further illustrate this procedure as a diagnostic technique, we shall draw upon three of our own recent examples—"An Action Plan for Pawtucket, Rhode Island," "A Downtown EIS for Newburyport, Massachusetts," and the "Advanced Urban Transit Technology" study for Denver, Colorado. These studies utilized several tools for diagrammatic analyses of cities:

Urban Diagnosis of a Small Historic Seacoast City (Newburyport, Massachusetts)
☐
The Historic Context
☐
Site Constraints and Historic Building Forms
☐
Water, Wharves, and Public Ways
☐
The Historic Urban Frame

Urban Diagnosis of a Medium-Sized, Highway-Oriented City (Pawtucket, Rhode Island)
☐
Are there Expressway Benefits?

☐
The Lay of the Land
☐
Existing Urban Frame
☐
Impacts of Highway Types
☐
Gestalt Groupings of Specific Land Use
☐
Unique Urban Form and Character of Space

Urban Diagnosis & Orienting a Large City to Mass Transportation (Denver, Colorado)
☐
An Alternative to the Automobile
☐
Denver's Urban Frame and Functions
☐
PRT System Fit—User Impact
☐
PRT Facilities—User Needs
☐
Guideway Selection

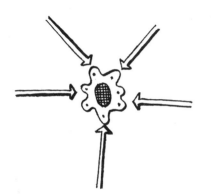

stage 1

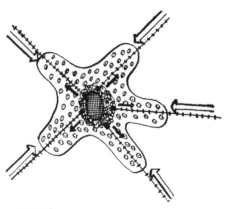

stage 2

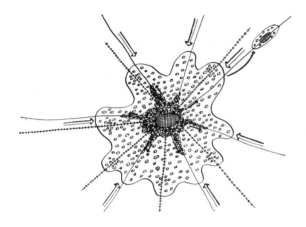

stage 3

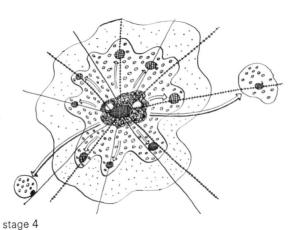

stage 4

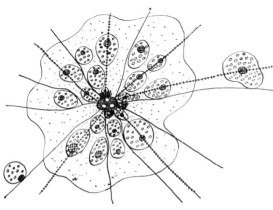

stage 5

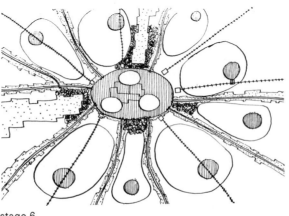

stage 6

Urban diagnosis. The key to analyzing a city is to think diagrammatically.

Stage 1: 1770–1820.
The modern city begins—industrialization as the magnetic impulse.

Stage 2: 1820–1900.
Concentration—some decentralization along railways.

Stage 3: 1900–1939.
Congestion—decay in the inner ring; unplanned decentralization.

Stage 4: 1945–?
Post-war planned decentralization to new and expanded towns. Comprehensive redevelopment of inner areas.

Stage 5: ?–?
The city recreated.

Stage 6: ?–?
The redeveloped center.

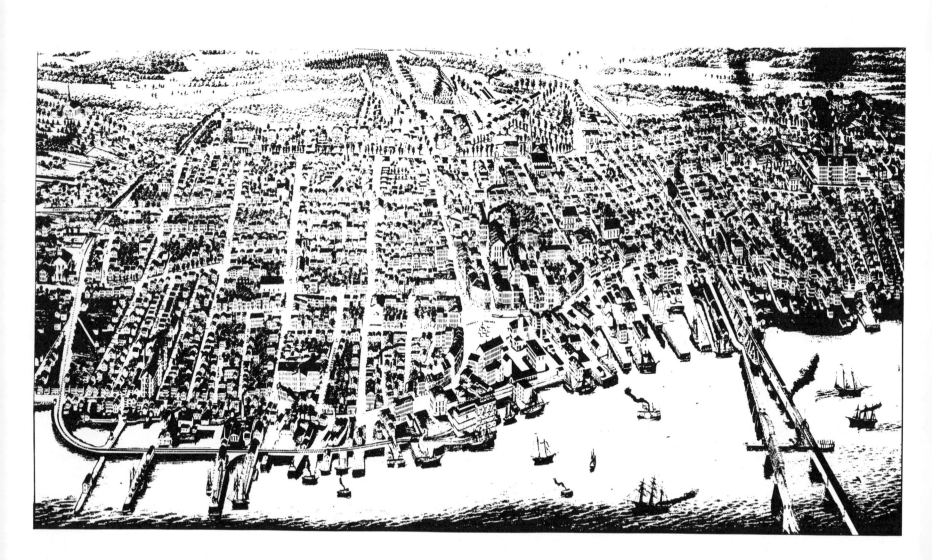

**Newburyport,
Massachusetts, 1880.**

Urban Diagnosis
of a Small Historic
Seacoast City

The Historic Context

What were the initial reasons for a city's settlement? Why did it take its particular course of growth and development through time? These questions can lead to an insight into the most significant events, buildings, and spaces within a city. This kind of appraisal can also be assigned certain values by the community, according to what elements are worth more or less than others to the community and to outsiders as well.

Newburyport as a case in point revealed many exciting facts from such an analysis and the historic context of the city certainly will play a most significant role in Newburyport's future.

Permanent settlement in the Newburyport area began around 1635, with Newburyport being established as an independent town in 1764. An important colonial port, it thrived as a center for trade, fishing, and shipbuilding into the nineteenth century. The early settlement had grown around a system of public ways that connected the wharves on the waterfront with the arterial thoroughfares.

The height of Newburyport's economic prowess occurred between the Revolution and the War of 1812, when the city led the country's shipbuilders in clipper ship construction, and was one of the four largest cities in America.

A disastrous fire occurred in 1811, destroying 16½ acres of the vital waterfront properties. Because Newburyport was still a major port at that time, however, the recovery was quick and resulted in an architecturally unified downtown in the Federalist

style. This was a most important point in time to the morphologic development of Newburyport.

Site Constraints and Historic Building Forms

The next two pages are an analysis of the physical properties of the old town plan of Newburyport, Massachusetts and the qualities of movement, scale, vistas, and space sequence it produced.

Simultaneous with these studies of the old town are considerations of existing site conditions such as sun and wind orientation, flooding precedents, and the existing land use presently adjacent to a cleared series of future waterfront development parcels.

The purpose of these diagrams is to determine what aspects of the layout of the old town plan were inherent to its sense of place and its special character and what aspects of that old plan should be retained in a new plan. Just as the new buildings should be compatible with the specific scale and rhythms of the remaining Federal-style buildings of the historic districts, so the scale and rhythms of the old open spaces and arrangement of streets should be reflected in a new plan.

Page 130 shows an approximation of historic building forms, taken from the Isometric of Newburyport in 1880.

Water, Wharves, and Public Ways

Beginning with a main artery parallel to the water, the wharves are extended perpendicular toward the water and that waterside district becomes the maritime industry (p. 131, right). Rights of way are

maintained to give public access to the wharves and to the water (p. 131). The perpendicular massing is typical of the waterside of the main artery because, as shown in Water Intrusion, the perpendicularity originally related to the wharves, which began right at the original harbor line, and the bulkhead lines were progressively extended. The main artery parallel to the original harbor line was inevitably and logically called "Water Street," and most New England coastal cities possess one.

The landward side of the typical Water Street became intensively and densely used as valuable, prime-frontage commercial property. Newburyport's 1880 massing clearly reflected this characteristic.

The massing and negative space of the old commercial section was compact and intimate, as is still evident on Inn Street. Toward the maritime district the scale of these "human-sized" spaces and the "wayes" widened as they approached the water, opened into the ship berths, and finally into the expanse of the river.

The buildings on the waterfront wharves telescoped from larger to smaller, allowing dock space for loading and other related activities. The wedge-shape, perpendicular massing of these dockside buildings also adjusted to the curve of the main Water Street artery.

At Market Square the main artery (Water—Merrimac Streets) merges with State Street, which connected the Maritime and Commercial section up to the elegant residential district along High Street.

The 1880 Isometric of Old Newburyport (p. 128) shows that Merrimac, State, and Water Streets

The site context.

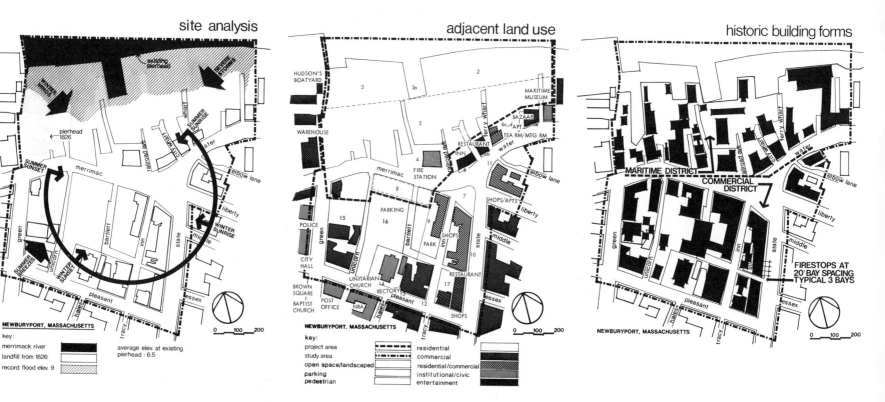

site analysis

HAZARD STORM
existing pierhead
SUMMER SUNRISE
pierhead 1826
SUMMER SUNSET
merrimac
wharf
water
railroad ave
city wharf
elbow lane
WINTER SUNRISE
liberty
bartlett
inn
state
middle
green
SUMMER SHELTER
WINTER SUNSET
unicorn
pleasant
essex
hales
tracy

NEWBURYPORT, MASSACHUSETTS
key:
merrimack river
landfill from 1826
record flood elev. 9
average elev. at existing pierhead : 6.5
0   100   200

adjacent land use

HUDSON'S BOATYARD
2
3
3a
MARITIME MUSEUM
WAREHOUSE
5
BAZAAR
6c, d APT
6e
TEA RM/MTG RM
RESTAURANT INN
6b
water
ferry wharf
merrimac
4
FIRE STATION
railroad ave
6
11
elbow lane
8
7
SHOPS/APTS
liberty
POLICE
15
PARKING
16
bartlett
9
SHOPS
inn
PARK
middle
state
CITY HALL
UNITARIAN CHURCH
unicorn
14
RECTORY 13
pleasant
10
RESTAURANT
17
12
essex
BROWN SQUARE
BAPTIST CHURCH
POST OFFICE
NRA
hales
tracy
SHOPS

NEWBURYPORT, MASSACHUSETTS
key:
project area .... residential
study area .... commercial
open space/landscaped .... residential/commercial
parking .... institutional/civic
pedestrian .... entertainment
0   100   200

historic building forms

MARITIME DISTRICT
COMMERCIAL DISTRICT
green
railroad ave
ferry wharf
water
elbow lane
liberty
unicorn
inn
state
middle
FIRESTOPS AT 20' BAY SPACING TYPICAL 3 BAYS
pleasant
essex
hales
tracy

NEWBURYPORT, MASSACHUSETTS
0   100   200

**Prototype of
urban morphology.**
Site constraints and historic
context.

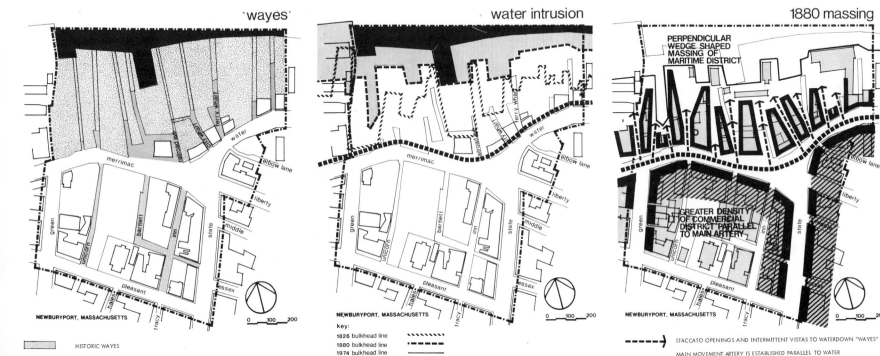

`wayes`

water intrusion

1880 massing

PERPENDICULAR
WEDGE-SHAPED
MASSING OF
MARITIME DISTRICT

GREATER DENSITY
OF COMMERCIAL
DISTRICT PARALLEL
TO MAIN ARTERY

NEWBURYPORT, MASSACHUSETTS

NEWBURYPORT, MASSACHUSETTS

NEWBURYPORT, MASSACHUSETTS

0   100   200

0   100   200

0   100   200

▨ HISTORIC WAYES

▨ FILL FROM ORIGINAL HARBOR LINE

key:
1826 bulkhead line
1880 bulkhead line
1974 bulkhead line
original harbor line

┅┅➤ STACCATO OPENINGS AND INTERMITTENT VISTAS TO WATERDOWN "WAYES"

■■■■■■ MAIN MOVEMENT ARTERY IS ESTABLISHED PARALLEL TO WATER

What constitutes historic urban character? The historic urban frame of an early seaport town revealed a unique scale and rhythm of the old open space plan.

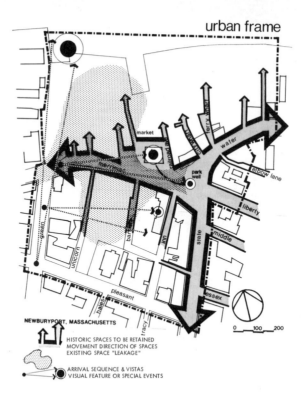

urban frame

NEWBURYPORT, MASSACHUSETTS

HISTORIC SPACES TO BE RETAINED
MOVEMENT DIRECTION OF SPACES
EXISTING SPACE "LEAKAGE"

ARRIVAL SEQUENCE & VISTAS
VISUAL FEATURE OR SPECIAL EVENTS

0 100 200

held their integrity as strong directional spaces—a pinwheel of commercial and maritime activity that widened at its center into Market Square. Frontage on these commercial streets was important retail property and intensely developed as such. The commercial side of Merrimac, in particular, was strongly articulated by three-, four-, and five-story "business houses."

The Historic Urban Frame: What Should be Retained?

The sequence character of space that resulted from this old town plan are expressed in the illustrations on page 130 and page 131. Just as retaining the "wayes" to the waterfront and the perpendicular massing between the main artery and the water retains so much of what was the unique heritage of a New England coastal town plan, so the compact massing along the commercial side of Merrimac Street reinforces this spine of the urban frame. The spatial sequence is thus one of solidity to the landside and staccato-like, intermittent vistas opening toward the water.

Just as the wayes were fingers reaching towards the river, so the water intruded into the maritime district (page 131). Much of this special character of the maritime section has now been lost by continual fill and extension of the bulkhead.

Finally, the Urban Frame diagram expresses the basic space of the old plan which should be retained and reinforced. It also indicates the existing "leakage" of that space due to the clearance of Waterfront Parcels and Parcel 8 (an area for development under question). This space leakage is currently unformed, whereas the original space

(above) was, in spite of its informal organic shape, very controlled space.

In order to retain the special character of this Urban Frame, it was essential to retain the perpendicular building orientation to the waterside of Merrimac Street and the horizontal orientation to the south. This analysis indicates that although a National Advisory Council on Historic Preservation Report was sensitive to the perpendicularity of orientation to the Waterfront, it did not appreciate the fact that it was an element unique to and evolving from the construction of wharves perpendicular to the original harbor line and that this type of perpendicularity did not extend past Merrimac Street. In this respect, the parallel orientation of a Parcel 8 building (parallel to Merrimac) would be consistent and supportive of its original space function—to define the tightness of the main artery before it opens out into the pin-wheel space, the Market Square Center.

Following this analysis of the historic qualities of the city (which was presented in a slide show to the community) and with the aid of the "Waterfront Urban Renewal: Citizens Preference Questionnaire" (See Chapter 4), ECODESIGN combined the desires expressed in the questionnaire with the important elements of the historic plan to be retained to develop a number of Selection Criteria. These criteria were thus a joint effort of the consultants' Urban Design expertise in urban morphology, and the citizens' expertise with respect to needs and desires and input from city officials.

The criteria of specific goals, economics, massing, land use, and circulation could then be charted and used to judge specific responses (or lack of them) to each proposed alternative scheme for downtown development, thus providing a more quantifiable and justifiable mechanism for selection. Degree of responsiveness to each selection criteria by each of seven alternatives was indicated in key below.

Aspects of each alternative which do not respond to Image and Goals and Massing of each Alternative are indicated by X marks on the comparative plans of the alternative proposals.

● Positive impact—compatibility with citizens goals, needs and good planning procedure, with tendency toward successful and defined conclusion of the project.

○ Negative impact on potential benefit—need or goal totally lacking expression or recognition in this plan.

N.S.
Not shown in Developers Proposed Material

⊜ Moderately positive impact— some effort made to address issue or maximize resource but could be better or more clearly done.

N.A.
Not applicable, out of range of development capabilities to show or implement.

Selection Criteria Charts.
Many schemes had been proposed for the Newburyport urban renewal area. For an urban design EIS, these had to be evaluated according to consistent criteria. Because selection criteria were based on dominant factors developed from the citizens' questionnaire, they responded to the particular impact areas important in this project.

image goals

Preserve heritage of old New England seaport city by:

Retaining massing concepts of New England coastal town plan

WATER
MARITIME INDUSTRY — WATERWAYS
MAIN ARTERY (Water Street)
COMMERCIAL SECTOR
Therefore, selected plan should:

SELECTION CRITERIA	Alternate I Park/No Action	Alternate II	Alternate III	Alternate IV	Alternate V	Alternate VI	Alternate VII EIS/Preferred Scheme
- retain massing perpendicular to river on water side of main artery (Merrimac-Water Sts)	○	○	○	●	○	⊖	●
- retain compact parallel massing (Parcel 8) defining the commercial land side of main artery	○	●	●	●	●	●	●
- retain historic rights-of-way and perpendicular massing to water	●	○	⊖	⊖	●	⊖	●
Preserve historic architectural structures with new structures in harmony and scale with old	⊖	○	●	●	⊖	●	●
Maximize water orientation by drawing public to water's edge by system of spaces, pedestrian walks and waterfront attractions	●	○	○	●	⊖	●	●
Maximize water orientation by encouraging waterside activities, clearly open to public -- docking facilities, boats, boatrides, launching, fishing, sketching, etc.	⊖	○	○	●	○	●	●
Encourage quality land uses and activities varied and integrated in nature - image of revitalized, bustling "new" downtown waterfront complex	○	○	⊖	●	○	○	●
Substantially increase city tax base, provide new jobs, and maximize economic development through tourism within image goals	○	⊖	⊖	●	⊖	●	●

economics & marketability

SELECTION CRITERIA	Alternate I Park/No Action	Alternate II	Alternate III	Alternate IV	Alternate V	Alternate VI	Alternate VII EIS/Preferred Scheme
Maximize history and heritage as magnet for attraction of commercial support for Newburyport -- retain urban form and character of seaport town	○	○	⊖	●	⊖	○	●
Encourage development of "thriving commercial" in downtown to benefit entire city, as opposed to "luxury waterfront condominium" type project which might bring the "burden" of schoolchildren to the city	○	⊖	○	●	○	●	●
Control extent and design of public open spaces, so as to not diminish potential tax base -- extensive and scattered "park" areas limit availability of prime commercial space and are a maintenance expense to city	○	●	●	○	○	⊖	⊖
Increase property available in waterfront, as this is potentially the city's prime commercial space and tax generator. Fire Station should be moved as it occupies the pivotal point in the center of the site (in most schemes, this was indicated as the main access point). This property is too valuable for non-tax producing uses	○	○	●	⊖	○	○	⊖
Avoid time delays due to citizens' resistance and aggravation by adapting plan to their demands that public still has legal claim to rights of way. These adjustments do not affect the cost projections of the project	●	○	○	○	○	○	●
Land uses should include "activities generators," "identity magnet," "must visit" activities to attract people to the project, such as a popular seafood restaurant, sight-seeing boatrides, a regional flea market, etc.	○	○	●	●	○	●	●
Land uses should also encourage "destination point uses" which would attract visitors year-round, such as hotel/conference center to set the tone of activity	○	○	⊖	●	⊖	●	●
There is a market for basic needs -- food, household goods, services -- for the residents that should be responded to, including new job opportunities	○	●	⊖	⊖	⊖	●	○

massing

134

SELECTION CRITERIA	ALTERNATIVES	Alternate I Park/No Action	Alternate II	Alternate III	Alternate IV	Alternate V	Alternate VI	Alternate VII EIS/Preferred Scheme
Newburyport's place on the Historic Register, as well as the preservation of the atmosphere of an old New England coastal town (which the citizens see as their image goal), is based not on the preservation of individual buildings but on the <u>coherence</u> of the whole -- the sense of space and movement inherent in it. The massing that forms these spaces is analyzed in Figures								
. Urban frame diagram shows the space and movement integral to the Market Square area. It was a veritable "pinwheel" of activity, and it was dependent upon the cross penetration of rights-of-way across the main artery.		○	○	○	●	○	○	●
. 1800's massing diagram shows the importance of retaining the tight dense 2 - 3 story massing of the old valuable commerical properties that once lined the land side of Merrimac Street (now Parcel 8). It clearly defined the land-oriented side of the street and accentuated the spatial effect of widening into Market Square. 2 - 3 story structures should continue between Green and Unicorn to maintain the spatial definition of the downtown hub.		○	⊖	⊖	⊖	⊖	○	●
. 1800's massing articulated the 18' - 20' bays not by a change in the building plane so much as by vertical architectural elements -- column spacing, lintel span, shutter line, etc.		○	●	(NS)	●	●	(NA)	●
. The old 1800's isometric of Newburyport showed the wedge-shaped massing which resulted from the telescoping of buildings toward the water, as they adjust to the curve of Merrimac and maintained a facade parallel to the north side of Merrimac and Water between the rights-of-way.		○	⊖	○	⊖	●	●	●

SELECTION CRITERIA	ALTERNATIVES	Alternate I Park/No Action	Alternate II	Alternate III	Alternate IV	Alternate V	Alternate VI	Alternate VII EIS/Preferred Scheme
. Water intrusion is what gave the old piers and waterfront areas their character as the compact massing of the maritime district opened suddenly onto expanses of water. Only one slip remains of the old, irregular pier line.		○	○	○	●	○	○	●
. Although original buildings were on either side of Bartlett Street opening, it would allow for more flexible and marketable space if the right-of-way in legal question (Bartlett Street) were articulated by breaking the roof line here and allowing a clear opening (no doors) passage of the "way" below.		○	○	●	⊖	○	○	●
. Potential adverse time and citizen reaction impact in the refusal of air rights over the disputed wayes. Minimizing adverse impact by separation of Parcel 8 structure at Bartlett Street.		○	○	○	○	○	○	●
Small retail space exists on project already. Requires some large contigious spaces for flexibility and variety.		○	⊖	○	●	⊖	⊖	●

land use (left)

SELECTION CRITERIA	ALTERNATIVES	Alternate I Park/No Action	Alternate II	Alternate III	Alternate IV	Alternate V	Alternate VI	Alternate VII EIS/Preferred Scheme
The citizens' own assessment of the land use needs of their downtown development correspond fairly closely to the market feasibility indicated by most developers' proposals.								
Their ranking of hotels (often described meaningfully as "inns"), conference centers, cultural/museum attractions, showed a sensitivity to the fact that Newburyport presently lacks the critical mass of a destination, activity, and prime shopping generator, a magnet for visitors. Conference centers, famous seafood restaurant, sidewalk cafe, regional flea market, and boatrides were suggested.		○	●	⊜	●	⊜	●	●
Parks, open space, ways to water, bike paths, ranked high not as land uses for major sections of the site but as the necessary ingredient, a network of atmosphere and activity that would tie the downtown complex together. Because Newburyport is well endowed with inland parks, this citizen preference was interpreted as a demand for waterside open space and pathways, specifically.		●	○	⊜	●	○	○	●
The mix of shops, office space, restaurant/bars, and appropriate parking, were middle ranking and left, in that sense, to the developers' assessment of marketability -- but, residents do want their basic needs, food, household goods, services, public toilets, as well as tourist and specialty shops. Quality of establishments was also stressed.		○	●	●	●	⊜	●	●
Marinas, for a single listed item, showed up as an area of concern as the means by which the waterfront is brought to life. There are problems of fast currents to be dealt with, but some method of encouraging the use of the waterfront as a public boat area was important.		●	○	●	⊜	⊜	⊜	●

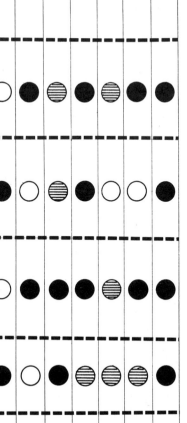

land use (right)

SELECTION CRITERIA	ALTERNATIVES	Alternate I Park/No Action	Alternate II	Alternate III	Alternate IV	Alternate V	Alternate VI	Alternate VII EIS/Preferred Scheme
There appears to be a market for moderate income housing. However, Newburyporters appear fearful that condominium development will take the waterfront from them. Even with extensive public walks, ground level housing taints the surrounding area with a sense of privacy which psychologically removes the waterfront from the public. From the market feasibility point of view, apartments above commercial, with downtown employees/proprietor/retiree, rather than family, orientation would be the best answer to the use of much second and third level space.		○	●	○	●	○	⊜	●
There are beneficial side effects of housing as recommended (option for housing open above ground level).								
-Gives 24-hour life to the downtown and provides nighttime activity								
-Provides the safety of surveillance that Jane Jacobs first identified in "Life and Death of the Great American Cities" referring to the eyes on the streets of the North End		○	○	●	○	●	●	●
-Parking it not totally accumulative with mixed uses. Some housing parking will be away days and used most intensively at night. Parking pressure is thus relieved.								
-More flexibility is allowed to potential developers in adapting to market capabilities								

circulation

SELECTION CRITERIA	ALTERNATIVES	Alternate I Park/No Action	Alternate II	Alternate III	Alternate IV	Alternate V	Alternate VI	Alternate VII EIS/Preferred Scheme
A headline in the Newburyport paper summarized attitudes towards circulation functions, expressed in the citizens' preference questionnaire, "Residents Favor Transit to Parking." This represents a uniquely forward-thinking attitude. Nevertheless, adequate parking must be provided. Accessibility to downtown shopping areas from major arteries is a locational advantage Newburyport has yet to capitalize on or even provide signage for. Parking must meet planning guidelines, but the formation, location, and access to parking need not and must not interfere with the downtown as the coherent and appealing pedestrian-oriented complex which marketability, economic feasibility, and citizens' image goals demand.								
Zoning requires one parking space per 300 sf exclusive of administration, maintenance, storage, and employee, and it is consistent with planning guide recommendations of 3 - 6 spaces per 1000 sf of rentable space. All schemes are required to provide parking accordingly. Provision within 300' of building, however, is an obsolete and inappropriate concept for contemporary shopping complex planning.		●	●	●	●	●	●	●
Citizens have requested the full range of public transportation -- between cities, within the city/to the downtown, and minibusing within the commercial core. Minibusing would also encourage use of several parking facilities south of Pleasant Street, diminishing traffic and parking congestion on Merrimack Street. No historic buildings will be removed.		NA	NA	NA	NA	NA	NA	●
Good planning, as well as citizen preference, requires that for successful shopping atmosphere, shops be tightly grouped within easy walking distance of each other and with only one parking effort (i.e., malls). This atmosphere can not be achieved when large expanses of parking separate shops and occupy vast parts of prime commercial/recreational property.		○	○	◒	●	◒	●	●

circulation

SELECTION CRITERIA	ALTERNATIVES	Alternate I Park/No Action	Alternate II	Alternate III	Alternate IV	Alternate V	Alternate VI	Alternate VII EIS/Preferred Scheme
The successful attraction of tourism may serve to accelerate implementation of intercity and downtown public transportation. Development of the waterfront as condominium - housing would tend to discourage this.		○	◒	◒	●	◒	◒	●
A bike path system from downtown into residential areas and from Plum Island would tend to relieve traffic and congestion (while still attracting tourism), especially during the critical summer months.		NA	NA	NA	NA	NA	NA	●
Parking provided for 2nd or 3rd level apartments is less than if commercial were required for this square footage. Some of this would be vacant for use by shoppers during the working hours of the day.		○	◒	◒	◒	◒	○	◒
Access to and egress from parking areas should be away from Market Square and all efforts made to siphon off automobiles before they reach the more pedestrian-oriented historic preservation areas.		◒	◒	○	◒	◒	◒	●
There is potential interference of mixed mode traffic (cars, bikes, pedestrian, buses) with safe operation of main Fire Station. Topics has arranged roads and lights to adjust to the station's emergency needs, but cars stalled in hot summer traffic cannot be controlled. Pedestrian traffic will also be most intense at this point. The station is badly located for auto circulation and discourages the most desirable pedestrian flow at the pivotal point connecting the downtown and the waterfront.		○	◒	◒	◒	◒	◒	●
The one-way clockwise circulator instituted by Topics does not allow the more appropriate "gateway" that a State Street counterclockwise direction would provide. However, the clockwise Green Street arrival could provide more immediate access to three major parking areas thereby eliminating these autos from Market Square. State Street would still be "gateway" walk for pedestrians parking south of Pleasant and walking towards the waterfront.		◒	◒	○	◒	◒	◒	●

Following page
Alternatives presentation and selection. Alternatives, including a no-build or "Park Alternative," are presented in consistent formats for "apples to apples" comparison.

circulation

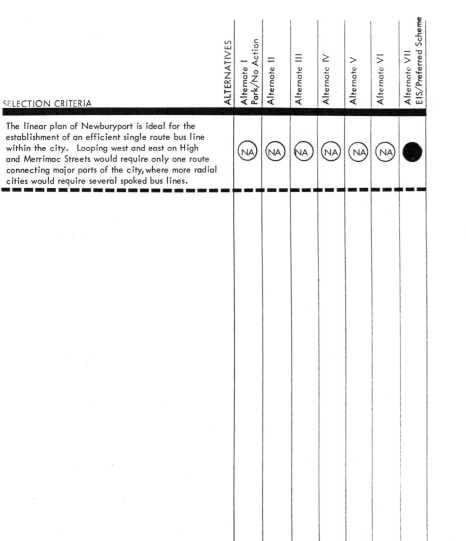

SELECTION CRITERIA	ALTERNATIVES	Alternate I Park/No Action	Alternate II	Alternate III	Alternate IV	Alternate V	Alternate VI	Alternate VII EIS/Preferred Scheme
The linear plan of Newburyport is ideal for the establishment of an efficient single route bus line within the city. Looping west and east on High and Merrimac Streets would require only one route connecting major parts of the city, where more radial cities would require several spoked bus lines.		NA	NA	NA	NA	NA	NA	●

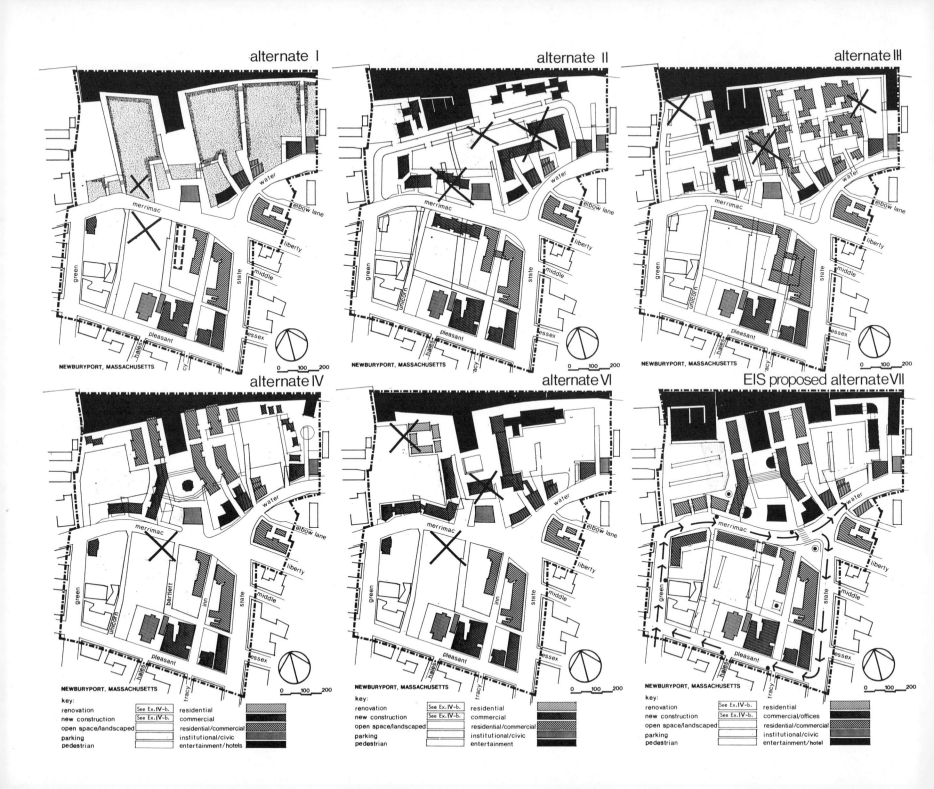

alternate I

alternate II

alternate III

NEWBURYPORT, MASSACHUSETTS

0 100 200

alternate IV

alternate VI

EIS proposed alternate VII

NEWBURYPORT, MASSACHUSETTS

0 100 200

key:
renovation   See Ex.IV-b.   residential
new construction See Ex.IV-b.   commercial
open space/landscaped   residential/commercial
parking   institutional/civic
pedestrian   entertainment/hotels

key:
renovation   See Ex.IV-b.   residential
new construction See Ex.IV-b.   commercial
open space/landscaped   residential/commercial
parking   institutional/civic
pedestrian   entertainment

key:
renovation   See Ex.IV-b.   residential
new construction See Ex.IV-b.   commercial/offices
open space/landscaped   residential/commercial
parking   institutional/civic
pedestrian   entertainment/hotel

Urban Diagnosis
of a Medium-Sized
Highway-Oriented City

Are There Expressway Benefits?

The construction of urban expressways in recent years has been plagued by increasingly militant resistance from local government officials and citizen groups who feel that an expressway through their respective community would harm them socially, economically, and/or environmentally. This resistance is fired by concern about the deteriorating urban environment, a resurgence in citizen participation and interest in local government affairs, and a generally greater awareness by all members of society of the full costs of developing a major expressway facility. These increasingly frequent confrontations between public and private highway building interests and the citizens have caused a great debate concerning the merits of having an expressway built in an urbanized area.

The federal government, therefore, had a legal and popular mandate to understand and act positively on the various impacts that an expressway can have on any community in which it is located. The problem is often worsened when a major expressway serving a regional interest must cut through a small or medium-size city, often breaking up a viable community and causing severe community-disruption problems. In such a case, the option exists to try to lessen the impact of disruption as much as possible, and to maximize the potential benefits of the expressway to the community.

As part of a joint DOT/HUD study, ECODESIGN undertook to diagnose the effects a highway cutting through the city of Pawtucket, Rhode Island, and to develop a "strategy for maximizing expressway benefits in a community of medium size."

Pawtucket Falls, Bridge and the mills.

The Lay of the Land

The elevated sections of the interstate highway that passes through Pawtucket, Rhode Island occur as the highway bends around the downtown core at the river, just prior to major egress points. This elevation, combined with the unique topography of the city, provides an opportunity to the highway user for a visual connection and understanding of the downtown area from the highway before descending to the local street network.

As the motorist makes the bend, he has a spectacularly clear view of downtown Pawtucket. He sees that it was a mill town that developed on a hillside along a river; he sees the towers of the old brick mills; he sees the historic Slater Mill, and the new renewal efforts along it. He also sees the major existing commercial generator—the Apex shopping complex. The egress is thus simple and direct. He has the "lay of the land."

This is the kind of clear invitation needed to attract commercial activity. The fortunate topography of Pawtucket and the existence of a single commercial generator at one end of Main Street indicate that a second polar commercial magnet could be offered with all of the amenities that attracted the Apex complex to Pawtucket—regional location, interstate highway access, visual connection and image, ease of egress, and clarity of arrival. Without doing an existing Urban Frame Analysis, this kind of comprehension of city elements would be difficult for planners to recognize and almost impossible for the general public to understand about their own environment.

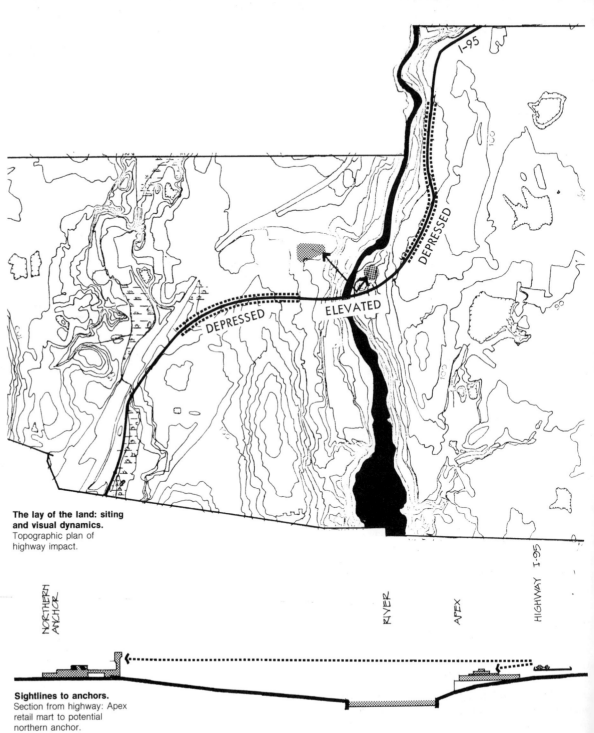

The lay of the land: siting and visual dynamics.
Topographic plan of highway impact.

Sightlines to anchors.
Section from highway: Apex retail mart to potential northern anchor.

Degenerating and regenerating forces.

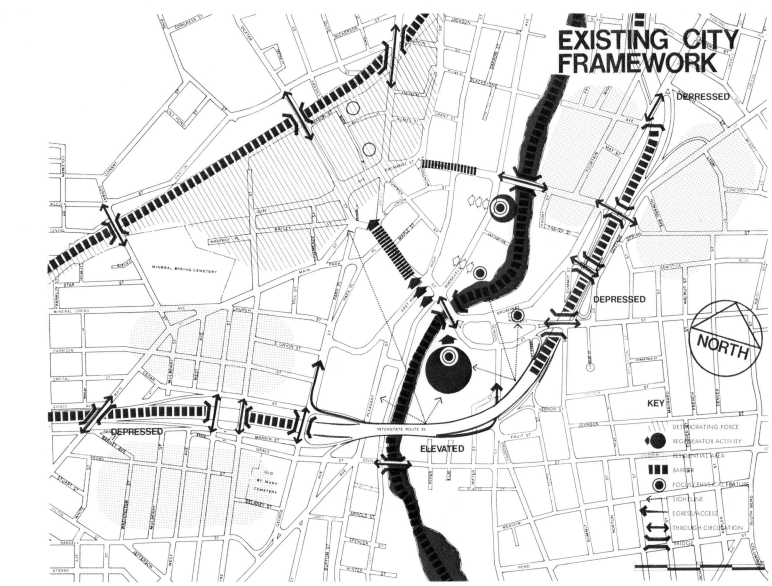

EXISTING CITY FRAMEWORK

DEPRESSED

DEPRESSED

NORTH

DEPRESSED

ELEVATED

INTERSTATE ROUTE 95

KEY

DETERIORATING FORCE
REGENERATOR ACTIVITY
RESIDENTIAL AREA
BARRIER
FOCUS/PHYSICAL FEATURE
SIGHTLINE
EGRESS/ACCESS
THROUGH CIRCULATION
BRIDGE

The Existing Urban Frame

The existing urban frame of Pawtucket has evolved as growth corridors, which developed from connection points that bridge certain barriers. In this case, the ''barrier forces'' are the railroad rights-of-way, the Blackstone River, and the I-95 expressway.

Where the river is crossed at Main Street and

Exchange Street, these streets have developed as growth corridors with distinct land-use functions— commercial uses along Main Street and civic uses predominate at Exchange Street. These relate to the major commercial and civic generators at the bridge points (Apex complex and the city hall).

From the elevated portion of the highway, passing cars can view these ''prime generators'' as well as

such pleasant focus elements as the Old Slater Mill and an historic church.

The railroad that cuts through the city once attracted the old brick mills and warehouses to its side. Now, economic obsolescence is obvious in this area, yet it now provides an area of land and buildings for potential recycling, if the existing commercial and civic growth corridors are to expand. The indi-

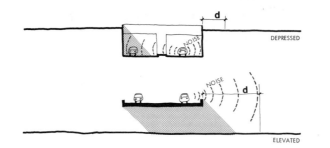

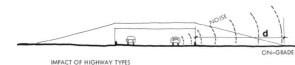

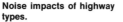

IMPACT OF HIGHWAY TYPES

Noise impacts of highway types.

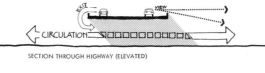

SECTION THROUGH HIGHWAY (ELEVATED)

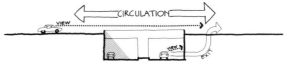

SECTION THROUGH HIGHWAY (DEPRESSED)

Access and view impacts of highway types.

cations are that these blocks can offer many of the requirements needed to attract an activity generator (a magnetic pole) to the northern end of Main Street.

Where I-95 cuts through the city, it also generates activity and growth at its access and egress points. The highway uses to its advantage the effects of depressed versus elevated highways, as diagrammed in the following Impacts of Highway Types.

Impacts of Highway Types

The depressed sections of I-95 work well with the neighborhood areas through which they pass. Connections that continue existing street patterns are more often successful when made by bridging a depressed highway because visual contact is maintained. When the highway is elevated, the shadow and the columns obstruct the views.

The Urban Frame analysis also indicates the one major negative impact of I-95, which is that the highway causes some population loss and necessitates relocation. Like all transportation corridors, the expressway has its perimeter negative effects such as shadow, noise, and pollution. These are minimized in Pawtucket's residential neighborhoods by use of a depressed highway. However, there is still a distance from a highway that is left unusable for residential purposes, except in a unique situation such as the famous Brooklyn Heights Promenade already discussed. However, this uninhabitable distance is substantially greater in the case of an elevated highway passing through residential fabric becase of its shadow and noise generation. Of course, the highway becomes a nearly total disruption to neighborhood street patterns when at grade,

because of the size of overpass connections and their ramps.

Gestalt Groupings of Specific Land Use

Other trends such as the evolution of clear commercial and civic corridors were determined through a kind of "gestalt grouping" of similar specific land uses. Studying the activity corridors identified in the Urban Frame in more detail, one discovers certain apparent patterns and opportunities.

The commercial spine along Main Street is heavily saturated with financial, service, and commercial activities. Another category including commercial businesses, banks, loan offices, and the electric company, lines almost the entire western side of Main Street. There specific uses are keyed by symbols and grouped.

The groupings show regeneration of the Main Street spine is already apparent in the new development related to and generated by the Urban Renewal Project. This is especially so in the sections closest to the southern "generator" or "anchor" facility—the Apex commercial complex.

There is also evidence through this exercise that a civic spine is developing parallel to Main Street along Exchange Street, generated by the locations of the City Hall, fire and police headquarters, Slater Mill, the Post Office, Social Security building, Municipal Welfare building, and other structures. Part of this civic secondary spine are the library and YMCA, which connect through to Main Street by way of Maple Street.

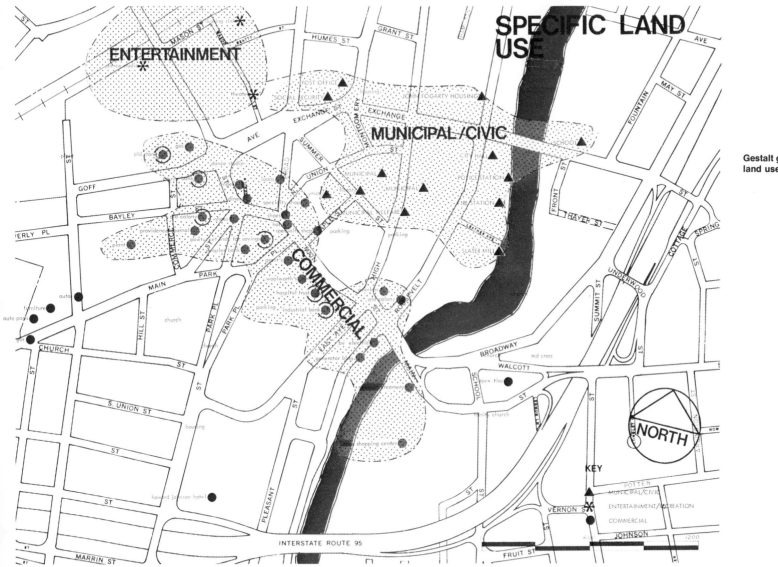

SPECIFIC LAND USE

ENTERTAINMENT

MUNICIPAL/CIVIC

COMMERCIAL

NORTH

KEY
MUNICIPAL/CIVIC
ENTERTAINMENT/RECREATION
COMMERCIAL

Gestalt groupings of specific
land use.

The existence of a civic grouping is an important contributor to a "sense of place." Town Halls, post offices, and libraries are the kind of downtown conveniences that a city's commercial competition—a shopping center or a shopper's mall—does not offer.

The two-year-old HUD-sponsored, enclosed skating rink, on the other hand, has been very successful in bringing activity and enthusiasm of the local hockey team's events downtown. In addition to the daytime activity of parents dropping children off at the rink and remaining downtown to shop, there is considerable nighttime use of the rink.

The combination of activities grouped in these blocks shows a growing need and opportunity for recreational/entertainment land use in this area.

These deteriorating and underused blocks might be renovated to allow for the planning of a park and additional entertainment facilities (such as bowling, movies, nightclubs, or pubs) and additional parking in conncection with the skating rink. Again a well-rounded collection of land uses and viable alternatives for attracting different age groups and lifestyles provides a particular character to a city that shopping centers have not yet acquired.

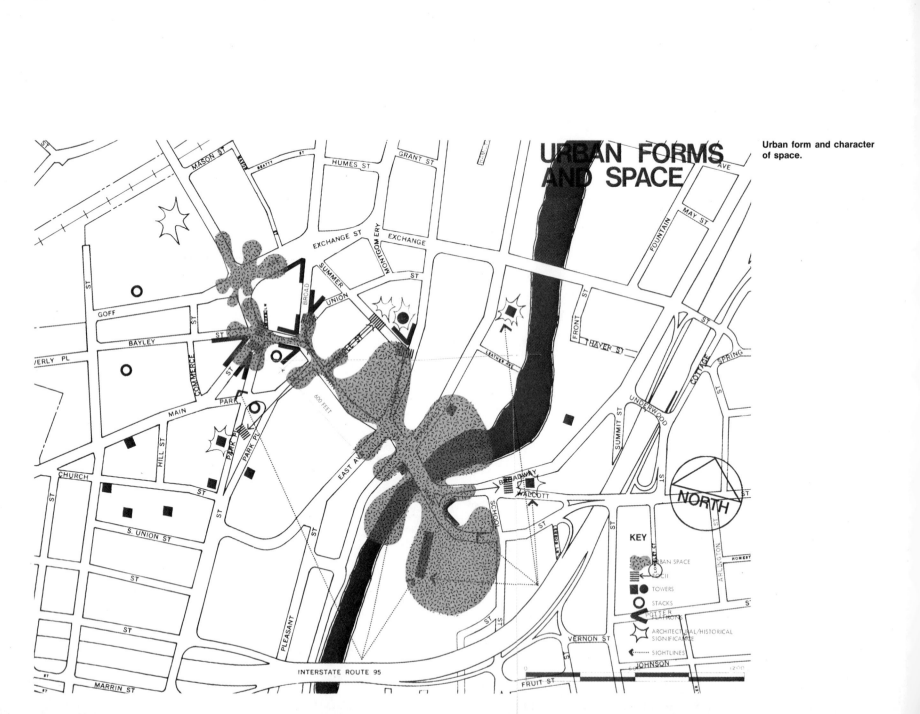

URBAN FORMS
AND SPACE

Urban form and character
of space.

145

Urban Form and Character of Space

In taking inventory of a city's physical assets, we have already described the effect of the topography in providing various high points from which to grasp the "lay of the land." It is from efforts to benefit from such an approach that the ideas developed for treatment of the downtown such as the closing of Main Street to create a nicely scaled pedestrian mall and the design of a highly visible retail center.

For example, from a high elevation point such as the Howard Johnson Motel, one can see the city hall tower, various church spires, other tower-like structures often related to old mill architecture, the Apex pyramid, and the river on its course. These towers, stacks, and spires, rising out of a relatively low-rise brick texture as it moves down the slopes on both sides of the river, make Pawtucket an individual and unique city with an inherent physical form and visual and historic interest, which no modern shopping center or mall can ever offer.

A typical building form that resulted from the old street pattern is the flatiron-shaped building. These triangular structures occurring at "Y" intersections act to "enclose" space along Main Street and the side streets linked to it. This, too, is a unique form, rarely found, and not easily reproduced economically today.

These same "Y" streets that run perpendicular to Main Street end visually, almost without exception, with a focal point—either a tower, a significant building, or a church spire. These focal points become visual events and enhance the experience of the downtown area and further define the Main Street space and Pawtucket as a place.

Main Street Square, 1936.

These special features—towers, stacks, and flatiron buildings, can be plotted on the downtown area base map. Then we superimposed over this map the sightlines afforded to these focal points and an indication of the flow of the resultant urban space and the dimensions of the compact Main Street core.

The type of spatial definition and enclosure that results reinforces the idea of actually closing Main Street and creating a pedestrian mall. The physical dimensions of Main Street are also in scale with this concept. It is approximately 1200 feet long from the Apex complex to the Broad and Bayley forked intersection. This makes the spine of the downtown core an easy five-minute walk—well within recommended lengths, and within budgeting limits for covering the entire length of the street with a plexiglass dome—the eventful "tour de force" of the project.

Orienting a Large City
to Mass Transportation

An Alternative to the Automobile

The opportunity to introduce a new transportation element that can restore the vibrancy of the downtown area without necessarily disrupting its character exists in any number of cities. Many of the problems faced by downtown America—declining retail activity or increasing commercial activity with its associated auto congestion, too much valuable land devoted to automobile parking or a lack of sufficient parking, as well as air pollution and sprawling development from the city core—could be alleviated by a new, attractive, safe and convenient alternative to the automobile. The knowledge, skills, and technologies are available—what remains is to assemble and organize them in an effort that might demonstrate the effectiveness of such alternatives as Personalized Rapid Transit (PRT), also known as "people movers."

The Regional Transportation District (RTD) of Denver attempted to do this in a study to provide the necessary environmental and physical design considerations for route selection to augment the engineering alignment of a route for a proposed PRT system. This study represents a cooperative effort between the urban designers, ECODESIGN, engineers, Nelson, Haley, Patterson, & Quirk, Inc., the client agency, RTD, and the community. It is based on a reconnaissance of the city, its transportation needs, a reevaluation of earlier studies including the Center City Transportation Project (1969–1970), and more recent studies prepared by the Joint Venture of Development Research Associates, Inc. and Wallace, McHarg, Roberts & Todd, Inc.

Controlling an Unlimited Potential for Sprawl

Denver, Colorado is a city that could become the prototypical American city of the future because of its heavy dependence on the automobile. This dependence is aggravated by the unlimited potential for sprawl that exists on the great plains that spread flatly for an area of 50 miles east and 200 miles north and south around this fast-growing city. To a city possessing a pleasant climate, and the most central location for access in the country (a fact already attracting many large corporations fleeing the congested east coast), there is literally no limit to growth but the edge of the Rocky Mountains themselves.

If one scribes a circle whose circumference lies 400 miles from Denver, the overall population densities are among the most sparse in the country, and no other metropolitan areas are within the circle. Yet within Denver's 339-acre central business district are concentrated most of the medical centers, major libraries, educational, theatrical, and museum institutions that serve that area as well as the centers for finance, retail, and government conventions, transportation and distribution services to a large sector of the country.

Denver's special character is that of a threshold* city. With only a small bus system in 1972 and with no planned attitudes toward growth, it has been forced by this dispersal and lack of transportation alternatives to become more and more dependent on the automobile.

*A "threshold" city is one which has a population of over a million, but is not more than three or four million, and is not truly an international city of world influence such as New York, Chicago, or San Francisco. It is more in the same class and ranking as Atlanta, Cleveland and Seattle.

Its current situation is as a city that has not yet completely committed itself to the auto and still has the opportunity of structuring its future growth around a rational balanced transportation system. It is toward this end that decisions made now to provide elements of a transit system could be an important asset to the future organization and structure of Denver and other large cities. Our study was designed to help resolve the urban design issues that must be confronted when a new transit system is proposed for downtowns and adjoining areas. In the case of Denver, the intent was to utilize the proposed PRT system to reinforce the existing urban frame and to consolidate a city that is sprawling as it grows.

These issues include determining the potential role of people mover transportation in the city, the impacts and opportunities (social, economical, and physical) of alternative route locations and system technologies, and the viable methods for selection of a specific route and of a specific PRT system "hardware" (guideway and vehicle). Links with Regional long-haul systems, possible parking intercepts for commuters, implications for employment, joint development and potential corridors as prototypical studies, street patterns and alignment—all of these are viewed against an Urban Frame that defines the functional areas of the downtown.

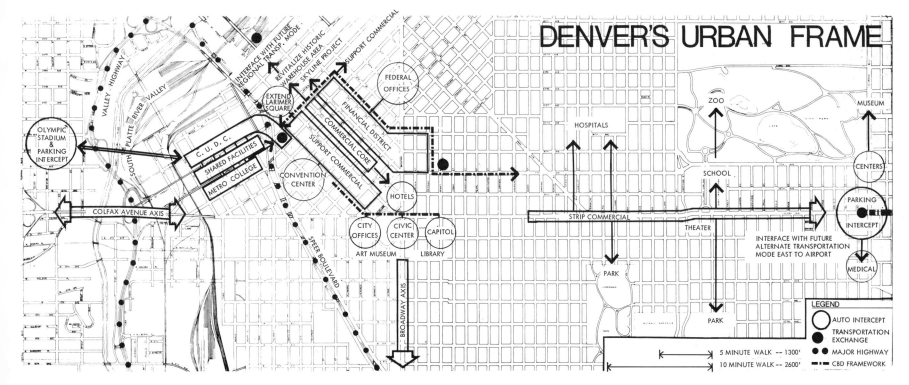

DENVER'S URBAN FRAME

**Linking cores, strips, and
nodes** on Denver's
Urban Frame.

PRT System Fit—User Impact

Any public transportation concept must address itself to the needs of an entire region and a downtown transportation system must be capable of being incorporated within a larger regional system, or better yet, form the very basis of one. A transportation system must evolve from a clear understanding of the location, numbers, habits, and needs of the users. In particular, what are the amenities that must be offered to dissuade the users from continuing to use their automobiles?

Who are the users? How does a specific technology fit with the users' own criteria and use characteristics? Many characteristics of transportation technologies relate to specific engineering details and equipment design details; others relate to basic functions of the technologies and their environmental, land use, or user impacts. The following factors provide general criteria for evaluating and comparing candidate PRT technologies in terms of user impact:

☐
Travel Times—the number and frequency of stops and right of way constraints
☐
Volume/Capacity—the volume of trips accommodated during a given time period
☐
Development Potentials—the ability to generate or concentrate development and the perceived significance of transit by participants in the development process
☐
Functional Variables—design characteristics relating to vehicle performance, such as free versus fixed guideway, separate versus combined rights of way, automatic versus manual controls
☐
Passenger Comfort, Ease and Comprehension—should exceed that of existing automobile, bus, and other transit in reflecting origin and destinations, walking distances, zone to zone trip, cost benefits
☐
Mode and Purpose of CBD Travel—existing and projected habits of present bus and auto riders, pedestrians, shoppers and workers, the old, the young, the handicapped, the independent and the dependent, high, medium, and low income groups, and so on
☐
Route Responsibilities—the routes fit with criteria above, its community acceptance, comprehension and imageability
☐
Modal Interfaces—interface with alternative transportation modes, such as a regional rapid transit system, bus lines, automobiles, mini-bus, dial-a-ride, speed belts, bikes, pedestrians, and so on
☐
Costs—the inevitable trade-off between operating and capital costs
☐
Flexibility—incorporating flexibility in routing, scheduling and alignment allows transit to respond to changing patterns of urban development and patronage
☐
Space Use—In the CBD's, carrying larger numbers in smaller volumes are preferable, and requirements of corridor alignments, rights of way, storage, parking or terminals, stations, etc. must be considered and located.

How does a proposed route fit with the users' existing patterns of trip purpose, origin, and destination, or employment? The fit of the proposed route was studied against these factors, and the illustrations show how the loop of the designed route serves the basic central business district intensified activity area. People are picked up from the suggested stadium parking intercept and delivered directly to the major downtown employment generators.

It is important that work and business centers be served directly from parking intercept to destination stop without further transfer. This is because timing for these trips is critical. Work hours must be adhered to, and transfers may bring unexpected delays. With shopping trips, on the other hand, timing is not so critical, and the trip patterns and shoppers carrying packages demand another mode for more closely spaced stops. The PRT system with station stop spacing at a minimum of four to five blocks cannot provide the kind of block-to-block service that shoppers' trips require. When shoppers are not provided with this block-to-block service, those with cars will inevitably drive into the CBD and use their cars for storing purchases rather than walk with packages more than 600 to 800 feet.

Because of these user tendencies, the east and west corridors forming the CBD loop were designed to define and serve the CBD without confining or restricting it. Under this scheme shoppers can be delivered to the commercial core by the PRT system but the shopper/user is provided with the block-to-block stop capability of a high frequency curb level mini-bus and as a future speed belt. Thus the proposed system is clearly tailored to the needs of both shopping and employment.

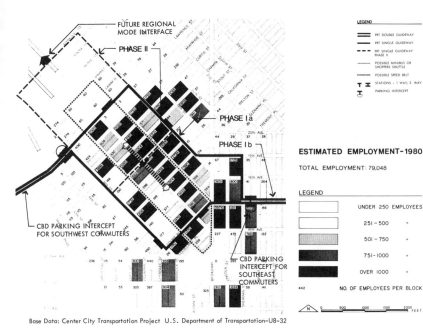

FUTURE REGIONAL MODE INTERFACE

PHASE II

PHASE I a

PHASE I b

CBD PARKING INTERCEPT FOR SOUTHWEST COMMUTERS

CBD PARKING INTERCEPT FOR SOUTHEAST COMMUTERS

LEGEND

═══	PRT DOUBLE GUIDEWAY
───	PRT SINGLE GUIDEWAY
─ ─ ─	PRT SINGLE GUIDEWAY PHASE II
·········	POSSIBLE MINIBUS OR SHOPPERS SHUTTLE
·········	POSSIBLE SPEED BELT
T Ⅰ	STATIONS - 1 WAY, 2 WAY
Ⅰ	PARKING INTERCEPT

ESTIMATED EMPLOYMENT–1980

TOTAL EMPLOYMENT: 79,048

LEGEND

	UNDER 250 EMPLOYEES
	251 – 500 "
	501 – 750 "
	751 – 1000 "
	OVER 1000 "

442 NO. OF EMPLOYEES PER BLOCK

N 0 500 1000 1500 2000 FEET

ALTERNATE MODE INTERFACE

HOURLY PARKING
JANUARY, 1970

LEGEND

	UNDER $ .40
	$ .40 – $ .59
	$ .60 – $ .79
	$ .80 – $ .99
	$1.00 AND OVER

N 0 500 1000 1500 2000 FEET

PRT—System impact/fit.

PRT—User impact/fit.

PRT Facilities—User Needs

The factors of convenience, comfort, and privacy afforded by the automobile are often attractive enough to compensate for the aggravation of traffic congestions for a significant number of drivers who have the option of transit. The simple addition of transit capacity, therefore, is not enough to produce the necessary radical reduction of motor vehicle traffic in older urban centers or forestall the unwanted traffic increase in newer rapidly growing metropolitan areas. In order to move toward the current urban environmental goals, a transit system must be developed and installed that will compete more favorably with the automobile in terms of convenience, comfort, and privacy, as well as overall trip time. Recognition of this need and opportunity to rescue our cities from the transportation dilemma has promoted research and development of transportation technologies aimed at making public transit an attractive alternative to the automobile.

The specific PRT technologies that could be used in the 1972 Demonstration Project for the Urban Mass Transportation Administration (UMTA) could not be determined at that time. Accordingly, the report was not technology-specific but, rather, it considered three generic prototypes, namely 1) a *suspended* vehicle on an overhead guideway, 2) an *air cushioned* vehicle supported from below, and 3) a *rubber-tired* vehicle also supported from below. The proposed demonstration route was designed to accept any of these three alternatives.

Regardless of the specific hardware or technology eventually chosen for the demonstration project, certain performance criteria must be met to assure

PRT FACILITIES IMPACT

KEY:

ENVIRONMENTAL IMPLICATIONS

SUPERIOR — GOOD — POOR

		A. SUSPENDED: 6 PERSON CAB		B. AIR CUSHION: 12 PERSON CAB		C. RUBBER TIRED: 40 PERSON CAB	
VEHICLE	WIDTH	5'-6"		7'-4"		7'-4"	
	HEIGHT	6'-8"		7'-0"		0-2"	
	LENGTH	8'-9"		13'-2"		21'-3"	
	WEIGHT	4000#		7000#		13,000#	
GUIDE	SINGLE	2½'		10' CONT. LEVITATION PAD – SOLID CUTS LIGHT IN CBD		9'-2" (WIDE, CUTS LIGHT IN CBD BUT CAN BE OPENED AT GUIDE CENTER)	
	DOUBLE	2½' – 10' OPEN – 2½'		20' CONT. LEVITATION PAD – CUTS LIGHT POSSIBLE "TUNNEL BLINDNESS"		20' (WIDE, BUT CAN BE OPENED AT GUIDE CENTER)	
	DEPTH	3'		3' – 4' (READS AS HEAVY BAND)		4' – 5" (READS AS HEAVY BAND)	
SUPPORT	BASE	1'-1½'		3'		4'-5'	
	ARM	1'		4'		5'	
STATION	LENGTH	85' FOR 4 VEHICLES		HIGH DENSITY LOADING CAPACITY – 4 DOCK STATION 75'		125' OR MORE FOR SIDINGS, ANGLES AND DOCKS	
	WIDTH	ADDITIONAL RAILS ALLOW OPEN STATION WITH LIGHT AND AIR		60' WIDE 2 WAY STATION BLOCKS LIGHT AND AIR BELOW FOR 200'		60' WIDE 2 WAY STATION BLOCKS LIGHT AND AIR BELOW FOR 200'	
RADII		URBAN 35' – GIVES GOOD MOBILITY AS CBD NETWORK		50' – STRUCTURAL PROBLEMS WITH CANTILEVERED CURVE		50' – STRUCTURAL PROBLEMS WITH CANTILEVERED CURVE	
WIND		SIDESWAY – ADJUST SPEED TO CONDITIONS		LOW CENTER OF GRAVITY		HIGH CENTER OF GRAVITY POTENTIAL SWAY	
WEATHER		GUIDERAIL COVERED – NO SNOW REMOVAL REQUIRED		SNOW REMOVAL REQUIRED OPERATION ON HEAVY SNOW, RAIN, AND ICE UNCERTAIN		SNOW REMOVAL REQUIRED SKIDDING WITH RUBBER-TIRED	
ESCAPE MECHANISM		REQUIRES SPECIAL EQUIPMENT		USE GUIDEWAY		USE GUIDEWAY	
VANDALISM		GUIDERAILS INACCESSIBLE TO VANDALS – NO WALKING SURFACE		HEAVY OBJECTS WILL NOT BE BLOWN OFF – GUIDEWAY CAN BE WALKED ON		HEAVY OBJECTS CAN BE PLACED ON GUIDEWAY – GUIDEWAY CAN BE WALKED ON	
CAPACITY & DEMAND		EXCELLENT AUTOMATED SELECTIVE ROUTING. MAKERS BELIEVE SMALLER CABS GIVE PERSONALIZED SERVICE (E.G., AUTO SIZED) BUT LARGE CARS CAN BE DEVELOPED		AUTOMATED SELECTIVE ROUTING. MAKERS OFFER 3 SIZED VEHICLES		LARGER VEHICLES LESS COMPATIBLE WITH AUTOMATED SELECTIVE ROUTING	
EFFICIENCY & FLEXIBILITY		LIGHT STRUCTURE INTEGRATES EASILY INTO EXISTING STREETS		HEAVY STRUCTURE HAS ENVIRONMENTAL CONFLICTS AS CBD NETWORK USE LINEAR INDUCTION MOTORS POSSIBLY INEFFICIENT AT LOW SPEEDS		HEAVY STRUCTURE HAS ENVIRONMENTAL CONFLICTS AS CBD NETWORK USE – POSSIBLE EXCEEDS DENVER'S CAPACITY REQUIREMENTS	

**PRT environmental
performance criteria.**

users' acceptance. From the users' point of view, the following criteria are important aspects of the physical design of the PRT system, and are used in evaluation of candidate transportation technologies:

☐
System Concept
Basic description

Best functioning situation

Linkage capabilities

Geometric and alignment capabilities

Operational flexibility: switching, storage, convertibility (e.g., off-hours freight handling

Headway

Station dwell time

Capacity—6-person, 12-person, 80-person, etc.

Speed—acceleration and deceleration

Service dependability—schedule adherence, maintenance frequency and standardization of components and parts

☐
Safety for Passengers
Entrance/exit, safety, barrier-free design, handrails, step heights, etc.

Emergency exit procedures and fail-safe features of vehicle

Security management

Fire and building code requirements

☐
Passenger Comfort
Ride quality—elimination of jerk

Ease of use—exits, entrances, crowd control, baggage handling, escalators

Acoustical levels—quietness in vehicle and in environs

Design dimensions—human engineering

Design quality—shape of seats, car, supports

Graphics—Clarity, comprehensibility, image

☐
Component Characteristics
Vehicle design specifications—suspension systems, power source, braking systems, etc.

Required guideway characteristics—maximum grade, minimum radius, etc.

Stations—spacing, surveillance, area and lanes required

☐
Environmental Characteristics
Appearance—scale, visual impact

Pollution levels—air, noise, odor, vibration

Nonuser reaction

Adaptability to the environment

Effects on neighborhoods

☐
Support Module and Guideway Sections
Suspended—small cabs and capacity, good demand routing

Air-cushioned—medium cabs and capacity, good demand routing

Rubber-tired—large cabs and capacity, no demand routing

Guideway and Support Selection

An experimental method was used to illustrate the striking differences in the visual impact of different PRT system hardware types. We used photographic slides of existing views of a route and superimposed the system in its actual context. Two rather typical, yet distinct, views have been chosen, illustrating two areas of particular concern:

How does one insert a system into an erratic, almost nonexistent fabric or low-rise situation where the required structure clearances might tend to give heights out of proportion with adjacent two- and three-story structures?

How does one "select" a system technology based on the environmental and aesthetic differences between two generic types—the suspended and the air cushion? The answers become more apparent in the actual settings.

Applied to East Colfax commercial strip, the light, unobtrusive steel structure of the suspended PRT looks almost lost in the environment of signs, chrome, and electric lights, while the air-cushioned, or rubber-tired vehicle guideway tends to act as a spine linking the pieces together. Here the more architectural concrete structure definitely improves an otherwise formless existing situation.

On the other hand, an almost opposite reaction is the result of the same experimental application in the low-rise 14th Street setting. The large, heavy air-cushioned concrete vehicle guideway imposes itself, and the delicate suspended steel forms are hardly felt, allowing light and air to the street almost as before the system was inserted.

Strong and form-giving versus nearly invisible.

a. Clark Kent approach—commercial strip

b. Superman approach—commercial strip

c. Superman approach—downtown

d. Clark Kent approach—downtown

GUIDEWAY DESIGN FOR SPECIFIC TECHNOLOGIES

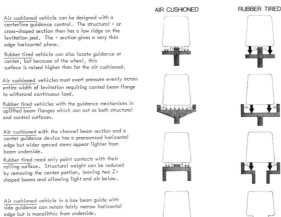

Air cushioned vehicle can be designed with a centerline guidance control. The structural + or cross-shaped section then has a low ridge on the levitation pad. The + section gives a very thin edge horizontal plane.

Rubber tired vehicle can also locate guidance at center, but because of the wheel, this surface is raised higher than for the air cushioned.

Air cushioned vehicles must exert pressure evenly across entire width of levitation requiring canted beam flange to withstand continuous load.

Rubber tired vehicles with the guidance mechanisms in uplifted beam flanges which can act as both structural and control surfaces.

Air cushioned with the channel beam section and a center guidance device has a pronounced horizontal edge but wider spaced stems appear lighter from beam underside.

Rubber tired need only point contacts with their rolling surface. Structural weight can be reduced by removing the center portion, leaving two Z-shaped beams and allowing light and air below.

Air cushioned vehicle in a box beam guide with side guidance can retain fairly narrow horizontal edge but is monolithic from underside.

Rubber tired vehicle could reset their wheels to narrow width of guide, but required side guidance planes with box beam depth would be substantial horizontal edge.

AIR CUSHIONED   **RUBBER TIRED**

Shaping the guideway.

One can see that there are two basic aesthetics for treating PRT systems in the urban context:

1
Clark Kent approach: To attempt to design the system to be the least intrusive and least visible structure in the environment (e.g., the bridges of Robert Maillart in Switzerland.)

2
Superman approach: To attempt to make the system an integral structuring element of the whole city (e.g., the magnificent aqueducts of Rome.)

The alignments and form of the guideway system depend, for the most part, on value judgments of the most intuitive kind, because, aside from everything, no PRT system has yet been attempted on a large-scale urban basis.

Ultimately the PRT aesthetics are based on personal opinions as to whether transportation systems should be "nearly invisible" or "strong structuring physical elements" of a city, as well as how they respond to the fact that the generic corridor situations through which they pass change in scale and form throughout the city.

"Guideway Design for Specific Technologies" shows a comparison of guideways cross-sections based on identical cab dimensions and weights for the two technologies requiring a supported guideway or air-cushioned/rubber-tired. When free from constraints, such as the side location of the guidance control surfaces, which could actually be located at the center for both technologies, the guideways can be reshaped in various ways.

The air-cushioned vehicle, for instance, requires a continuous levitation pad, but because it sets lower,

the guidance and control surfaces can also be lower. This decreases the horizontal silhouette of the guide.

The rubber-tired vehicle sets higher because of the wheels. This tends to raise the heights of the guide wall control surface. On the other hand, the wheels are only point loads to their rolling surface, not continuous as with the air-cushioned vehicle. This allows areas at the center of the guide, which are not serving as rolling surfaces, to be removed, reducing both the dead load and the bulk of the guideway, as well as allowing light and air through to below.

It is clear that, by analyzing the city through diagrams, one is not only able to comprehend its essential growth needs and framework, but one can also begin to make technological and socio-economic diagnostic evaluations and treat the city as a doctor treats his patient. Not to say that doctors can think diagrammatically, but only that a city is perhaps more complex even than a human patient with an ailment which has a more limited number of cures. The number of alternatives open to the urbanist as potential "solutions" are limitless, and

no one of them is ever truly correct. Refining the complex urban area into generalized systems and its component parts can bring the urbanist closer to the most correct solution. At the very least, more questions become apparent through this technique and an earlier diagnosis can be made.

Analysis of an Urban Function

The use of the Urban Frame diagram has been shown as a diagnostic instrument used with each city studied and treated. Such graphic problem solving can also be used to isolate and examine specific Urban Functions and to confront critical issues from new and more direct angles.

However, because Urban Functions are so many and complex in their interactions, it is a special time-consuming "laboratory test," which is not practical to perform unless indications point to a problem in a particular area of functional interaction. Pedestrian and vehicular interaction in congested, chaotic Harvard Square, Cambridge, Massachusetts, for example, is not usually acknowledged to be one of its most desirable characteristics! Although there exists a certain dynamic quality associated with pedestrian/vehicular interaction, beyond a certain intensity, the interaction becomes uncomfortable or even dangerous.

Cities are constantly counting their cars, seldom their pedestrians.

In diagramming Harvard Square's status quo (prior to the construction of a proposed major tourist attraction), ECODESIGN felt that Harvard Square was at that critical point where the pedestrian's position must be reexamined and reasserted. The proposed project's impact on the urban frame depended to a large extent on estimated visitor projections and increased pedestrian activity levels in Harvard Square.

In order to project the additional pedestrian activity, the existing pedestrian activity had to be known. The City Planning Department, which would normally have the responsibility to conduct such a study in order to do adequate planning for Harvard Square, seemed to have only a sketchy view of

Typical pedestrian spacing.
The basic terminology developed by E. Hall for determining the amount of space people want or need was put into graphic form and expanded upon by ECO-DESIGN to include space criteria for specific user needs, i.e., moving and waiting, street vendors and musicians, the effect of street furniture.

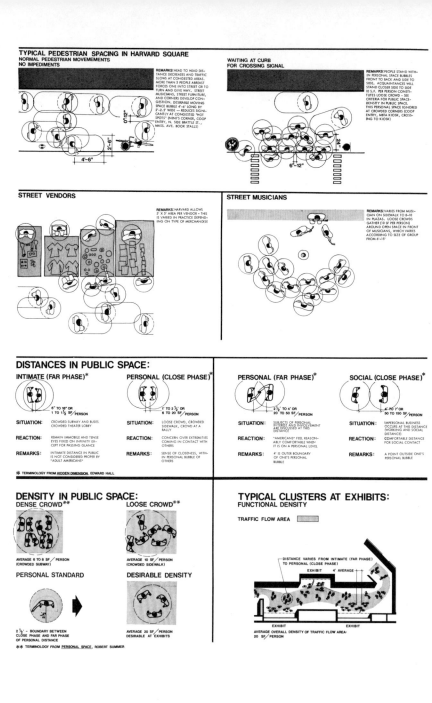

the existing pedestrian situation. Some privately sponsored counts were available on pedestrian capacities and flows in Harvard Square and although this data was made available, the team found that additional work was required in two areas. First, the figures only contained pedestrian count information for Harvard Square as a whole. Specific areas were not broken down within the total capacity figures. Second, because the study was undertaken for the project developer, the material might require corroboration in order to be totally acceptable to the community. The only other existing data adequate for evaluating the pedestrian activity in Harvard Square was just completed by a special MIT student workshop, and documented only specific areas.

In order to supplement and corroborate this existing information, ECODESIGN conducted pedestrian counts in the critical areas around the Square. The critical areas were defined as those areas where, through observation and experience, the existing situation was felt to be already approaching a critical level of congestion, and would be the most severely affected by the injection of a tourist attraction. Both 15-minute and 30-second counts were done in the noontime hours (11–2), on both weekdays and weekends. Instantaneous counts were done in the parks and open spaces, and crowds watching special occasional attractions (musicians, puppeteers, etc.) were also observed and counted.

Due to budget and time constraints, these spot counts were most useful as a supplemental data check as they could not entail a more extensive counting procedure over long periods of time. Such comprehensive pedestrian counts should be an ongoing function of a city's planning department,

but although cities are constantly counting their cars, they seldom count their pedestrians or consider pedestrian habits and characteristics.

A simultaneous view

Our pedestrian/vehicular interaction studies were an attempt to take a unique simultaneous look at intensities and conflict in circulation modes. Vehicle flow data was available from traffic engineering studies. Pedestrian counts were conducted not to determine the total number of people in Harvard Square, but rather to give indications of the pedestrian activity—particularly in those areas most likely to be affected by additional traffic.

The base for comparison was the existing condition against which the projected impact of the tourist attraction on the street pattern and pedestrian network of Harvard Square could be evaluated. A late spring Saturday at 2:00 P.M. was selected as the maximum existing activity base time, while the projected critical impact period to be evaluated against the existing conditions was a summer Saturday at 2:00 P.M. (The seasonal difference was unavoidable due to the time schedule of the EIS.)

Comparing functional activity and interaction at two specific points in time required careful selection of those points in time:

☐
The critical impact period is the time when the impact of the proposed project would be the most severe. It is important to evaluate the critical period, rather than an average period, because the impacts may be severe enough in the critical period so as to destroy the quality of life in the area studied before the leveling off. Also, combinations of other

events happening simultaneously (i.e., construction of a new subway line and temporary inefficiencies) can also have a severe effect.

☐
As the *peak year visitor projections* for a tourist attraction are applicable for two to three years after the project is built, it must be assumed that major changes in response to those visitors could occur. Permanent changes in traffic systems, type of retail operations, change in land values would occur in response to the peak year load, not necessarily with stable year projections in mind.

☐
Peak Day. Considering the great numbers of people in Harvard Square on Saturdays (comparable to weekday capacity and twice as much as on Sunday) and the fact that a higher proportion of that number is using the sidewalks and streets (shopping, as opposed to working inside and off the street), it seems reasonable to assume that various urban systems (circulation, parking, open space, etc.) will be operating close to or above reasonable capacity on that day.

☐
Time. While during weekdays vehicular traffic is heaviest at morning and evening rush hours, on Saturday the heaviest traffic occurs in the afternoon, between noon and 4:00 P.M. This coincides with the heaviest pedestrian use of Harvard Square and with the projected heaviest use of the proposed tourist attraction. While peak arrival hours for such a facility are from 1:00 P.M. to 3:00 P.M., the largest number of people will head toward Harvard Square between 2:00 P.M. and 4:00 P.M.

Viewed separately, the vehicle flow per hour and the pedestrian activity were simply raw figures that did not seem to be a true reflection of the circu-

The fallacy of the "Traffic Engineering" approach in such a case of increased circulation volume would be to chart numerical vehicular flows, velocities, origins and destinations, and deal with the pedestrian separately in terms of the time sequence on traffic lights. We felt the fallacy lay in the fact that this approach considers auto and pedestrian traffic as separate entities whereas it is the interaction of the two that often causes congestion and safety hazards on the urban streets. The true situation is better represented in these two figures where the interaction between the lines of the vehicular and the dots of the pedestrian traffic reveals the degree of interaction between these modes.

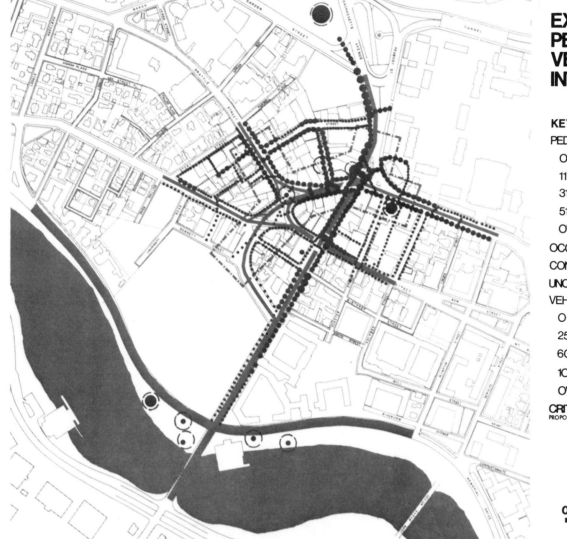

EXISTING PEDESTRIAN & VEHICULAR INTERACTION

KEY

PEDESTRIAN ACTIVITY (30 SECONDS)

0-10	•
11-30	•
31-50	●
51-80	⬤
OVER 80	⬤

OCCASIONAL ATTRACTION ◯

CONTROLLED CROSSING

UNCONTROLLED CROSSING

VEHICLES PER HOUR

0-250	——
251-600	——
601-1000	——
1001-1400	——
OVER 1400	——

CRITICAL IMPACT AREA —·—·—·—
PROPOSED PRIMARY PEDESTRIAN FLOW

NORTH

0 200 400 800
FEET

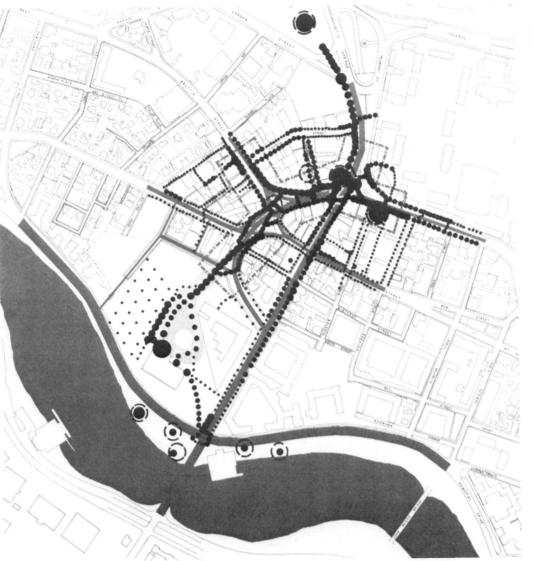

PROJECTED PEDESTRIAN & VEHICULAR INTERACTION

KEY

PEDESTRIAN ACTIVITY (30 SECONDS)

O–1O

11–3O

31–5O

51–8O

OVER 8O

OCCASIONAL ATTRACTION

CONTROLLED CROSSING

UNCONTROLLED CROSSING

VEHICLES PER HOUR

O–25O

251–6OO

6O1–1OOO

1OO1–14OO

OVER 14OO

CRITICAL IMPACT AREA

PROPOSED PRIMARY PEDESTRIAN FLOW

NORTH

O 2OO 4OO 8OO

FEET

lation activity and conflicts, either existing or projected, in Harvard Square. Individually, they were merely a cataloguing of a single mode of an intrinsically multimodal function. Superimposing the pedestrian activity graphically over the vehicle flow presented a clearer picture of the situation.

A measure of the intensity and of problem areas in the interaction of pedestrians and vehicles was the most immediate accomplishment of comparing theoretical (pure traffic engineering vehicle counts) vehicle capacity of streets and intersections to the actual observed mixed capacity.

The difference between the ideal and the actual use is due to a combination of jaywalking pedestrians, bicycle traffic, unsignaled pedestrian crossing, double-parked cars and delivery trucks, cars cruising slowly and searching for on-street parking, and finally, on-street parking itself (as door openings and parallel parking inhibits traffic flow). For example, the Harvard Coop intersection operates at 75 percent efficiency.

These pedestrian/vehicular interaction diagrams pointed out a basic fallacy in most traffic planning— why solutions to improve traffic flow are sought, such as widening streets or creating one-way circulators, when the emphasis is on pedestrian uses, as it was in Harvard Square. Any improvement to traffic conditions must come as a result of improvement of pedestrian amenities.

For example, the question is not merely how many more people might be in Harvard Square during the critical impact period. This number is only of relative significance because it depends on the extent of control exercised over the pedestrian/

vehicular interaction. The places where pedestrian crossing is signalled are located on the Existing Pedestrian/Vehicular Interaction Diagrams map. Jaywalking (uncontrolled crossings) is also indicated, as are other particular problems and lack of pedestrian amenity.

This method of mapping the interaction of activity also showed that the increased pedestrian activity in the Square due to the new tourists would not be felt uniformly throughout Harvard Square. The visitors will tend to concentrate in certain areas of the Square because they would have some common wants and needs: eating, some limited sightseeing and small purchases (postcards, souvenirs). The natural flow from one attraction to another, i.e., from the new attraction to Harvard Yard, will also tend to concentrate traffic between those points. Most, too, will also limit themselves to a five-minute walk (1200 feet). Thus, the critical impact area, or "proposed primary pedestrian flow" can be determined by the concentration of services available and desired, probable routes, understanding of the area, and distance from the project site.

7

The Treatment

"Would you tell me, please, which way I ought to go from here?" asked Alice.

"That depends a good deal on where you want to get to," said the Cat.

—Lewis Carroll, *Alice in Wonderland*

We have seen that in order to understand the urban environment and what its evolving form is becoming, one must first examine its structural characteristics and begin to grasp the underlying purposes and theories behind the physical reality—the need for the place at all, the reason for a certain building type in a particular location, and why an area will get overdeveloped or will remain underdeveloped.

We then can visualize the potential physical outcome of the recycling repair work and begin to operate as ecosurgeons, cutting away at and unclogging the systems in order to get "where we really want to get to."

Perhaps utilizing the term "recycling" for every aspect of the treatment of urban problems is almost as important as the treatment itself in this day of media overkill. At the very least, any positive urban action would get the same notice that "recycled jeans" get, or the fanfare the Liz Taylor/ Richard Burton "recycled lovers" does. For half the battle is getting the people together in united action to preserve and revitalize their civic centers. A popular phrase attributed to Tiny Tim (the singer) was, "You are what you eat," and a variation on this theme, which is frequently stated by our six-year-old son Max Cutler is, "You are what you say you are!" Following this logic, if treatment is undertaken or even just proposed, and if the city can get people believing it enough to state it—then there is an excellent chance that it will actually happen.

Some examples of particular treatments or solutions to specific urban problems are illustrated here.

Saving a Place:
The Heritage of
a Main Street

The Small City

In recent years, downtown Gardiner, Maine, like so many small New England towns, has experienced a decline in economic activity and patronage. Inaccessible parking, poor traffic circulation, unresponsive merchandising, together with the general physical and aesthetic deterioration of the downtown core were contributing factors to this problem. The natural asset of the town's location at the juncture of the Kennebec River and the Cobbosseecontee Stream had not been capitalized upon for many years. The historic heritage of the old main street and its warm brick buildings had never been appreciated.

Some citizens of Gardiner believed that the completion of the new I-93 highway section through Gardiner to the Maine Turnpike would provide them with the opportunity to regenerate their economy by allowing an outside developer to construct a shopping center at the interchange on the outside of town. However, others feared that competition from the developing commercial areas around the interchange would result in the further decline of the downtown commercial business district. The question then became: How to revive the downtown? And what are the uniquely Maine answers to restoring natural assets such as the presence of the Cobbosseecontee Stream and developing a new urbanistic plan that would invigorate a flaccid merchandising economy?

People and Their Problems

At the onset of this project, some merchants of Gardiner, Maine had already made their own diagnosis of the problems of their main shopping street.

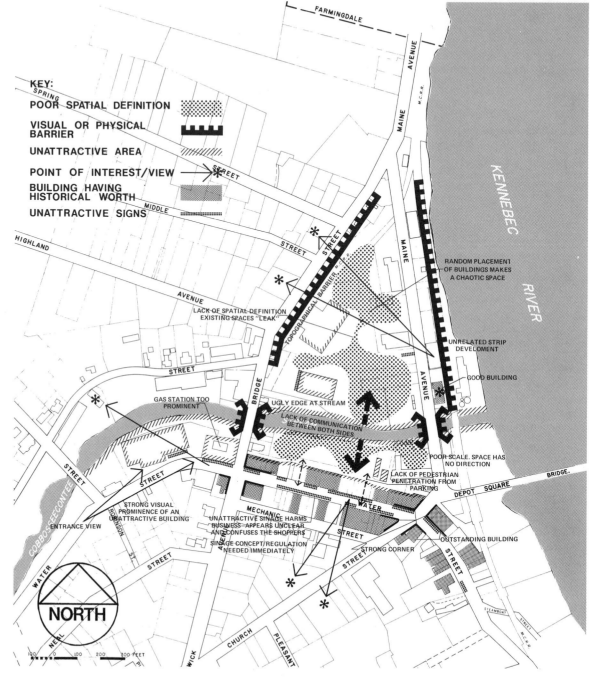

KEY:
POOR SPATIAL DEFINITION
VISUAL OR PHYSICAL BARRIER
UNATTRACTIVE AREA
POINT OF INTEREST/VIEW
BUILDING HAVING HISTORICAL WORTH
UNATTRACTIVE SIGNS

RANDOM PLACEMENT OF BUILDINGS MAKES A CHAOTIC SPACE

LACK OF SPATIAL DEFINITION EXISTING SPACES "LEAK"

UNRELATED STRIP DEVELOMENT

GOOD BUILDING

GAS STATION TOO PROMINENT

UGLY EDGE AT STREAM

LACK OF COMMUNICATION BETWEEN BOTH SIDES

POOR SCALE. SPACE HAS NO DIRECTION

LACK OF PEDESTRIAN PENETRATION FROM PARKING

STRONG VISUAL PROMINENCE OF AN UNATTRACTIVE BUILDING

ENTRANCE VIEW

UNATTRACTIVE SINAGE HARMS BUSINESS—APPEARS UNCLEAR AND CONFUSES THE SHOPPERS

SINAGE CONCEPT/REGULATION NEEDED IMMEDIATELY

OUTSTANDING BUILDING

STRONG CORNER

KENNEBEC RIVER

TOPOGRAPHICAL BARRIER

COBBOSSEECONTEE

NORTH

100 0 100 200 300 FEET

Poor spacial definition.

First of all, it was old—how could their small old brick shops compete with what they saw as modern concrete block structures proposed for the shopping center on the city's perimeter?

Second, they felt there was inadequate parking—after all, it was no longer possible to park right out in front and run in for their provisions. And certainly the chaotic cross-purpose circulation and general physical and aesthetic deterioration of this old-fashioned downtown were contributing factors to the problem.

Finally, there was the uncertainty about an impending bridge replacement across the Kennebec River. If it were to be replaced, wouldn't the mammoth modern ramps of the new bridge wipe out the end of their Water Street?

The solution, some of the merchants resolved, was to simply tear down one entire side of Water Street and replace the old brick shops with inexpensive concrete block structures and put the parking right there in the middle.

A Fresh Look

The purpose of our study was to take a fresh look at the nature and extent of these problems and the feasibility of the proposed solution. For example, is it the amount or is it the distribution and accessibility of automobile parking that is inadequate? Are there alternative bridge locations with less disastrous impacts on the old shopping street? And based upon the analysis of needs and problems, what are the realistic plans for the downtown Gardiner business district? Obviously, the plan of development should be economically feasible. It should

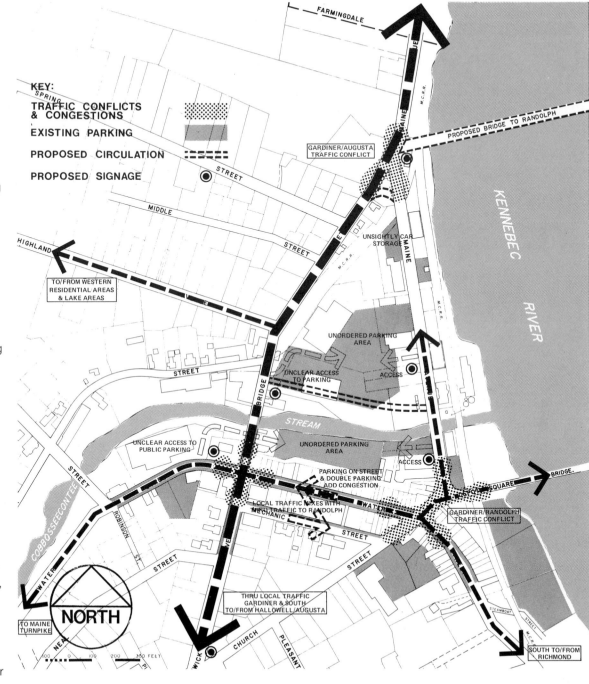

KEY:
TRAFFIC CONFLICTS & CONGESTIONS
EXISTING PARKING
PROPOSED CIRCULATION
PROPOSED SIGNAGE

Traffic conflict and congestion.

also capitalize upon and restore the natural assets, such as the presence of Cobbosseecontee Stream, in developing an urban plan. The plan should make the downtown Gardiner area a convenient place to visit for its shoppers. Therefore, it should make a positive contribution toward alleviating its circulation and parking problems, and provide the area with an identity and a merchandising image capable of sustained customer attraction.

To understand the new, real needs of the city's main shopping street required that the community take a fresh look at itself and its objectives. Were their objectives compatible with the city's original roots and with its present market? Was there consensus? This fresh look raised questions that could only be anwered by the intensive community involvement program including both merchants and shoppers, which was covered in Chapter 5.

Reviving self-confidence to revive a physical place

The challenge was the prototypical issue at stake, that is, the fear that an impending new highway with its magnetic attraction for commercial growth at the interchange to be located near the city could actually kill an already subdued and depressed downtown.

It was our intent to try and revive the flagging spirits of the town—revitalize self-confidence as well as a physical place. It was also our intent to illustrate several alternatives to the people and to illustrate the fact that the best scheme need not be the most expensive. We also attempted to reveal to some of the people of Maine that ''new'' is not by definition ''better''; that ''old'' can be even more

feasible through reuse and recycling from an economic standpoint. Heritage has a value, too, which the people had altogether neglected.

In this as well as in many other small towns, it was innovative planning that dealt with an intuitive approach to the people and their problems, rather than suggesting new zoning or other legislation. For example:

□

Deft ecosurgery. Analysis and surveys showed that it was not a lack of sufficient parking, but rather that existing parking was inaccessible behind a long row of buildings. A simple solution required only the removal of one unsafe structure at the center of the row in order to provide a convenient pedestrian link. This precluded the need to raze other sections of the street for additional parking, and provided a link to and across the stream from the main commercial spine.

□

New is not by definition better than old. It had to be explained to the people diplomatically, patiently, and in dollars and cents that ''their'' scheme was not the most economical, and the reasons why there was a hidden value they might not yet see in the heritage of an old shopping street. Indeed, many of the new citizens were people who came to the town for that same ''quaint'' quality that some merchants found an embarrassment. Questionnaires began to indicate some of these differences in attitude and slide shows of successfully revitalized (economically) old sections of other cities were used to show that reuse was a trend in the mainstream cities and demolishing of these old structures and of the old street might be something

Gardiner might regret in later years. They would be destroying not just some buildings, but a ''place'' and its sense of place. Communities are often their own worst enemies and need protection from themselves.

□

Another intuitive technique was that of dealing with a poorly contrived solution that some members of the community had come up with, which, in effect, suggested the destruction of one side of the main street in the town to provide more parking. We illustrated this notion and compared it to two other alternatives, providing an equal analysis of three schemes including progressive phasing and costing with clear pros and cons described. Because of the construction interruption and the steep hillside site, the ''destruction'' Scheme III turned out to exceed both the town's budget and the total cost of the two other schemes by a large margin. This helped us greatly in achieving credibility for the more significant preservation schemes (Alternatives I and II) which we had proposed and which were ultimately accepted by the community as Phases I and II.

□

Our Scheme II proposed a new kind of shopping mall that is uniquely ''Maine'' in character. It would attract both Maine residents and tourists alike as customers and capitalize on the historic character of the main street. It involved new merchandising concepts for a uniquely ''Maine Town'' attraction. In order to justify a preservation scheme, reuses had to be proposed for the apparently out-dated structures, and flexibility for new types of retail space had to be built into the scheme. We proposed a cluster of ''factory outlet'' or ''mill end'' type

Renovation of old
Gardiner.

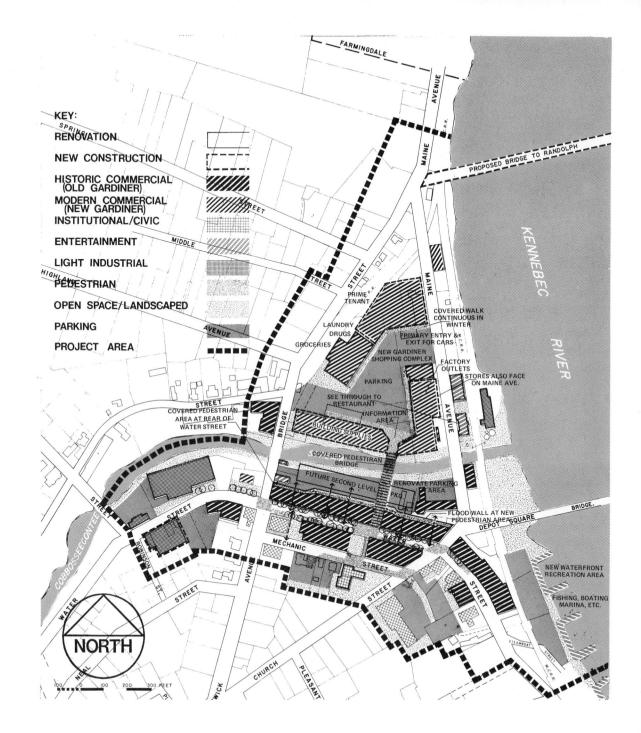

KEY:

RENOVATION

NEW CONSTRUCTION

HISTORIC COMMERCIAL
(OLD GARDINER)

MODERN COMMERCIAL
(NEW GARDINER)

INSTITUTIONAL/CIVIC

ENTERTAINMENT

LIGHT INDUSTRIAL

PEDESTRIAN

OPEN SPACE/LANDSCAPED

PARKING

PROJECT AREA

FARMINGDALE

MAINE AVENUE

R.R.

PROPOSED BRIDGE TO RANDOLPH

KENNEBEC RIVER

SPRING STREET

MIDDLE STREET

HIGHLAND AVENUE

PRIME TENANT

COVERED WALK
CONTINUOUS IN
WINTER

LAUNDRY
DRUGS
GROCERIES

PRIMARY ENTRY &
EXIT FOR CARS

NEW GARDINER
SHOPPING COMPLEX

FACTORY
OUTLETS

STORES ALSO FACE
ON MAINE AVE.

PARKING

SEE THROUGH TO
RESTAURANT

INFORMATION
AREA

MAINE AVENUE

STREET

COVERED PEDESTRIAN
AREA AT REAR OF
WATER STREET

BUILDING SUPPLIES

COVERED PEDESTRIAN
BRIDGE

BRIDGE STREET

FUTURE SECOND LEVEL

PKG

RENOVATE PARKING
AREA

FLOOD WALL AT NEW
PEDESTRIAN AREA SQUARE

BRIDGE

DEPOT STREET

COBBOSSEECONTEE STREET

ROBINSON ST

STREET

MECHANIC STREET

STREET

NEW WATERFRONT
RECREATION AREA

FISHING, BOATING
MARINA, ETC.

WATER STREET

NEAL STREET

NORTH

100   0   100   200   300 FEET

WICK

CHURCH

PLEASANT

STEAMBOAT STREET

M.C.R.R.

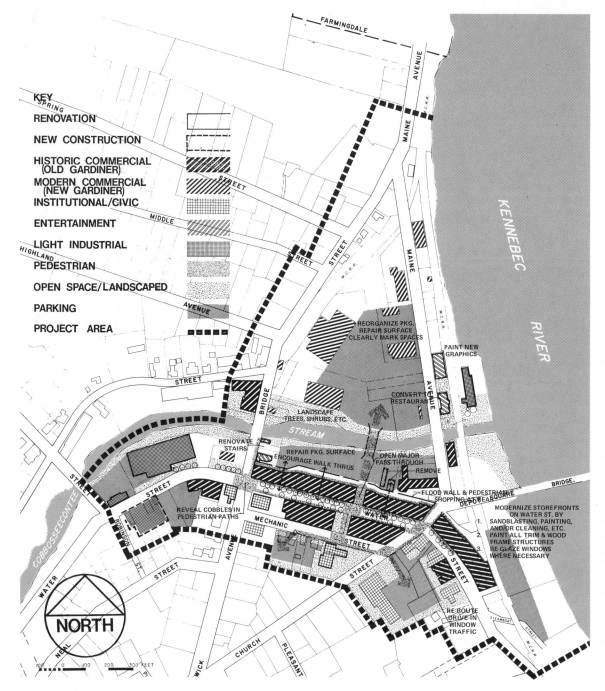

KEY

RENOVATION

NEW CONSTRUCTION

HISTORIC COMMERCIAL
(OLD GARDINER)

MODERN COMMERCIAL
(NEW GARDINER)

INSTITUTIONAL/CIVIC

ENTERTAINMENT

LIGHT INDUSTRIAL

PEDESTRIAN

OPEN SPACE/LANDSCAPED

PARKING

PROJECT AREA

FARMINGDALE

KENNEBEC RIVER

REORGANIZE PKG.
REPAIR SURFACE
CLEARLY MARK SPACES

PAINT NEW
GRAPHICS

CONVERT TO
RESTAURANT

LANDSCAPE
TREES, SHRUBS, ETC.

STREAM

RENOVATE
STAIRS

REPAIR PKG. SURFACE
ENCOURAGE WALK THRUS

OPEN MAJOR
PASS THROUGH

REMOVE

BRIDGE

FLOOD WALL & PEDESTRIAN
SHOPPING

GEDOTEASQUARE

REVEAL COBBLES IN
PEDESTRIAN PATHS

MODERNIZE STOREFRONTS
ON WATER ST. BY
1. SANDBLASTING, PAINTING,
   AND/OR CLEANING, ETC.
2. PAINT ALL TRIM & WOOD
   FRAME STRUCTURES
3. RE-GLAZE WINDOWS
   WHERE NECESSARY

RE-ROUTE
DRIVE IN
WINDOW
TRAFFIC

NORTH

100 0 100 200 300 FEET

A theme for new Gardiner.

stores selling Maine products such as shoes, shirts, canoes, wood products, and other popular Maine items; such factory discount stores are becoming popular in Maine (following the successful "just off the highway" and "mail order" model of L. L. Bean). By grouping these popular outlets, Gardiner would achieve a "critical mass" in attracting shoppers and tourists, would provide additional off-season commerce through traditional mail order sales, and Maine would be benefited by a modified control of this latest sprawl element on her highways.

□

A final innovation was establishing a precedent of do-it-yourself "ecosurgery"—the removal of newer structures, unattractive cladding material, and tawdry signage because they are inconsistent with the visual environment rather than removing older structures simply because they are old.

The "Fix-Up Guidelines" may look simplistic in terms of big city urban design and preservation, but to convince a storeowner from a small depressed city in inland Maine to remove the stucco and the 1950s signage to reveal the elegant brick building beneath at his own cost for no reason but the attractiveness and continuity of the town, we felt was a giant step in urban environmental preservation. This feeling of accomplishment was verified by ECODESIGN's receipt of a 1975 *Design and Environment* Award for Excellence in Environmental Design, a citation: "for an important contribution to the nationwide urban landmark preservation movement".

PRELIMINARY FIX-UP GUIDELINES TO MERCHANTS AND OWNERS OF BUILDINGS IN PROPOSED HISTORIC DOWNTOWN DISTRICT

The pleasant quality of old commercial main streets in the U. S. rested heavily on the consistency of texture, colors, and materials of the buildings. It is this quality that the following "fix-up" guidelines would attempt to restore in a very cursory and inexpensive manner. If these very preliminary guidelines were successfully and enthusiastically adapted, then a more detailed set of specifications for rehabilitation work in the historic commercial area of Gardiner should be written and signage legislation drawn up.

BUILDING SURFACES AND MATERIALS

- **Existing brick and other masonry buildings** which have been surfaced over with stucco, asphalt, metal or wood siding, etc. should be stripped to reveal brick surfaces.

Existing natural red brick surface should be cleaned. Brick repairs and additions must utilize matching brick and mortar.

- **Existing or newly revealed brick surfaces** should be brick red color. If natural red brick color is either painted over or of the inconsistent yellow brick type, this can be done by removing old paint by sandblasting/cleaning or by painting over nonconforming colored brick building with brick red paints. The brick red paint is particularly important on the rear elevations of buildings on both sides of Water Street where buildings have been painted a variety of colors. Paint should be flat or nongloss type.

- **Existing concrete block buildings,** such as the Truitt Shoe Plant, Bowling Alley, and exposed sides of the Cottles complex, should be either faced in brick or painted in a dark color to cause these surfaces to recede.

Colors to be brick red, dark brown, or forest green on Water Street.

- **Existing and proposed clapboard siding.** Existing clapboard in Water Street area should be painted. If building is only partially clapboard (i.e., brick building with clapboard additions, etc.), then color should be brick red or dark brown. If entire building is clapboard, such as house and barn structures, the color may be of the traditional New England farmhouse type — white, yellow, red, as well as dark green (such as Harvey's Hardware).

- **Other siding types.** Metal and asphalt siding materials are inconsistent with the historic buildings of downtown Gardiner and should be removed or covered over with clapboard siding. Shingles and Texture 1-11 are borderline materials; existing uses can remain, but future materials should be restricted to red brick and clapboard.

CUT ON DOTTED LINE

FOLD ON DOTTED LINE

CORNICES, MOULDINGS, WINDOWS, AND DOOR FRAMES

All old cornices, mouldings, windows and door frames and historic storefronts should be retained, restored, and repainted, where necessary. Colors, again, should be in the traditional brick reds, greens, browns, or white painted in either gloss or semi-gloss paints.

AWNINGS

The beginning of consistency is apparent in the green and white canvas awnings on the north side of Water Street, and awnings should be used rather than other sun screen devices (built-on overhangs, metal and plastic awnings are definitely disruptive to the character of the old street). Canvas awnings should remain with the green and white and green and yellow stripes or bright yellow solids.

GENERAL REPAIR AND HOUSEKEEPING

General repairs that many buildings appear to be in need of include:

- Broken windows fixed.

- Recaulking

- Repointing

- Old sheds removed.

- Paper and cardboard signs taped to windows should be removed as they degrade all the neighboring stores as well.

- Exposed shiny metal should be painted black or to match building wherever possible (e.g., aluminum vents, air conditioners).

- Dirty curtains in dirty windows are also depressing for all who pass by them. If street level curtains must be hung, they should at least be consistent with historic tone of the street (e.g., Gardiner Water District building) as shiny fabrics and patterns are distracting.

SIGNAGE

Although there are several raised gold letter signs that are reminiscent of the signs that used to line Water Street, bad signage is obviously the most disrupting aspect of Water Street's visual impact today. Sign regulations consistent with the street's heritage would prohibit use of back-lit, porcelain, tile, plastic, and neon signs, as well as free "advertising signs" (Coca Cola, etc.).

Signs could be either parallel or perpendicular to the building or both, but placed to relate to the building's window bays, cornices, doors, etc.

FOLD ON DOTTED LINE

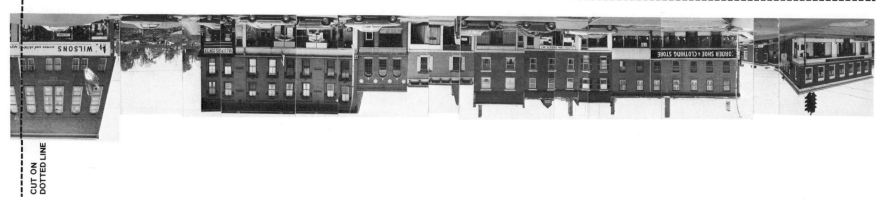

CUT ON DOTTED LINE

FOLD ON DOTTED LINE

Recommended prototype sign:

The traditional sign of this period was the long narrow horizontal wooden sign painted dark (usually black, or dark green or red) with lettering in either raised gold (e.g., National Bank of Gardiner, Eastman's Book Store) or flat painted in white or black (e.g., Eagle Publishing Company). Copy on the signs was limited to the name and business of the establishment (e.g., Harvey's Hardware) and perhaps the date established and the street number. Width of these signs was generally about 12 — 15 inches, and the length might run to the distance of the building. Placement was important, and the signs usually fit in neatly between store front tops and the first floor cornice moulding (e.g., Cushing's Farm Products Market, Shepard's Auto Parts). They began and ended in relation to windows on the first floor or were centered over doors.

With perpendicular signs, the sizes were generally controlled by the metal angles cantilevering the signs from the building. The shapes were normally rectangles or circles and often included painted-on graphic symbols.

It is important to remember that a first priority for the Town is to utilize efficiently the large existing public parking area along Cobbosseconttee Stream. In addition to purchasing a property along the north side of Water Street to break through a pedestrian access to the shopping street (this is essential), the back of these buildings should be treated as the arrival point to Downtown Gardiner. This means that signage on the back of the buildings is important. Presently, only one or two merchants have recognized the importance of their "back door."

MERCHANDIZING

The critical element in the commercial success of Downtown Gardiner will ultimately be the responsiveness of the shops' merchandizing attitudes. The fix-up guidelines above, together with the proposed landscaping of Water Street, the river and stream banks, etc., are intended to restore the warm background of reds, browns, and greens to the historic area. Then, the addition of the bright, colorful window displays of merchandise oriented to contemporary tastes gives new life to the street. Bright color accents and display devices are placed in the window displays and call attention to the products to be sold rather than to the building or the signs. Charles Street and Newbury Street (Boston), Ghiradelli Square (San Francisco), Larimer Square (Denver), Market Square (Newburyport) are examples of old towns across the country that are proof of the success of this formula — historic background complementing contemporary merchandise.

FOLD ON DOTTED LINE

A New Generator:
A Will to Live

The Medium-sized City

Developing a strategy for maximizing the benefits that an interstate highway can bring to a medium-sized city faced with a new highway becoming a dominant aspect of community life—this was the directive for a joint DOT/HUD study for which ECODESIGN developed an action-oriented plan.

The major objective was to identify in an action-oriented plan the possibilities for both solving the most pressing problems and for taking advantage of the positive potentials for development in a city that is part of a larger metropolitan area traversed by an already constructed urban expressway.

The subject city was Pawtucket, Rhode Island, a city with a 1970 population of 76,984 persons. Land area is 8.8 square miles, which gives a population density of approximately 8,500 persons per square mile. Of special interest is the central business district of the city, which is approximately 78 acres in size and has an assessed evaluation of 20 million dollars.

According to the 1970 Bureau of Census population figures, there are some 122 cities that fall within this particular study's definition of a medium-sized community. Approximately 67 communities (just over 50 percent) have a transportation corridor (namely, an interstate expressway) passing through them. Thus, this study and the action plan it produced does not apply only to Pawtucket, or for that matter a handful of communities, but also to a significant number of existing communites of this size today and to definitely more by the end of this decade.

Some major expressway benefits to be expected, as identified in Chapter 6, included the visual dynamics of the siting of the I-95 highway, the fortunate relevance of the elevated and depressed sections of the highway, the existence of a major commercial attraction visible from the highway, direct access and egress to the downtown circulation from the highway, the compactness of the downtown Main Street, and so forth.

The Importance of Enthusiasm in Achieving Goals

The most important positive consideration for Pawtucket was the attitude of enthusiasm and a will to fight to save a depressed downtown that existed in the leadership levels as well as in the community itself. Problems and deficiencies were confronted head on, and goals were developed with the intention of maximizing the opportunities available.

Goals—Developing Opportunities:

☐
To improve and revitalize the character and environment of Pawtucket's downtown by fully developing its commercial—retail, recreational, and entertainment—potential; to encourage development of the area as a well-rounded commercial, recreational, residential city.

☐
To benefit from the existence of a major retail attraction (Apex) to the south of Main Street, to provide northern anchor attractions with convenient and attractive linkage between anchor uses, to encourage and protect existing development, and to stabilize and upgrade these property values of the Main Street spine.

☐
To clarify auto access, circulation, parking, and pedestrian circulation, and to provide direct accessibility and convenient parking.

☐
To reinforce visible image of "Pawtucket as a unique place"—preservation and continuance of its inherent urban forms and spaces (specific buildings, areas, topography, forms, texture, and materials) by encouraging renovation of such existing structures when functionally and economically compatible with new growth and needs.

☐
To eliminate physical and economic blight by removing deteriorated and functionally obsolete structures of no historic or aesthetic value.

☐
To encourage future renewal action in adjacent areas by providing renewed sections from which adjacent areas can draw new strength.

The following "accounting" of the problems (deficiencies in achieving goals) and opportunities (potentials for an action plan) was then compiled:

Problems—Eliminating Deficiencies:

☐
Presently there is no anchor or axial relationship to the north.

☐
Main Street axis is a tenuous "spine" at bridge crossing to Apex.

☐
CBD circulation traffic and standing traffic from semipublic and industrial uses are mixed.

☐
Housing stock is deteriorating (I-95 is a prime cause of population loss).

3-1

A new generator. The plexiglass-covered main commercial spine links the two activity/commercial generators, as if the city were "glass-covered," and it makes the place work.

☐
Fragmented uses of parcels.
☐
Inadequate circulation, intercept parking and specific short term and all day parking serve existing retail uses.
☐
Bad connections to and lack of recreational and entertainment activities; downtown park deficiency
☐
Downtown conveniences—comfort station, bus terminal, public transport service within downtown, convenience shopping—are all lacking.

Opportunities—Components of a Plan
☐
Clarity of access, circulation, and arrival.
☐
Parking—highway intercept, long term, short term.
☐
Increased land utilization.
☐
Improved CBD image, desirability, and strengthened concentrated central core with its dual retail-civic spines
☐
Ambient land redevelopment potential—redevelopment needs: parking, community facilities, housing, open space, entertainment/recreation (new land use); potential availability of large contiguous blocks through obsolescence as well as small specific lots possibly available for specific semi-public (library, YMCA) use.
☐
Historic atmosphere of mill town, topography, river spaces and land, notable buildings and foci, preservation of structures of unique historic or architectural interest.

☐
Pedestrian connections, reinforcing co-spine of civic and semi-public uses (library, city hall, welfare, post office, etc.).
☐
Attractions of: large land area, access and highway visibility to "northern anchor" retail to induce attractor-generator function of the conceptual model. Inducements/controls to the missing link.

The Prototype Concept

The principle of "shopping center generators," which has been proven across the country, is implied in the goals. When a single magnet or two polar magnet facilities (department stores, major discount chains, etc.) are located in a situation offering direct regional access from a major highway, clear arrival points, adequate parking, and ease of pedestrian circulation, it will attract and support facilities, such as specialty shops, satellite recreational activities, and convenience shops. We felt that the same principle could be applied in the case of an existing strip of such specialty shops, and that a "generator" facility could be introduced to stimulate economic revitalization.

The classic contemporary shopping center develops outside of the downtown area and offers such amenities as enclosed all-weather malls, minibus circulation within the complex, and entertainment in addition to the basic requirements of access, circulation, and parking. It is this shopping center competition against which our downtown main streets across the country must fight for survival.

A concept model was drawn to illustrate the idea to the city client. Then, by overlaying these working

parts on the existing downtown plan of Pawtucket, we were able to demonstrate which parts are already existing and which are lacking and should be provided for in a proposed action plan based on this concept.

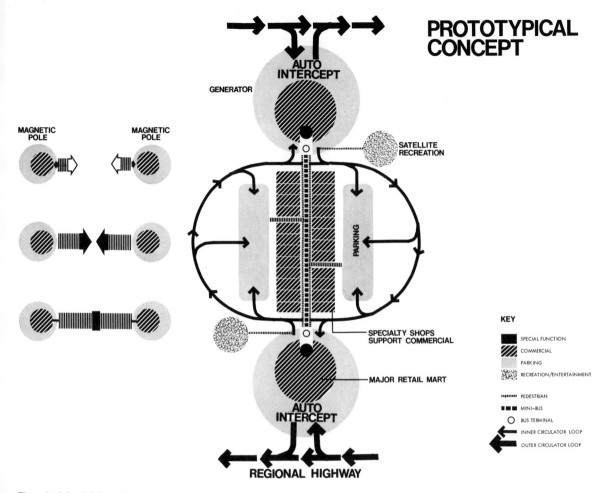

PROTOTYPICAL CONCEPT

MAGNETIC POLE   **MAGNETIC POLE**

GENERATOR

AUTO INTERCEPT

SATELLITE RECREATION

PARKING

SPECIALTY SHOPS SUPPORT COMMERCIAL

MAJOR RETAIL MART

AUTO INTERCEPT

REGIONAL HIGHWAY

KEY

SPECIAL FUNCTION
COMMERCIAL
PARKING
RECREATION/ENTERTAINMENT

PEDESTRIAN
MINI-BUS
BUS TERMINAL
INNER CIRCULATOR LOOP
OUTER CIRCULATOR LOOP

The principle of "shopping center generators" is parallel to the concept for revitalizing Pawtucket.

The Concept Fit and the City-wide Fit

In the Concept Fit diagram, (page 172), we superimposed the shopping center concept model of generating and attracting poles on Pawtucket's existing framework and land use patterns. Certain amenities and attractions far beyond the possibilities of an isolated shopping mall become apparent.

The Concept Fit (page 173) has been diagrammed to "fit" Pawtucket, and yet, it is still considered a *diagram,* not a plan. The retail mart complex (Apex), with direct connection from the highway off the access loop, becomes the southern anchor generating activity on Main Street's commercial/financial spine.

The City Hall and the historic Slater Mill (a tourist attraction) occupy a similar location on the access loop at the base of the municipal/civic spine.

A northern anchor or generator is shown as a tripod connection that serves several functions:

☐
The tripod pulls a proposed "anchor" retail facility closer into the Main Street spine with a direct overhead (air rights) connection to this entire facility. Air rights use often presents a far more economical solution to location and space problems than right-of-way land taking.

☐
The base of this tripod provides a central location for several presently nonexistent downtown conveniences: bus terminal, connection of mall, minibus, comfort station, and so on.

☐
The need and opportunity for a satellite recreational and entertainment complex is acknowledged. This

172

Superimposing the concept on the city and making it ''fit'' points up the real possibilities.

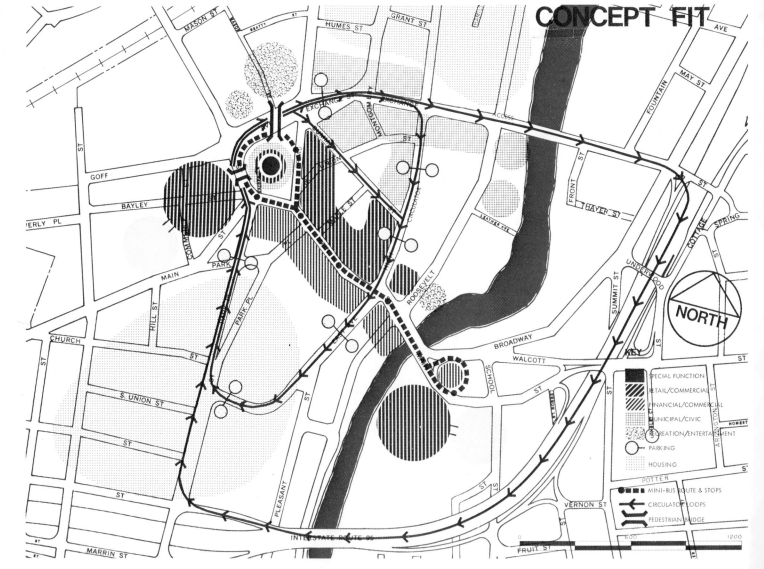

CONCEPT FIT

NORTH

SPECIAL FUNCTION

RETAIL/COMMERCIAL

FINANCIAL/COMMERCIAL

MUNICIPAL/CIVIC

RECREATION/ENTERTAINMENT

PARKING

HOUSING

MINI-BUS ROUTE & STOPS

CIRCULATOR LOOPS

PEDESTRIAN BRIDGE

The larger scale "fit"
is equally important for such
a concept to function.

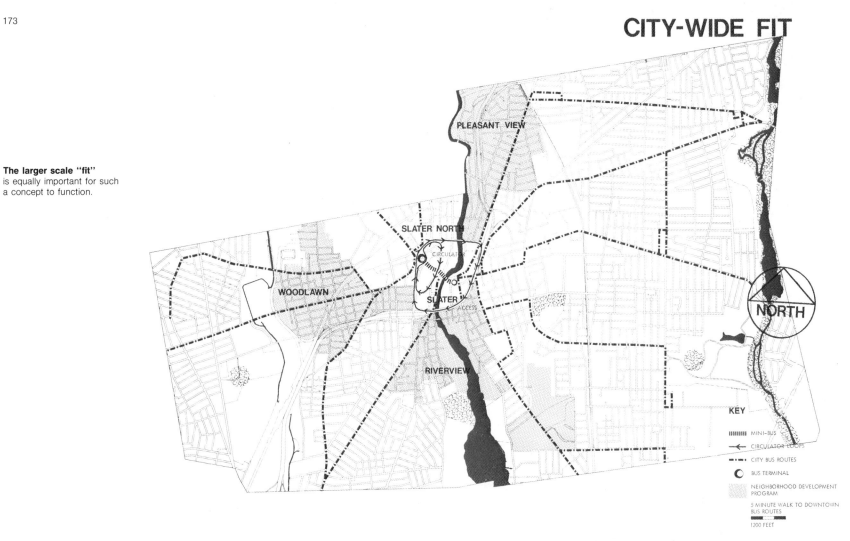

PLEASANT VIEW

SLATER NORTH

CIRCULATION

WOODLAWN

SLATER

ACCESS

RIVERVIEW

NORTH

KEY

|||||||| MINI-BUS

← CIRCULATOR LOOPS

·—·—· CITY BUS ROUTES

◐ BUS TERMINAL

NEIGHBORHOOD DEVELOPMENT PROGRAM

5 MINUTE WALK TO DOWNTOWN BUS ROUTES

1200 FEET

would bring much-needed activity and nightlife to the downtown area. Again, an overhead connection is shown here bridging the wide, confusing Goff-Exchange Street.

The Concept Fit diagram also illustrates:

☐
Adaptation of the Concept diagram to include both the Main Street commercial spine and the parallel, developing secondary civic spine.

☐
The essential direct egress from the highway to the two retail generators or anchors, which is provided by an outer *access loop*. A clear traffic pattern directing motorists to desired points in the downtown core and to intercept long- and short-term parking is provided by an inner *circulator*.

☐
Parking (without regard for parking ownership in this functional diagram) is indicated schematically to show ease of access off the inner circulator loop to major parking areas.

☐
The minibus, serving the mall and connecting the anchor facilities (retail and recreational), interchanges at the ends of the mall with the city-wide bus system, which is rerouted about the inner circulator loop.

The City-Wide Fit shows how the access, the circulator, and the mall with minibus service fits within the city's existing bus system.

The linkages of new with old and the creation of a ''city room'' highlight this place.

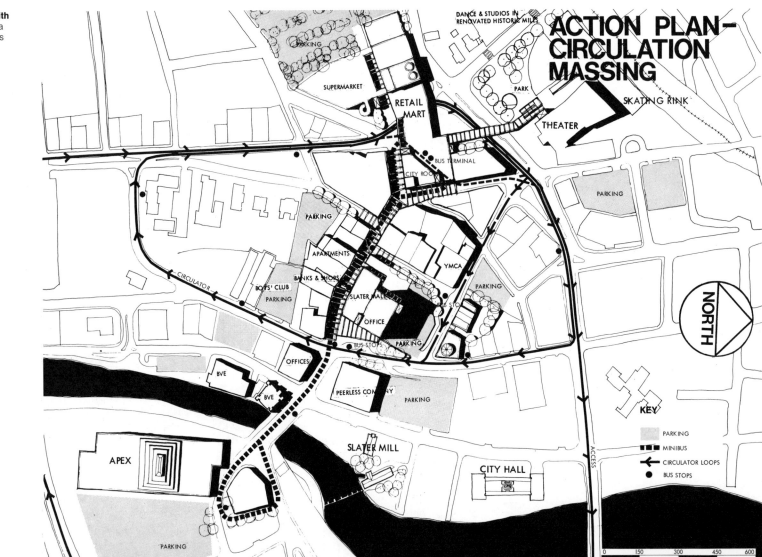

ACTION PLAN–
CIRCULATION
MASSING

DANCE & STUDIOS IN
RENOVATED HISTORIC MILLS

PARKING

SUPERMARKET

RETAIL
MART

PARK

SKATING RINK

THEATER

BUS TERMINAL

CITY ROOM

PARKING

PARKING

CIRCULATOR

PARKING

APARTMENTS

BANKS & SHOPS

BOYS' CLUB
PARKING

YMCA

PARKING

SLATER MALL

BUS STOP

OFFICE

BUS STOPS

PARKING

OFFICES

BVE

BVE

PEERLESS COMPANY

PARKING

SLATER MILL

CITY HALL

APEX

PARKING

ACCESS

NORTH

KEY

PARKING

MINIBUS

CIRCULATOR LOOPS

BUS STOPS

0   150   300   450   600

The Action Plan

The Action-Oriented Plan for downtown Pawtucket, which developed from the concept model and the Concept Fit diagram, proposes a twelve-acre shopping mart to form an opposite northern pole to a successful existing commercial complex to the south. The interaction of these two poles at either end of Main Street and the provision of additional parking will create a downtown area that functions according to the proven shopping-center formula.

The new retail facility would form a natural opposite pole to Apex and the Slater Urban Renewal area, with existing Main Street shops forming a connecting "spine" to bring the entire downtown into an integrated whole.

The retail mart is pulled closer and connected to the Main Street commercial spine by an air-rights extension over Dexter Street to an enclosed "city room" or central public area, which includes toilets, bus station, benches, and convenience shop booths.

The revitalization of the existing Main Street shopping area is further enhanced by a clear dome-type plastic enclosure, which extends its full length, transforming it into an enclosed shoppers' mall, including East Avenue and partly up Maple and Park Place East, which run perpendicular to Main Street. These cross streets will be closed to all but service traffic and become the pedestrian walkways, giving access east on Maple to civic and municipal buildings, the library and YMCA, and west to the proposed mall parking structure.

The active downtown complex is contained within an outer access loop and an inner circulator loop.

The reversing of traffic to clockwise was recommended so as to permit entrance and egress from cars and buses on the inner, or shopping side of the street.

Among the advantages suburban shopping centers have created are the direct accessibility from major thoroughfares and the convenient parking provided to the shopper. These same concepts have been applied to downtown Pawtucket in the action-oriented plan.

The proposed Dexter Street retail center would provide "balance" to the business district, where the center of gravity is now located at the Apex Discount Shop at the southern end. The two anchor retail facilities—the northern and southern poles—are connected by minibus service, which would operate along the Main Street shopping mall and link up to an existing transit system network and regular buses within terminal facilities inside the "city room."

The recreational complex north of Goff Avenue is also shown with the skating rink and the existing theater, operating as a twin cinema, with bowling alleys, restored mills for shops and studios, and nightclubs, to come.

The physical dimensions of pedestrian Main Street are in scale with the idea of creating a mall by closing the street to traffic. It is approximately 1200 feet long from the Apex complex to the Broad and Bayley forked intersection. This makes the spine of the downtown core an easy five-minute walk—well within recommended lengths. (People tend to turn to their cars when shopping walks exceed these limits.)

The existing circulation and proposed traffic pattern would allow the closing of Main Street only north of East Avenue. The proposed mall would then be 600 to 800 feet long—a length that would also be economical to cover with an all-weather clear canopy.

The street width of 48 feet is appropriate for all the functions of a shopping mall—two 8-foot lanes for pedestrian traffic, two 10-foot lanes for minibus traffic, and one 12-foot landscaped center seating area. The street is not overly wide, which would create wasted space and lack a sense of enclosure in a place.

Perhaps, only by such appealing measures as all-weather malls can our declining commercial areas compete with the suburban shopping malls. Pawtucket is fortunate in that the length, width, interest and containment of Main Street make it ideal economically and attractively for conversion to an enclosed mall.

**The glass-covered
pedestrian mall** provides
environmental protection and
links the activity generators
with a minibus.

**Enclosed views from the
mall** toward the secondary
(institutional) spine.

**People mover system—
Structuring land use.** PRT
context in the urban fabric.

Putting a Skeleton
Into the Flesh:
People Movers

The Large City

Denver, Colorado, is a threshold city. By threshold we mean it is not as big as Chicago, New York, or San Francisco, but it is like other large American cities on the scale of Atlanta, Pittsburgh, and Seattle. As a threshold city, Denver is also prototypical of many American cities with its singular dependence on the automobile in order to survive. The story of the increasing dominance of the automobile as the preferred transportation mode and the resulting decline in use of public transit is well known. Equally well known is the fact that this

preference results in urban traffic congestion and pollution on a scale increasingly unacceptable in the context of urban environmental goals. These environmental considerations notwithstanding, this preference continues in spite of the ability of existing and more advanced transit systems, on reserved rights-of-way, to maintain average running speeds equal to or better than the automobile over parallel urban routes.

Controlling "Californication" in Colorado

The most important realization about urban growth in the United States in the last hundred years is that

the nature of the growth almost uniformly is directly related to the nature and quality of the transportation network system. New advanced urban transportation systems can, in fact, control, limit, and define growth for tens of years in the future by structuring the urban frame to resist sprawl.

In our Advanced Urban Technology Study for Denver, we inserted a personalized rapid transit system (PRT), more commonly known as a "people mover," into the urban fabric as if it were the skeleton being inserted into the flesh of the city.

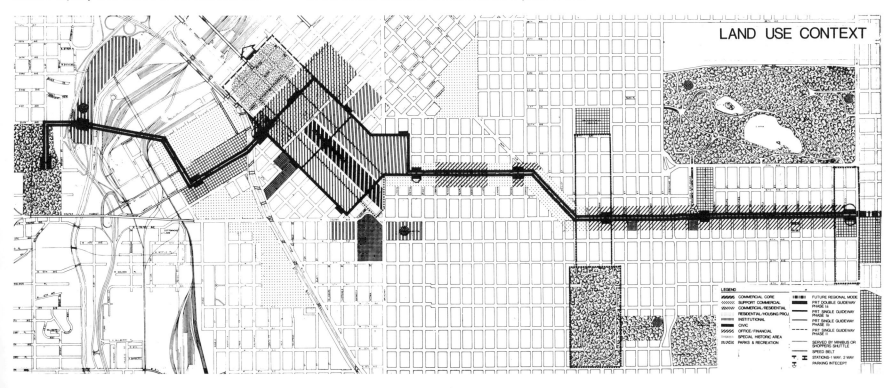

LAND USE CONTEXT

Then, depending on the land use context of the urban fabric, how the route corridors were selected, and where the stations are located, the system will determine many aspects of future growth and the urban form of the future. Likewise, the type of technologies used for the "people mover" would also affect the character of the city.

By the same token, the physical design of the PRT system will interact with and respond to the inherent organization and form of the city. (This was discussed for Denver in Chapter 6). Areas of interaction include:

☐
Patterns of city development—their interfaces and potential corridors that could be used for PRT system
☐
Organizational fit between city and system—efficient geometry of lines and points, the structuring of land use
☐
Continuity or consistency of massing, materials, and building types of blocks of buildings
☐
Change—flexibility in responding to potential change and possibilities evident in hard, soft, or transitional areas
☐
Space and form—both man-made, natural, and future spaces and forms that help structure the urban frame with associated edges, linkages, and barriers.

In proposing a route and a technology for a new transportation system, the opportunity is great to enhance the quality of the core city and to change the present image. The alternative to a strong trans-portation policy is a decline in the physical environment, the economic health and the accessibility of the core city—to the detriment of the entire region.

Realizing that Denver is prototypical of the directions of the future American city, and is one of the series of so-called threshold cities (in size and potential) our study was concerned with both the particular needs of Denver as well as the general needs of other metropolitan areas. Clearly, a PRT demonstration project such as that proposed in Denver could not only benefit the immediate Colorado citizens, but indeed could benefit the whole nation as a laboratory of urban transit scenarios.

Corridors as prototype urban transit scenarios

Denver offers itself as a perfect testing ground in that there are a variety of generic corridor situations through which the system could travel: therefore, the corridors could be studied as both prototypical test case examples and as part of a total network.

The results of the Corridor Analysis indicated that a PRT demonstration system in Denver could, in one project, illustrate by corridor the following experiments:

a
A major auto parking intercept at CBD periphery. Integrating with the present highway system, propose strategic auto-intercept parking locations. Denver's Mile High Stadium is typical of a recreational area with sporadic peak usage, which could utilize auto parking spaces jointly as an intercept for the PRT. Here the auto mode would interface with the terminus of the downtown PRT system.

b
Flexibility for changing land use. The Centennial Park Parallel Run is an example of a system in an area undergoing transition, from present rail yards and industry to future park and institutional use (new US Mint). This corridor also permits incorporation of PRT system within a new divided highway.

c
Stations as linkage elements. The Auraria Education Center is an urban renewal context where the PRT can unite separate but integral parts. Mixed use structures in the station design could create a special node of shared facilities and a generator of activities and development related to the two colleges.

d
Revitalization of an historic area. With better accessibility, an historic district such as Denver's old stockyard and warehouse area is potentially more feasible for renovation and reuse of its old buildings. In addition the seed of such successful commercial restoration already exists in the colorful Larimer Square restoration.

A regional transportation terminal and modal interchange. The route is located in such a manner that several modes of travel are brought together in one central location in preparation of a possible extension of the system to connect with the regional transportation system utilizing the old railroad station and railroad rights of way. This requires the North CBD loop area to be designed with the flexibility for future expansion.

e
PRT system design. Demonstrate that through quality urban design and environmental controls, this new mode of transport is acceptable to the public. The North CBD Loop, for example, is an opportunity to install the PRT within new structures, while the

Proposed route and corridors.

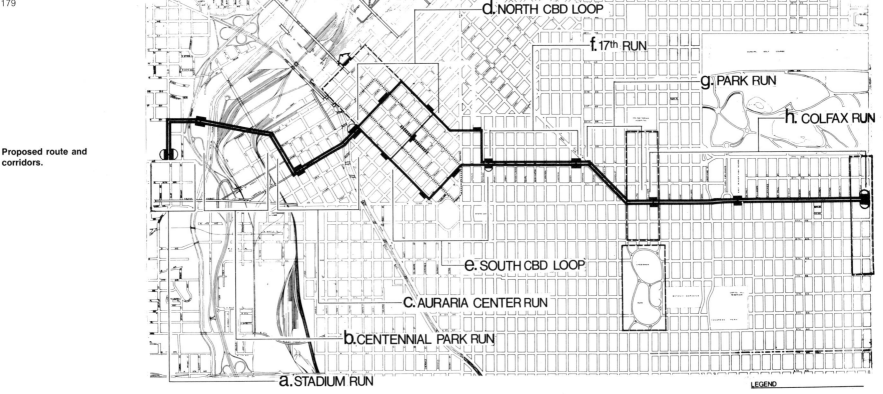

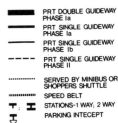

South CBD Loop could become a typical inner city commerical district reinforced by the system, with potential for strengthening the area.
Enhancement of opportunities for minorities and disadvantaged communities. Through deft location of stations and route and station design criteria, give greater accessibility and service to those communities in need of a stimulus.

f

Linear development corridor. The location and fit of the PRT is designed as an infrastructure to influence and service land use. The 17th Avenue Run, Park Avenue Run, Colfax Avenue Run are examples of dual guideways transversing through long strip developments and different land use situations, with opportunities for encouraging more cohesive development of existing strip commercial areas.

g

Alteration of the pedestrian / rider environment.
Through the use of innovative technology and by sensitive design studies of the guideway structure, integrate with the changing scales of the communities through which the route passes.

h

Integration with new development. Coordinate PRT systems and future development into a unified package and in some cases (such as proposed in building a station at 18th Street and a parking intercept at the Colfax Terminal) into the same structure. At the Colfax Terminal a parking intercept would serve medical centers, and it would also interface with a future transit system connecting or extending to the airport.

LEGEND

PRT DOUBLE GUIDEWAY PHASE Ia
PRT SINGLE GUIDEWAY PHASE Ia
PRT SINGLE GUIDEWAY PHASE Ib
PRT SINGLE GUIDEWAY PHASE II
SERVED BY MINIBUS OR SHOPPERS SHUTTLE
SPEED BELT
STATIONS-1 WAY; 2 WAY
PARKING INTECEPT

Corridor analysis.

CORRIDOR	PHYSICAL DATA			LAND USE		
	STREET & BLOCK DIMENSIONS	TRAFFIC SPEED	PRT CLEARANCE	LAND USE & EVENTS	TYPICAL DENSITY BUILDING HEIGHTS	USER NEEDS & STATION LOCATIONS
a. OLYMPIC STADIUM	CLAY STREET 60' WIDTH	AUTO: 30 MPH ACCESS STREET TO PARKING PRT: 30 - 40 MPH	DOUBLE GUIDE RUN 16'6" ON CLAY	▪OLYMPIC STADIUM & ARENA ▪INTERMITTENT PARKING REQ'D ▪KISS & RIDE CBD INTERCEPT	▪LOOSELY KNIT NEIGHBORHOOD ▪UNSTABLE PRESENT LAND USE ▪RESIDENCES, JUNK YARDS,	▪CONNECT CBD WITH WEST SIDE SPORTING EVENTS, AND MINT EMPLOYEES ▪EXISTING PERIPHERAL PARKING INTERCEPT ▪NEW COMMERCIAL USES AROUND STADIUM
	VALLEY HIGHWAY INTERSTATE HIGHWAY	AUTO: 60 MPH HEAVY PRT: 30 - 40 MPH	DOUBLE GUIDE RUN CROSSES OVER I-25	▪NEW MINT WILL BE HEAVY EMPLOYMENT CENTER AND REQUIRES SERVICE ACCESS	▪EXISTING MEDIUM INDUSTRY ▪CONCRETE PLANT ▪MINT SITE UNSTABLE	
b. CENTENNIAL PARK	MARKET BLAKE PARKWAY PROPOSED NEW PARKWAY 6 - 12' LANES, 12' SHOULDER, 20' LANDSCAPED MEDIAN STRIP	AUTO: 50 - 60 MPH PEDESTRIAN & BIKE TRAFFIC IN MEDIAN PRT: 30 - 40 MPH	DOUBLE GUIDE RUN 23' CLEARANCE REQUIRED FOR EXISTING RR YARDS	▪PROPOSED PARK - RECREATIONAL USE ▪EXISTING AS RAILROAD YARDS ▪RIGHT OF WAY RETAINED FOR REGIONAL TRANSPORTATION MODE	▪POSSIBLE LOW CAMPUS-TYPE OFFICE BUILDINGS - SUPPORT ▪UNSTABLE W. COLFAX - DRY GULCH -- CONNECTION SHOULD BRING EQUILIBRIUM	▪MAY DEVELOP SUPPORT FACILITIES TO MINT AS WELL AS PROPOSED CENTENNIAL PARK ▪CONNECTS WITH HIGH DENSITY CAPITOL HILL NEIGHBORHOOD
c. AURARIA EDUCATION CENTER	8TH STREET ALSO TO BE DEVELOPED AS PARKWAY WITH LANDSCAPED MEDIAN STRIP	AUTO: 50 MPH PEDESTRIAN: LIGHT PRT: 30 MPH	DOUBLE GUIDE RUN 16'6" CLEAR IN MEDIAN - PEDESTRIAN OVERPASS NOT REQUIRED	▪UNIVERSITY ▪SHARED FACILITIES ▪CONVENTION COMPLEX TIES ▪HOUSING (MEDIUM DENSITY) PROPOSED	▪HIGH DENSITY EDUCATION, SOME HOUSING ▪HIGH RISE SLABS CLOSE TO SPEER BOULEVARD, OLD WAREHOUSES FURTHER OUT	▪INTOWN AUTO INTERCEPT FOR CBD - ALSO STUDENT PARKING ▪STUDENT ACCESS FOR A METRO-POLITAN UNIVERSITY FROM EAST AND WEST ▪UNIVERSITY COMPLEX SHOULD BE LINKED AND COMMUNITY ENFORCED BY SYSTEM
	LAWRENCE STREET 60' WIDE, 12 - 15' WALK 250' BLOCKS	AUTO: 20 MPH PEDESTRIAN: OVERPASS PRT: 30 MPH	DOUBLE GUIDE RUN 16'6" CLEARANCE			
d. NORTH CBD LOOP	LAWRENCE STREET 80' WIDE, 12 - 15' WALK 450' BLOCKS	AUTO: 25 MPH PEDESTRIAN: UNDERPASS PRT: 20 MPH	SINGLE GUIDE 26' CLEARANCE ALLOWS CBD PEDESTRIAN 2ND LEVEL WALKWAYS	▪CONNECTS TO LARIMER SQUARE ▪SHOPS AND RESTAURANTS ▪DURA SKYLINE PROJECT	▪DURA HIGH RISE OFFICE AND COMMERCIAL BUILDINGS WITH PARKING AND PEDESTRIAN LEVEL OVERPASSES INTEGRAL	▪INTEGRATE STATION IN A NEW BUILDING COMPLEX ▪REVITALIZE WAREHOUSE DISTRICT ▪PROMOTE LOW INCOME COM-MERCIAL AREA TO NORTHEAST
	18TH STREET 80' WIDE, 12 - 15' WALK 250' BLOCKS	AUTO: 20 MPH PEDESTRIAN: UNDERPASS PRT: 20 MPH		▪FINANCIAL OFFICE BUILDINGS ▪FEDERAL CENTER ▪POST OFFICE	▪HEAVY EMPLOYMENT, 5 - 20 STORY WITH PARKING STRUCTURES INTEGRAL	▪EMPLOYMENT CENTER NEEDS EASY SHOT TO EAST AND WEST
e. SOUTH CBD LOOP	14TH STREET 80' WIDE, 12 - 15' WALK 250' BLOCKS	AUTO: 20 MPH PEDESTRIAN: LIGHT PRT: 20 MPH	SINGLE GUIDE 16'6" CLEARANCE	▪CONVENTION CENTER ▪DENVER POST ▪CONNECTS TO CIVIC CENTER, CAPITAL, ART MUSEUM	▪SUPPORT COMMERCIAL MEDIUM - HIGH RISE SLABS ▪PARKING LOTS	▪CONNECT CONVENTION CENTER FROM STADIUM, PARKING, HOTELS ▪STATION AT CIVIC CENTER
	STOUT STREET 80' WIDE, 12' WALK 450' BLOCKS	AUTO: 20 MPH PEDESTRIAN: UNDERPASS PRT: 20 MPH	SINGLE GUIDE 26' CLEARANCE ALLOWS 2ND LEVEL WALKWAYS	▪CROSS CBD CORE LINK ALTERNATE LOCATION IS CALIFORNIA STREET MALL PROPOSED	▪5 - 20 STORIES WITH PARKING INTEGRAL ▪CONNECTS COMMERCIAL AND FINANCIAL AREAS	▪STATION AT 16TH STREET INTER-SECTION INTERFACES WITH SHOPPERS SHUTTLE, ETC.
	COURT PLACE 60' WIDE, 12' WALK 450' BLOCKS	AUTO: 20 MPH PEDESTRIAN: UNDERPASS	SINGLE GUIDE 26' TO CLEAR EXISTING "SKYWALK"	▪LARGE "NAME" HOTELS ▪DEPARTMENT STORES ▪"SKYWALK"	▪5 - 20 STORIES WITH PARKING INTEGRAL	▪STOP SERVES HOTELS AND LINCOLN STREET BANK AND OFFICE TOWERS
f. 17th AVE.	17TH AVENUE 80' WIDE, 12 - 15' WALK	AUTO: 20 MPH HEAVY RUSH HOUR - POSTED 30 MPH PRT: 30 MPH	DOUBLE GUIDE RUN	▪MIXED USE ▪AT LINCOLN STREET CONTINUES BANK AND FINANCIAL DISTRICT	▪1 STORY COMMERCIAL & SMALL OFFICE BUILDINGS ▪HIGH DENSITY APARTMENTS AND OFFICE BUILDINGS GOING UP	▪BIKE TRAFFIC ON INCREASE ▪ACCESS TO HOSPITALS TO NORTH
g. PARK AVE.	PARK AVENUE 100' WIDE LONG DIAGONAL BLOCKS	AUTO: 30 MPH PRT: 30 MPH	DOUBLE GUIDE RUN TO NORTH SIDE 16'6"	▪HOMES FOR ELDERLY ▪RESIDENTIAL ▪HOSPITALS TO NORTH	▪RESIDENCES MIXED WITH MEDICAL OFFICES ▪PARKLETS ▪OLDER BRICK 2 STORY BUILDINGS	▪RETAIN RESIDENTIAL CHARACTER
h. COLFAX AVE. TERMINUS	COLFAX AVENUE 150' - 6 LANE WIDTH SWITCHBACK - TURNABOUT DIFFICULT	AUTO: 35 - 40 MPH HEAVY, AUTO NEED, UNLIMITED LEFT TURN PRT: 30 - 40 MPH	DOUBLE GUIDE RUN AT CENTER 26' CLEARANCE FOR PEDESTRIAN UNDERPASS	▪COMMERCIAL STRIP ▪PARK, MUSEUM, PLANETARIUM ▪MEDICAL CENTER - HOSPITAL AND SCHOOL	▪3 - 8 STORIES DECREASES HEIGHT GOING EAST MAINLY 1 - 2 STORY STRIP COMMERCIAL AND GAS STATIONS	▪POSSIBLE PARKING STRUCTURE INTERCEPT FOR CBD/EAST SIDE COMMUTERS AND MEDICAL IN-OUT

DOUBLE GUIDEWAY
TO BE DESIGNED INTO
MEDIAN OF PROPOSED
HIGHWAY -- WHICH
WILL ALSO INCORPORATE
BICYCLE PATH

MODE INTERFACE
WITH FUTURE REGIONAL
TRANSPORTATION SYSTEM

A STATION INTEGRATED
INTO NEW BUILDING
COMPLEX -- DENVER
URBAN RENEWAL AUTHORITY
PROJECT

TRANSPORTATION
MUSEUM

CENTENNIAL
PARK

HIGH DENSITY
HOUSING

MAJOR AUTO INTERCEPT
EXISTING FACILITIES
DOUBLE FUNCTION
PARKING SERVICING
STADIUM, ARENA, OLYMPIC
SITE. DURING WEEK IS
INTERCEPT FOR CBD AUTOS.

SINGLE GUIDEWAY WOVEN
THROUGH EXISTING HIGH
DENSITY CBD

INSTITUTIONAL

HOUSING

MARKET   BLAKE   PARKWAY

COMMUNITY
COLLEGE
OF
DENVER

SHARED

NEW MINT
WILL BE MAJOR
PERIPHERY
EMPLOYMENT
GENERATOR

PARK

ARENA

PARKING TERMINAL

MUSIC
HALL   ARENA

CONVENTION
CENTER

MIXED USE STRUCTURE
EXCHANGE NODE

AURARIA
HIGHER EDUCATION CENTER

METRO
STATE
COLLEGE

COLFAX AVE.

SERVING AND LINKING
THE PROPOSED EXPERIMENTAL
AURARIA EDUCATIONAL CENTER
WITH SHARED FACILITIES AT THE
TRANSPORTATION NODE

EVOLVING LAND USE
BELOW PRT -- RAILROAD
YARDS TO REMAIN IN
USE UNTIL CENTENNIAL
PARK CREATED

THIS CORRIDOR WOULD BE OF
PARTICULAR USE AS A "DE-BUGGING"
AREA FOR THE WHOLE PRT SYSTEM.

"COMMERCIAL STRIP" PRESENTLY
AUTO DOMINATED CAN BE GIVEN
NEW FORM AS 22' DOUBLE
GUIDEWAY INCORPORATED INTO
THE CENTER CAN ACT AS SPINE
FOR COMMERCIAL SPRAWL
[SEE PERSPECTIVE]

**Denver's PRT prototype
experiments.**

Linking Activity Centers and Building Flexibility into the Urban Frame

The organization of movement corridors should connect activity centers in an easily perceptible way. The visitor, in particular, should be able to perceive a basic organization in the downtown, which includes gateways to the downtown, major and minor movement corridors, as well as the linking of primary activity centers.

Since the system proposed for Denver is linear, directly linking a number of types of activity centers, its organization should be easy to comprehend. It will be easy to use and will encourage interaction between the Civic Center, retail district, hotels, office district, Convention Center and Auraria Higher Education Complex. For example, visitors to the major hotels area can utilize the linking PRT to gain easy access to the Convention Center. The workers in the Civic Center can easily get to the federal offices complex.

Most important, in locating corridors the major land use activity centers fall tangential to the CBD downtown PRT. The PRT transit system then acts as a linking chain tying the various urban components together.

In introducing a new transportation system into an existing environment in Denver, studies of alternatives and of the sequences of activities were made. Diagrammatic sections of proposed station and corridor types (over-street, off-street, integrated into buildings, etc.) were developed to show the synthesis of PRT with associated existing and suggested land use (educational facilities, transportation exchange, parking structures at auto intercept stations, etc.).

These sequence diagrams show corridor sections and stations drawn to the actual dimensional requirements of the existing technologies. For example, stations for air-cushioned vehicles presently require three lane widths: 1) one through lane, 2) one siding and by-pass lane, 3) one docking lane for maximum throughput in stations with more than two loading/alighting locations.

These requirements generally mean that single stations alone will span the entire downtown street width and that the effect for the motorist and pedestrian would be as if passing through a 200-foot long tunnel. For this reason, it is advisable wherever possible to place station facilities in buildings or over open parking lots, as shown on 14th Street in the sequence section diagram. The proposed Denver route provides several other opportunities for unique treatments of the station incorporated within buildings with a variety of mixed uses.

Good spatial organization of these sections communicates information to the user, such as the impending arrival of entrances. The PRT system's supporting architecture should respond to differences in existing architectural treatments. The system parts should be designed to best fit the specific urban fabric traversed.

Sequence sections of the route through the city.

1. OLYMPIC STADIUM

THE OLYMPIC STADIUM AND ARENA STOPS WOULD SERVE AS THE P R T SYSTEM WESTERN TERMINUS. THE 12,000 PARKING SPACES SURROUNDING THESE OLYMPIC FACILITIES WILL DOUBLE FUNCTION ON WEEKDAYS AS A COMMUTERS' AUTO INTERCEPT. AS THE ROUTE TURNS EAST TOWARDS THE C B D IT WILL CROSS OVER BOTH VALLEY HIGHWAY AND MARKET BLAKE. THE FIRST INBOUND STOP WILL BE AT THE PROPOSED NEW MINT, WHICH WILL BE A MAJOR EMPLOYMENT GENERATOR ON A SITE WHICH MIGHT ALSO INCLUDE COMPLEMENTARY ACTIVITIES IN CAMPUS-STYLE OFFICE BUILDINGS.

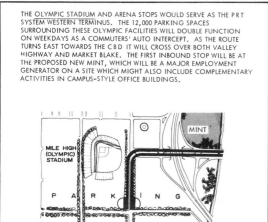

SUSPENDED

AIR CUSHIONED

2. CENTENNIAL PARK

THE DOUBLE GUIDE P R T WOULD THEN PASS OVER THE SOUTH PLATTE RIVER AND THROUGH THE CENTENNIAL PARK, WHICH WILL BE CREATED OUT OF THE PRESENT RAILROAD YARDS. AS THE RAILROAD YARDS WILL BE FUNCTIONING FOR SOME TIME AFTER THE P R T HAS BEEN BUILT AND BECAUSE A RIGHT OF WAY WILL STILL BE RESERVED THROUGH THE PARK FOR A FUTURE REGIONAL TRANSPORTATION MODE, IT IS NECESSARY TO MAINTAIN 23' CLEARANCE BELOW THE GUIDEWAY. AT THIS HEIGHT, THE GUIDEWAY WILL SLIP THROUGH THE TOPS OF THE TREES OF THE FUTURE PARK AND OF THE MEDIAN OF THE MARKET BLAKE, WHICH WILL ALSO INCLUDE A BICYCLE PATH NETWORK.

SUSPENDED

AIR CUSHIONED

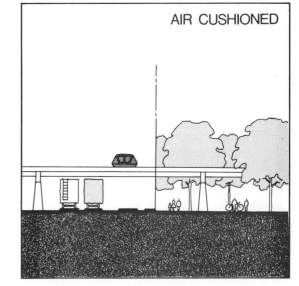

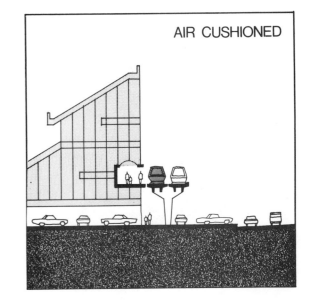

3. 8th STREET MEDIAN

8TH STREET – THE ROUTE TURNS SOUTH AT THE WESTERN EDGE OF THE AURARIA HIGHER EDUCATION CENTER AND FOLLOWS 8TH STREET'S LANDSCAPED MEDIAN STRIP TO LAWRENCE STREET. THIS STREET WILL PROBABLY NOT RECEIVE THROUGH PEDESTRIAN TRAFFIC TO JUSTIFY UNDERPASSES OR OVERHEAD WALKWAY FOR SOME TIME. THE PRT GUIDEWAY CLEARANCE, THEREFORE, WOULD BE THE HIGHWAY CLEARANCE OF 16'6". AT THIS HEIGHT, THE VEHICLE WOULD CONTINUE INBOUND THROUGH A TUNNEL FORMED BY THE MEDIAN'S TREES.

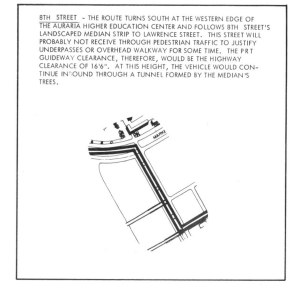

SUSPENDED

AIR CUSHIONED

4. AURARIA EDUCATIONAL CENTER

THE AURARIA HIGHER EDUCATION CENTER PRESENTS A UNIQUE OPPORTUNITY TO USE A PRT STATION STRUCTURE AS A SPINE OF AN EDUCATIONAL SHARED FACILITIES COMPLEX SUCH AS PROPOSED BETWEEN COLORADO UNIVERSITY AND THE METRO STATE COLLEGE THE SHARED FACILITIES WOULD BE MULTIMODAL -- OCCURRING AT THE THREE CONSECUTIVE EDUCATION AND CONFERENCE ORIENTED STATIONS. STUDENTS WOULD MOVE FROM THE AURARIA STATION, WITH ITS SHARED LIBRARIES, AUDITORIUMS, GYMNASIUMS, LABORATORIES, ETC., TO JOINT CLASSES AT C.U.D.C. WITHIN THE LAWRENCE STREET/14TH STREET EXCHANGE STATION, OR TO THE CONVENTION CENTER STOP FOR A CONCERT AT THE MUSIC HALL.

THIS AURARIA STATION DIAGRAM INDICATES HOW THE STATION COULD TIE THE VARIOUS COLLEGES OF THE CENTER TOGETHER TIGHTLY AROUND A TRANSPORTATION NODE.

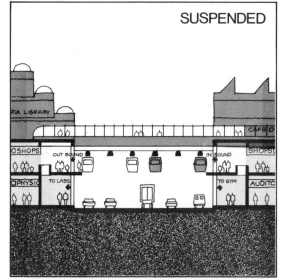

SUSPENDED

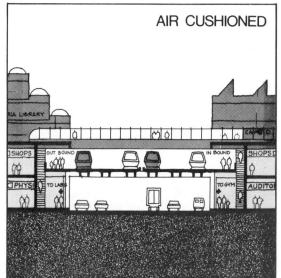

AIR CUSHIONED

5. EXCHANGE STATION

CBD EXCHANGE STATION - AT THIS CBD EXCHANGE STATION, THE DOUBLE TWO-WAY GUIDE SPLITS TO CONTINUE INTO THE CBD AS THINNER SINGLE GUIDES. THIS IS THE STATION AT WHICH THE PRT PASSENGERS COULD EXCHANGE ROUTE DIRECTION TO REACH VARIOUS POINTS ON THE NORTH OR SOUTH CBD LOOPS. IT ALSO BORDERS PART OF THE COLORADO UNIVERSITY DOWNTOWN CAMPUS.

AS THE NEXT LINK IN THE EDUCATION CAMPUS CHAIN, THIS SECTION COULD PROVIDE AN AIR RIGHTS CLASSROOM BUILDING ABOVE THE STATION AREA. THE LOWER PART OF THIS MIXED USE PROJECT MIGHT INCLUDE PARKING, WHICH WOULD NOT ONLY SERVE THE CENTER BUT ALSO WOULD BE A "LAST CHANCE" AUTO INTERCEPT FOR MOTORISTS TO PARK AND RIDE BEFORE ENTERING THE CBD WITH ITS MORE EXPENSIVE AND LESS AVAILABLE PARKING. SMALL CONVENIENCE SHOPS SERVING STUDENTS AND PRT RIDERS WOULD ADJOIN THE STATION PROPER.

SUSPENDED

AIR CUSHIONED

6. CONVENTION CENTER

CONVENTION CENTER STATION - THE DIRECT CONNECTOR BETWEEN THE STADIUM AND ARENA AND ITS ASSOCIATED PARKING WILL STRENGTHEN DENVER'S ALREADY SUPERIOR CONFERENCE FACILITIES. THE STATION, ALTHOUGH ONE-WAY INBOUND, LOOPS IMMEDIATELY CROSSTOWN AT STOUT STREET, INTERFACES AT 16TH STREET, AND ENABLES THE CONVENTIONEERS TO RETURN TO PARKING AT STADIUM BY CONTINUING ON THE NORTH CBD LOOP, 18TH STREET, AND LAWRENCE STREET WEST-BOUND CORRIDORS.

THE STATION FACILITY COULD ACTUALLY AUGMENT THE CONVENTION CENTER PLAZA BY CONTAINING THE PLAZA OPEN SPACE THAT PRESENTLY "LEAKS" INTO THE MANY OPEN LOTS OF 14TH STREET.

SUSPENDED

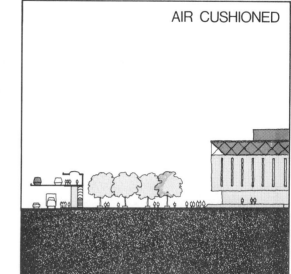

AIR CUSHIONED

7. 14th STREET STATION

14TH STREET WAS SELECTED AS THE WEST CORRIDOR OF THE C B D NETWORK BECAUSE OF THE CONVENIENT AND COMPREHENSIBLE TWO-WAY SERVICE WHICH THE CONVENTION CENTER COMPLEX REQUIRED AND BECAUSE IT DEFINES WITHOUT RESTRAINING THE C B D. 14TH STREET ALSO PRESENTLY OPERATES AS AN INTOWN AUTO INTERCEPT WITH MANY LOTS LINING THE WEST SIDE OF THAT STREET. DIAGRAM 7 ON 14TH STREET SHOWS A TYPICAL INTOWN STATION SOLUTION WHERE THE 60' WIDE ONE-WAY STATIONS ARE PULLED OFF STREETS ABOVE PARKING LOTS WHEREVER POSSIBLE, RATHER THAN BLOCKING STREET LIGHT FOR THIS WIDTH, AS STATIONS FOR GUIDEWAY TECHNOLOGIES REQUIRE.

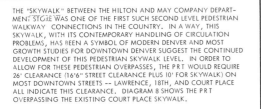

SUSPENDED

AIR CUSHIONED

8. SKYWALK-HILTON/MAYS

THE "SKYWALK" BETWEEN THE HILTON AND MAY COMPANY DEPART- MENT STORE WAS ONE OF THE FIRST SUCH SECOND LEVEL PEDESTRIAN WALKWAY CONNECTIONS IN THE COUNTRY. IN A WAY, THIS SKYWALK, WITH ITS CONTEMPORARY HANDLING OF CIRCULATION PROBLEMS, HAS BEEN A SYMBOL OF MODERN DENVER AND MOST GROWTH STUDIES FOR DOWNTOWN DENVER SUGGEST THE CONTINUED DEVELOPMENT OF THIS PEDESTRIAN SKYWALK LEVEL. IN ORDER TO ALLOW FOR THESE PEDESTRIAN OVERPASSES, THE P R T WOULD REQUIRE 26' CLEARANCE (16'6" STREET CLEARANCE PLUS 10' FOR SKYWALK) ON MOST DOWNTOWN STREETS -- LAWRENCE, 18TH, AND COURT PLACE ALL INDICATE THIS CLEARANCE. DIAGRAM 8 SHOWS THE P R T OVERPASSING THE EXISTING COURT PLACE SKYWALK.

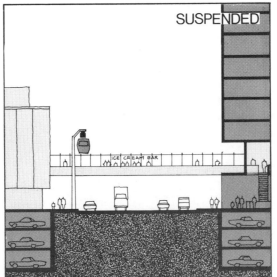

SUSPENDED

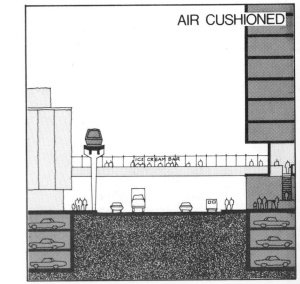

AIR CUSHIONED

9. D.U.R.A. SKYLINE STATION

DURA SKYLINE PROJECT INCLUDES SEVERAL BUILDING COMPLEXES JUST BEGINNING THE DESIGN PHASE, PRESENTING AN IDEAL OPPORTUNITY TO INCLUDE THE P R T STATIONS WITHIN THE NEW STRUCTURE. IT IS PARTICULARLY DESIRABLE TO INCLUDE STATIONS WITHIN STRUCTURES BECAUSE OF THE STREET AREA WHICH THEY OTHER-WISE REQUIRE COVERING. THE COVERING OF STREETS IS DETRIMENTAL FROM MORE THAN THE ENVIRONMENTAL POINT OF VIEW. THE DARK A REAS CREATED BY STATIONS OCCURRING AT CLOSE INTERVALS OVER THE STREETS CAN CAUSE DANGEROUS "TUNNEL BLINDNESS" FOR MOTORISTS DRIVING ALONG THESE STREETS.

DIAGRAM 9 SHOWS A STATION PLATFORM INCLUDED WITHIN A BUILDING PRESENTLY IN DESIGN PRELIMINARIES.

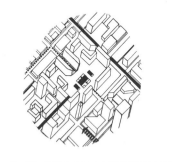

SUSPENDED

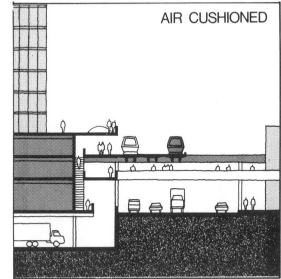

AIR CUSHIONED

10. 18th STREET STATION

18 TH STREET , ANGLING DIRECTLY EAST, IS EVOLVING AS A HIGHRISE OFFICE AND FINANCIAL DISTRICT WHICH IS THE MAJOR EMPLOYMENT AREA OF THE C B D . THIS AREA ALSO PROVIDES AN OPPORTUNITY FOR A STATION TO BE INCLUDED WITHIN A NEW BUILDING PROGRAM AND STRUCTURE. THERE ARE ECONOMIC ADVANTAGES AS WELL AS ENVIRONMENTAL AND SAFETY BENEFITS. THE TRIPLE GUIDEWAY AND STATION PLATFORM, INSTEAD OF FORMING A TUNNEL OVER THE STREET, ENCLOSE AN AREA WHICH, WHEN OCCURRING WITHIN A BUILDING, BECOMES PROFITABLE LOWER LEVEL COMMERCIAL SPACE. HOWEVER, IF THE STATION WAS OVER THE STREET IN FRONT OF THIS S AME BUILDING, THAT FIRST LEVEL SPACE WOULD REALLY ONLY BE APPROPRIATE FOR UNDERGROUND GARAGE, AS THE 200' LONG COVERED SECTION WOULD NOT BE EITHER SAFE OR APPEALING FOR PEDESTRIAN TRAFFIC.

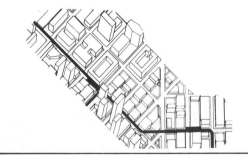

SUSPENDED

AIR CUSHIONED

11. 16th STREET

16TH STREET - THE C B D NETWORK BASICALLY CONSISTS OF A NORTH LOOP AND A SOUTH LOOP. THE CROSSTOWN STREETS NOT ONLY CONNECT THE EAST AND WEST EMPLOYMENT CENTERS BUT, MOST IMPORTANTLY, THE THREE STATIONS ON 16TH STREET AT LAWRENCE STREET AND STOUT STREET (OR ALTERNATE, CALIFORNIA STREET) AND COURT PLACE PROVIDE AS GOOD SERVICE TO 16TH STREET AS COULD ACTUALLY BE PROVIDED RUNNING A LINE DOWN THAT STREET. (IT WOULD BE IMPRACTICAL TO PROVIDE ANY MORE THAN THE THREE STOPS -- EVERY 3 OR 4 BLOCKS.) THIS SOLUTION PROVIDES THESE WELL PLACED STATIONS AT 16TH STREET, BUT DOES NOT RUN THE P R T STRUCTURE OR STATIONS DOWN THIS IMPORTANT SHOPPERS STREET WHICH IS SCHEDULED TO BECOME A PEDESTRIAN MALL. THESE 16TH STREET STATIONS WILL INTERFACE WITH THE PROPOSED SHOPPING MODES PROVIDING THE REQUIRED BLOCK TO BLOCK SERVICE TO THE COMMERCIAL CORE. THESE MODES MIGHT BE A MINIBUS LOOP ON 15TH OR 17TH STREET. SHOPPERS SHUTTLE MIGHT ACTUALLY RUN ON AREAS OF THE MALL ITSELF, ON LARIMER STREET OR CALIFORNIA STREET, OR OTHER AREAS THAT RECEIVE HEAVY SHOPPING TRAFFIC AT CERTAIN TIMES.

ANOTHER POSSIBILITY MIGHT BE A PEDESTRIAN SPEEDWALK CONNECTING ESPECIALLY INTENSE SHOPPING AREAS.

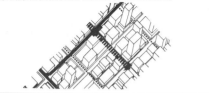

SUSPENDED

AIR CUSHIONED

12. 17th AVENUE

THE P R T LOOP'S SINGLE GUIDES COME TOGETHER AGAIN AT 17TH AVE. AND THE DOUBLE STATION AT 17TH AND GRANT WOULD BE A TWO-WAY EXCHANGE STATION WHERE RIDERS CAN CHANGE DIRECTION TO REACH VARIOUS POINTS IN THE C B D NETWORK.

DIAGRAM 12 SHOWS THE DOUBLE GUIDE IN A CROSS-SECTION TYPICAL OF 17TH AVE AND PARTS OF PARK AVENUE BUILDING DENSITY AND LAND USE INCLUDE MEDIUM SIZE RESIDENTIAL BUILDINGS MIXED IN WITH ONE AND TWO-STORY SUPPORT COMMERCIAL AND SOME MEDICAL OFFICE SPACES.

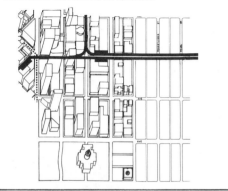

SUSPENDED

AIR CUSHIONED

13. COLFAX AVE.

COLFAX AVENUE CARRIES THE PRT ROUTE TO ITS EAST TERMINUS AT THE INTERSECTION OF COLFAX AND COLORADO AVENUES. THIS AREA, WITH ITS HOSPITALS, MEDICAL CENTERS, AND ITS ADJACENCY TO THE CITY PARK, MUSEUM, AND THE DENVER ZOO, MARKS THE EDGE OF "DOWNTOWN" ACTIVITIES. THESE ACTIVITIES ARE COMPARABLE TO THE OLYMPIC STADIUM IN THEIR ABILITY TO OFFER DOUBLE FUNCTIONS TO A LARGE NUMBER OF PARKING SPACES WHICH MIGHT BE CONSTRUCTED TO ACT AS AN AUTO INTERCEPT FOR COMMUTERS COMING INTO THE CBD FROM THE EAST AND SOUTHEAST. THIS STATION WOULD ALSO SERVE AS AN INTERFACE AND TRANSPORTATION EXCHANGE WITH A FUTURE FASTER MODE WHICH MIGHT LINK UP WITH THE DENVER AIRPORT, LOWRY A.F.B., AND THE EASTERN AND SOUTHEASTERN REGIONS.

THE HIGH SPEEDS AND UNLIMITED LEFT TURNS ON THE PRESENTLY AUTO-DOMINATED COLFAX AVENUE REQUIRES PEDESTRIAN UNDERPASSES AND THE 26' CLEARANCE WHICH THEY ENTAIL. BECAUSE OF THE SPRAWL AND SIGN CLUTTER OF THIS TYPE OF "COMMERCIAL STRIP," ONE FINDS THAT BY INCLUDING A DOUBLE GUIDE PRT AT THE CENTER HERE THAT THE VISUAL EFFECT IS ACTUALLY IMPROVED BY GIVING A FORM OR SPINE TO THE DISPERSED DEVELOPMENT.

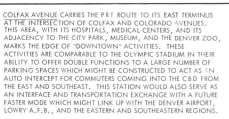

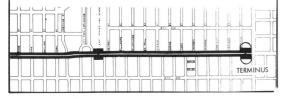

TERMINUS

SUSPENDED

AIR CUSHIONED

LAKE PONTCHARTRAIN

A new lifestyle for old New Orleans.

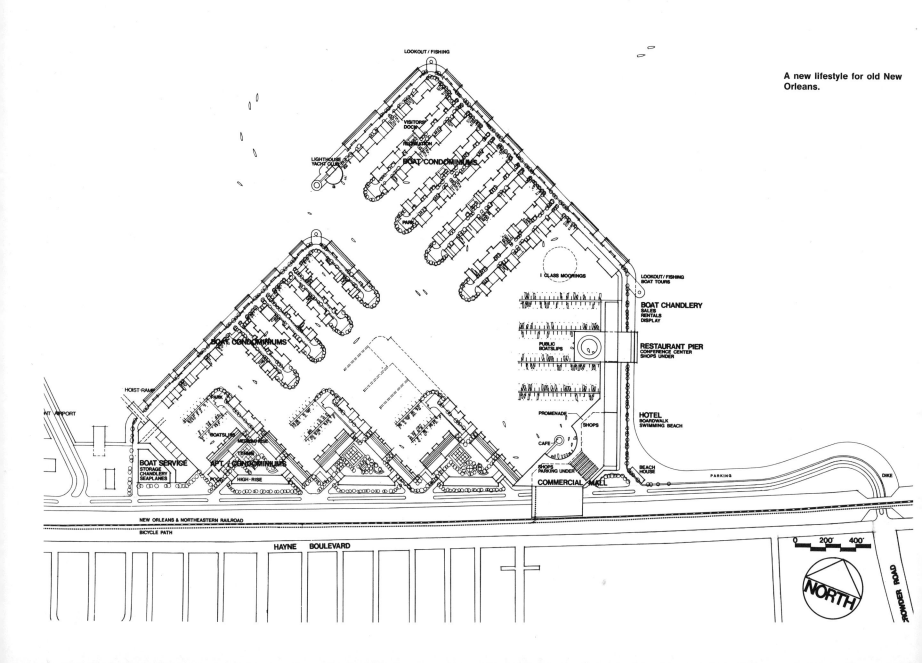

LOOKOUT / FISHING

VISITORS' DOCK

RECREATION

LIGHTHOUSE
YACHT CLUB

BOAT CONDOMINIUMS

PARK

I CLASS MOORINGS

LOOKOUT / FISHING
BOAT TOURS

BOAT CHANDLERY
SALES
RENTALS
DISPLAY

BOAT CONDOMINIUMS

PUBLIC
BOATSLIPS

RESTAURANT PIER
CONFERENCE CENTER
SHOPS UNDER

HOIST-RAMP

NT AIRPORT

PARK

BOATSLIPS

MEDIUM RISE

TENNIS

PROMENADE

SHOPS

HOTEL
BOARDWALK
SWIMMING BEACH

CAFE

BOAT SERVICE
STORAGE
CHANDLERY
SEAPLANES

APT. / CONDOMINIUMS

SHOPS
PARKING UNDER

BEACH
HOUSE

PARKING

DIKE

POOL   HIGH-RISE

COMMERCIAL MALL

NEW ORLEANS & NORTHEASTERN RAILROAD

BICYCLE PATH

HAYNE   BOULEVARD

0   200'   400'

NORTH

ROWDER   ROAD

New Lifestyle for an Old City

How to respond to the desire for a new kind of lifestyle in New Orleans that would utilize the recreational potential of this unique, colorful old city surrounded by lakes, bays, rivers, canals, and oceans?

This desire to create a leisure-with-work living environment is not unique to this city. However, it is unique in this swampy section of our coastline because during the early years of its history, New Orleans turned its back on the lakes and bays that surrounded it. Old New Orleans was clustered on a small area of high ground to gain protection from the floods and diseases with which these water bodies plagued the early city. The contemporary city has learned to control the floods with levees and has controlled malaria and yellow fever by the filling and spraying of mosquito-breeding swamps.

Now the citizens of New Orleans are beginning to avail themselves of a lifestyle based on the water-oriented recreation and living environments that these water bodies offer. Few cities have such an opportunity to live in the second-home recreation atmosphere of a lakefront house while living in a major city. The potential for live/play/work environments is great here and the desire to maximize this was the prime motivation behind the unique plan for the Lakefront Marina Community project.

Live/work environment based on water-oriented recreation.

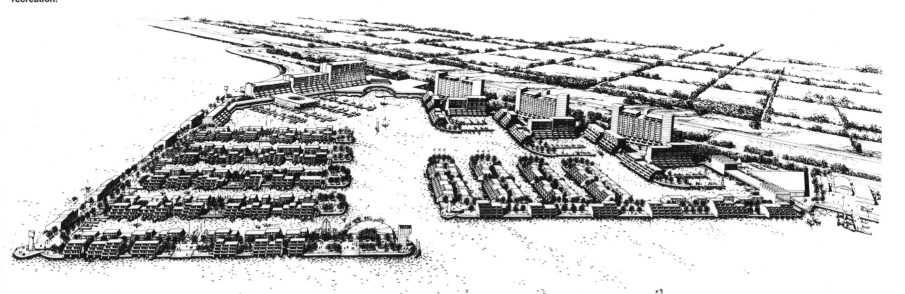

A water-oriented new town in town

This marina community was based on an innovative living element—a special boathouse/townhouse that evolved out of the old metal sheds that had begun to line the shores of Lake Pontchartrain. Originally built to house boats, their owners began to envy their boats' ideal location and moved in with them! Piecemeal at first, the owners began to build homes inside the boat sheds until finally many became substantial permanent homes.

The basic boat condominium utilized in the Lakefront Marina is in response to the community's demands for this type of dwelling. These units are set on piers in the water requiring expensive fill only for the building of the narrow road and service "moles" (linear land fill areas) to which they connect.

The project location near the airport and only six miles from central New Orleans and the famed French Quarter indicated a potential for sharing this unique living situation with visiting businessmen and tourists while building in some financing and local employment possibilities. A Hotel/Conference Center was designed with this in mind, with overhanging piers for popular fish restaurants, leading onto a boardwalk that follows the marina boat slip groups. A further mix of live/play/work is the inclusion of a small shopping center, office space, and accommodations for various aspects of the boat business—chancellory, sales, schools, rental, tours, and so on.

Modular growth to avoid sprawl and urban ghettoes

Housing is clustered around small usable recreational complexes including pools and tennis courts, as well as visitor boat and car parking. Bike and pedestrian paths tie the community together following the entire perimeter park.

The new recreational land use and building type developed here has definite implications as a luxury housing community as opposed to the trend of recent years where most housing communities in downtown areas have tended to be low-income projects only. If our downtowns are to be revived, we must create amenities and living conditions that will attract the full range of income levels, age groups, family size and backgrounds that bring vitality to a city. Only by attracting the middle classes back from the suburbs will we halt the tendency of our cities to become urban ghettoes of lower income and minority groups.

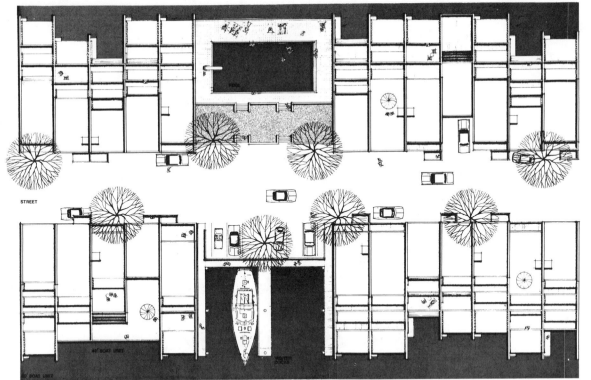

Typical cluster plan of boat condominiums.

STREET

Boat condominiums from pool area.

An innovative living element—boathouse/ townhouse.

Landing between townhouses and boat condominiums.

Providing the Gateway

Bridges are links between two points, and they are events within a city. Sometimes they are the most important single event because they provide the very gateway to a city. However, bridges have traditionally been designed solely by structural engineers and located by municipal engineers with little sensitivity as to their significance in providing the first impression for a visitor to a city. A bridge provides a sense of arrival and a sense of departure. It is a linkage between two sectors or two parts of a city, two neighborhoods, two villages. It is passage through and across for pedestrians and vehicles, and yet, it is rare that planners or urban designers are ever called upon to create solutions for the design of a bridge structure. A bridge is looked at from above, from beyond, and sometimes while passing below. It is by definition picturesque, a place where pictures are taken from and pictures taken of.

In New Haven, Connecticut, a deteriorating, rusting but sculptural old truss-cantilever pivot bridge spanning the Quinnipiac River is to be replaced by a four-lane bascule-style bridge. The old bridge with the diagonals and angles of its high trusses had for many years provided a dramatic gateway—similar to the effect of a covered bridge—from one sector of the city to another, and it served as the linkage to the main commercial spine entering the very heart of the Central Business District. The New Haven Redevelopment Authority realized that the new bridge, because of its wider roadbed and uneventful silhouette would have trouble filling the urbanistic role of the old bridge, although it was clear that a better functional fit was necessary. ECODESIGN proposed utilizing the old granite support structures for a new restaurant/cafe, a clam shack, playground, and docking facilities for pleasure craft.

In the new bridge that evolved, the urban designer's hand is noticeable, as well as the structural engineer's. The superstructure is of weathering steel, a material that has enjoyed wide architectural application in New Haven because of its aesthetic appeal as well as its maintenance-free characteristics. Even the choice of materials was made by the urban designer in conjunction with the structural engineer. The control tower and the corresponding piers are constructed of brick-faced reinforced concrete, and they are designed to visually express the movement and muscle inherent in the nature of a bascule-bridge. The proposed bridge now fits well within the cityscape of small brick buildings and fits as a landmark. Its success urbanistically is due to consistency of materials and colors and the way it services the city as a connector—and visually, as a gateway, emphasizing entrance into New Haven from East Haven and vice versa.

Consistent color, scale and geometery unify a community

Through consistent scale, geometry, color, and materials, the bridge is able to blend successfully with its background neighborhoods. Low lighting standards, rather than the out-of-scale expressway lighting types, are used along with pedestrian-scale railings. Seating areas are provided on projections from the bascule piers and can be used for fishing or just sitting and viewing. Stairs and ramps on the side of the bridge lead to a riverside park below. The bridge utilizes these elements as "givers of scale," for the bridge has meaning for both the driver and the pedestrian.

With the old bridges, too, the bridge furnishings, control tower, lighting, commemorative plaques and materials can make a prideful landmark within a city, but the contemporary bridge, in recognizing and utilizing the river over which it passes, can surpass that.

This important project is using the bridge as a unique opportunity to bring the community down to the water's edge so that they can enjoy a park alongside a reclaimed river. It is the full integration of a bridge into its setting.

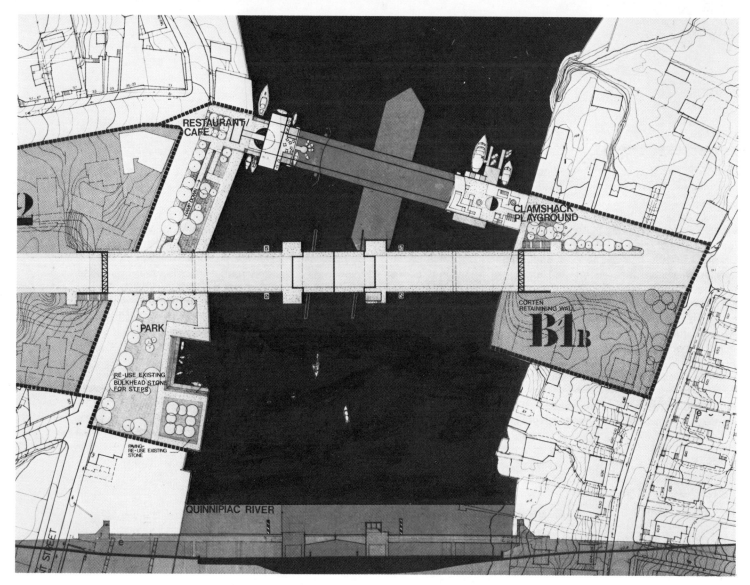

Text labels within the figure:
RESTAURANT/CAFE
CLAMSHACK PLAYGROUND
PARK
RE-USE EXISTING BULKHEAD STONE FOR STEPS
PAVING- RE-USE EXISTING STONE
CORTEN RETAINING WALL
B1ʙ
QUINNIPIAC RIVER
STREET

Recycling the old Grand Avenue Bridge. A restaurant/ cafe is proposed to be built at one end with boat access and a clam shack/playground at the side.

Blending with the neighborhood. The control tower and the corresponding piers are constructed of brick-faced concrete which has the same basic coloring as the church and neighborhood beyond.

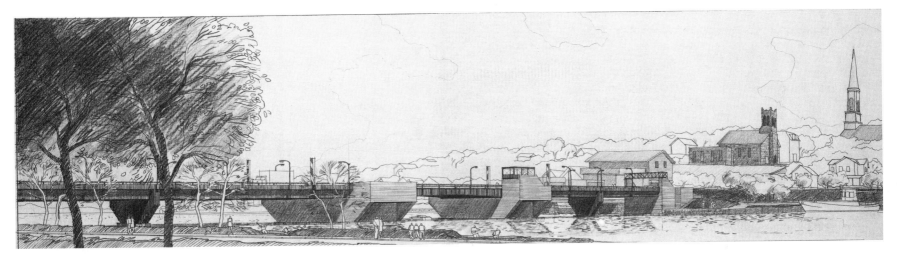

Consistent scale and geometry. A riverside park is created with pedestrian access to the bridge fully integrating the bridge into its setting.

Highlighting Urban Events in the Soft City

Fall River, Massachusetts, is certainly a soft city if any city can be described as soft. Once a thriving industrial seacoast city in southern Massachusetts, full of textile mills and factories, Fall River, like many other New England communities, has undergone changes in its basic economy that have caused rapid deterioration in the urban fabric.

Again like so many other cities, Fall River decided to undertake a major renewal program for the 75-acre commercial core. Included in this renewal project was the renovation of a number of historic warehouses, mills, new housing schemes, new commercial, light industrial and recreational land uses. Yet there is no single focus nor any tour de force that would tie the city together or act as a focus and rallying point for the community.

Select a focus and create a symbol

In this case, one could see a major problem developing unless some focus element was selected, and selected fast, as a symbol. We chose to highlight a civic event—the major downtown tourist attraction, the battleship USS Massachusetts. The battleship is located on axis with the main commercial spine, which runs parallel with the slopes of a hill, which unfolds to the waterfront. We linked the battleship by platforms and a funicular to the new commercial spine. The spine is terminated to the north by the new city hall complex. In this manner, a previously somewhat disjointed location of the battleship can be linked commercially and physically to the main spine street, which acts as a catalyst for recycling.

Select a focus—The battleship USS Massachusetts. Pedestrian linkages from a new housing sector across the main commercial mall through stores and by cafes to the river and the ship.

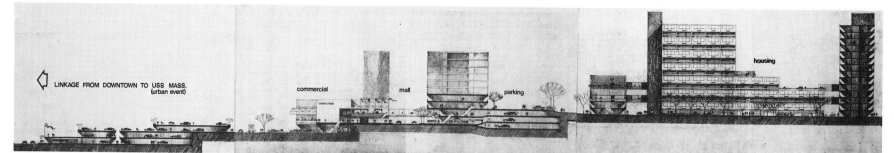

LINKAGE FROM DOWNTOWN TO USS MASS.
(urban event)

commercial mall parking housing

Polishing the Stars

**Seeing some of the city's highlights begin to shine:
a zoo, a racetrack, a civic center . . .**

Sometimes it is difficult to determine what buildings
and what places are actually "the stars" in an
urban context. But certainly the buildings and areas
that provide public events, meeting places, or are
significant in terms of size either by being a very big
place or a very small, important place can be described modestly as "the stars." The stars, then,
are the arenas, the racetracks, the zoos, T.V. stations, the symphony halls, town halls, and museums.
If one is looking to recycle the city in a small way
with modest expenditures, then polishing the stars is
certainly the best way to do it from a public relations standpoint.

Take zoos, for instance. More people attend zoos in
the United States each year than all spectator sports
put together. So a modest investment in rehabilitating a zoo by reorganizing the spaces with better
enclosures for the animals and meaningful exhibit
design will get more exposure than any group of
other projects one could envision. It would provide
exposure to the greatest number of people for the
least amount of money.

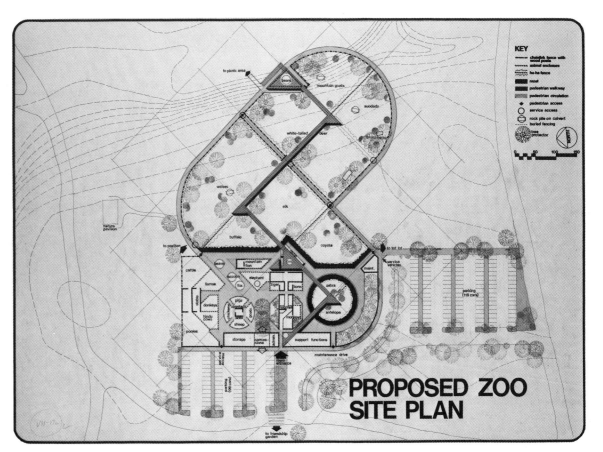

**PROPOSED ZOO
SITE PLAN**

**Recycling an underutilized
old municipal zoo in a city
park.** A totally new zoo idea
stresses the interaction between urban visitors, the
natural environment, and the
animals. The rehabilitated
zoo is integrated into the 193-
acre Slater Park so that both
can respond more fully to the
community's recreational
needs.

A new image of youth for a racetrack. At Suffolk Downs, the basic structure was retained and stripped of years of additions and renovations in order to emphasize the clear lines of the building. The building now can house boat shows, flower shows, art festivals, industrial exhibits, and other events in a recycled environment.

Civic Center and Jai Alai Fronton. By combining building uses, this project can function as a recreational and cultural resource for the city through utilization of the large open space for civic events as well as spectator sports.

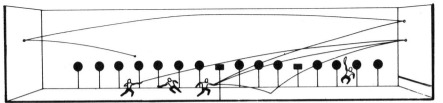

Diagram of Jai Alai.

Development packages and site plan. Phasing diagrams indicate how the commercial (private) portions of the project would develop at an early stage with recreational activities coming in part three of the scheme.

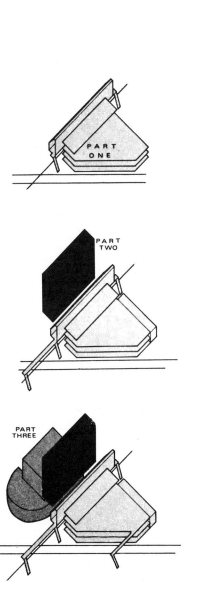

PART ONE

PART TWO

PART THREE

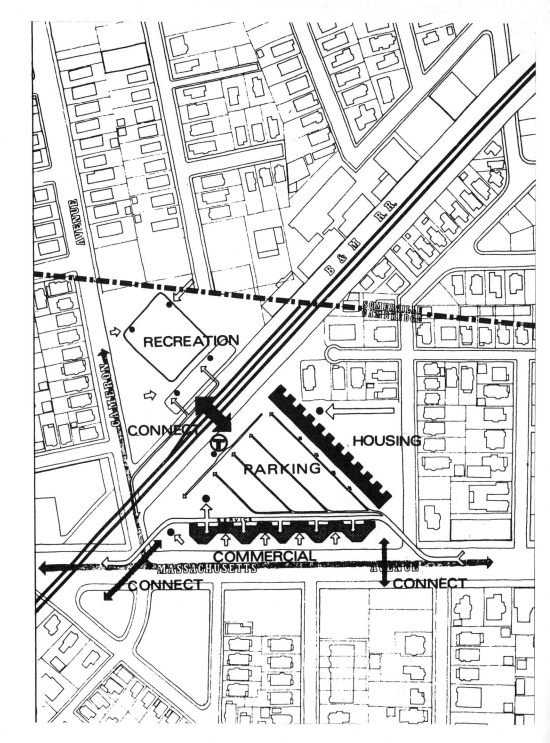

RECREATION

CONNECT

HOUSING

PARKING

COMMERCIAL

CONNECT

CONNECT

MASSACHUSETTS

AVENUE

CAMERON

AVENUE

B & M R.R.

SOMERVILLE
CAMBRIDGE

The Tools for Repair Work

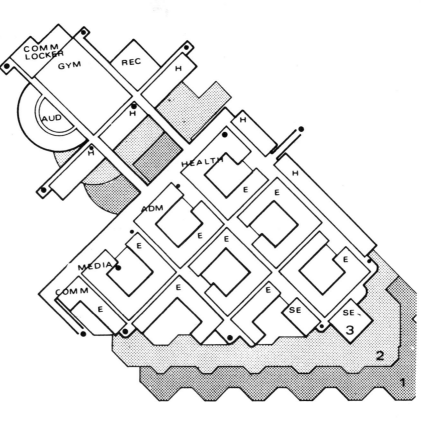

The city as a coherent unit: a public/private partnership

Over the past fifteen years, Cambridge, Massachusetts, has witnessed an ever-increasing number of changes in its physical environment. Many new office buildings and housing projects have been built under private investment along its major access way, Massachusetts Avenue, through the heart of the city between Harvard Square and MIT. The housing supply has been unable to keep pace with the tremendous market demand. The academic institutions have found it increasingly difficult to provide the necessary facilities they require due to lack of land and the social pressure put on them by the community to maintain the existing housing supply. For these reasons, it became clearly necessary for the city to develop a strategy that would project the city as a coherent unit: a development plan based on data and analysis from three major factors—physical design, true real estate value, and market demand. An analysis of the interrelation of these three factors determine future needs.

The availability of a particular site for the development of a public use, such as a school, should depend in large part on the relative economic and social benefit to the community of the existing and proposed land uses. So in this case, a tool was developed in order to study and examine alternative combined building programs and mixed land use schemes for the particular site in question. This variation on a development theme for a particular site was, in fact, the tool invented. For instance, there are many alternative combined building programs that are feasible for any particular site, some of which may incorporate shops, offices, recreational and educational facilities within a single structure or may be variations on that theme.

Diagrammatic plan of combined public/private use building. Level three contains academic uses, the surrounding community can also utilize the gym, auditorium, and other facilities.

There is also the possibility of adapting such juxtapositions of land uses to different site situations depending on the interrelation of the three factors—physical design, real estate values, and market demand. And so, for Cambridge, Massachusetts, a new tool was developed for land use planning that not only ascertained the conceivable school sites within the urban context, but also proposed schematic designs for these sites based on mixed land use programs, which could continue to benefit the tax base and also answer local, social, commercial, and recreational needs. This kind of "development package tool" assists local authorities in being responsive both to the needs and the particular characteristics of any site within the city.

Urbanscaping the Superblock

In Rome, New York, a rather ordinary town with relatively nondescript architecture and a large downtown urban renewal project with many different developers, contractors, planners, and architects all working in a broad area, it is extremely difficult to "pull everything together." The question then becomes, "How can one make the new commercial area a coherent place?"

An integration of dispersed old with new buildings

In this case, a major parking facility was located beneath a central place with the main plaza being the intersection of two streets in a four-block area. The streets were closed off and pedestrian malls and playgrounds, greenhouses, terrace/grass areas, and fountains, which become focuses for civic gatherings, were created for the community's use. A space frame canopy links the new projects with older buildings, providing coverage for rough weather protection and from the sun on hot, or rain on wet, summer days. Consistent designs for street furniture, signage controls, benches, paving patterns, lighting, sales kiosks, bollards, and waste receptacles were all a part of this four-city-block study to create a totally integrated environment of dispersed old buildings and a few new ones.

The Plaza—looking toward Fort Stannix. Linking old projects and new projects is done by a space-frame canopy above, and coherent texture, colors, and materials on the pavement.

East Promenade looking east. Fountains act as focus points and also serve as snow removal depots in the winter. Consistent street furniture and signs are another important element.

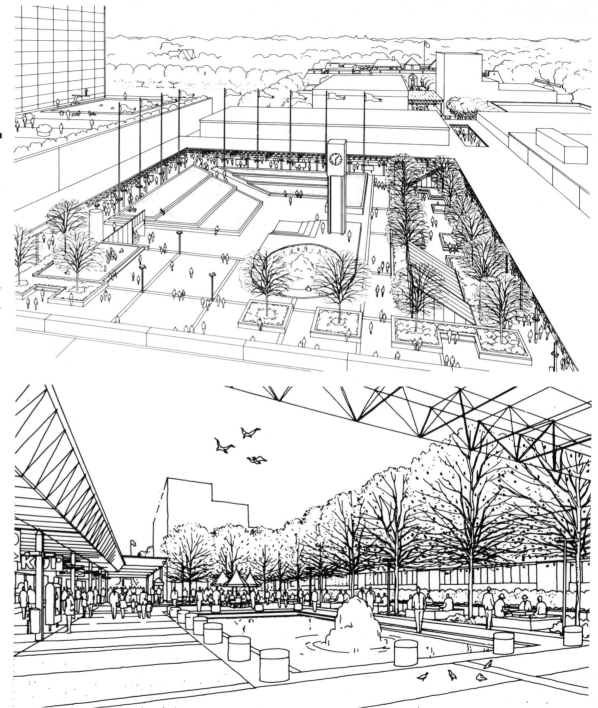

Repairing the Fabric Buildings

In almost every major city and most intermediate-sized cities in the United States, there are public projects in need of major repairs. Whether these projects are public facilities, such as subway stations, post office buildings, fire and police headquarters, or fabric buildings such as housing projects built in the early 1930s, almost all of them are in dire need of modernization. These projects make up the major three-dimensional form of the urban fabric because they exist at consistent locations and over broad areas within each of our cities. Illustration of how a modest amount of money and input can go a long way in repairing the fabric buildings of our cities is illustrated here.

Residents can be inspired to significant accomplishment

In Boston, the Boston Housing Authority undertook a projected three-phase modernization program to reestablish 1600 units built approximately thirty years ago under federal sponsorship as a substantial residential environment. The first phase called for renovation of all the bathrooms and kitchens throughout two housing projects. Other phases were to include recreation area development, landscaping, and community facilities. In each of the projects, the clients were an elected group of residents called the Modernization Task Force. This task force was empowered to make decisions at all levels from design to budget and to provide program content to the architect/planners. The project itself was funded through state and federal programs, which included the total modernization program for over 10,000 dwelling units throughout the city. An interesting aspect of this project was the relationship of the residents to the Boston Housing Authority and the consulting architects, as most of the decision-making power was in the hands of

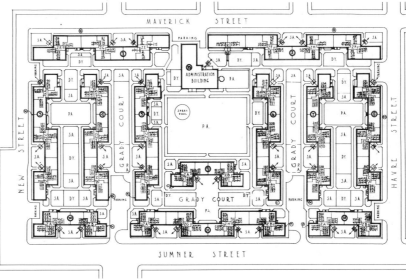

Repairing the fabric buildings from within. In every major urban center there are numbers of fine-grain textures of building-blocks (as seen from the air) and the blocks make up the urban fabric.

the tenants themselves. As a result of this working relationship, the residents were inspired to make significant improvements out of their own pocketbooks to their dwellings, even though they were public housing project tenants, and not owner/occupants.

Consequently, an extremely large percentage of dwelling units throughout both the East Boston and Charlestown projects were substantially improved at a very modest cost to the government and with great enthusiasm on behalf of the tenants.

Under a limited program, the repairing of at least some fabric buildings was undertaken; similar innovative financing techniques, such as urban homesteading, can be utilized to repair other fabric buildings and housing projects.

Public housing kitchens
which had not been
renovated in over three
decades.

Illegal washer and dryers
and other tenant-provided
appliances proliferate.

Isolating the Historic Ambience

One of the most provocative questions to be dealt with by community groups and architectural historians alike is the question: Where does one stop the time clock when going through history to isolate the particular period of history that best reflects the nature of the architecture of a particular town or city?

The second part of this question is whether or not one should reproduce that particular period or era, and thus create a "Disneyland" kind of atmosphere, or whether one should rehabilitate and reconstruct buildings of a particular period as faithfully as possible and design and construct structures that answer new needs in a scale and rhythm harmonious with the old.

Unique in situation, but not in theory

Newburyport, Massachusetts, had such a problem. Although Newburyport is unique in situation, it is not unique in theory. In fact, its problem is shared by many of the older New England towns. The question here is: How can a town resolve seemingly contradictory needs of new development, historic preservation, and a changing social environment in a manner that not only satisfies the representative factions in the community, but also does not interfere with the social, political, and physical functions of the existing community? And, of course, how does one isolate the historic ambience of this particular place, Newburyport? There are, of course, certain indicators such as the compatible architectural treatment, dimensioning of streets, ways, open space, and land use allocation—some of which were discussed in Chapter 6.

The issue of architectural compatibility with the existing Federal-style commercial buildings of Newburyport's Historic District had truly disintegrated into the personal opinions of the individual members of the selecting authority and their advisers.

The Renewal Authority's *Developer's Handbook* listed the elements of compatibility as design criteria, but precisely what the compatible height, proportion, rhythm, spacing, material, color, roof shape, and so on are had not been spelled out and "correct" answers to these elements of compatibility were left to subjective tastes and attitudes.

In order to make these elements answerable in more definitive and measurable terms, we defined the qualities and quantities of Proportion and Rhythm, which related specifically to the historic Federalist buildings in question. Actual dimensions and specifications could be assigned to building widths and heights, projections, bay spacing, materials, colors, glass, entrances, balconies, doors, windows, roof types, wall façades, and signage, but, for what relationships of these elements create harmony and scale, no scientific judgment had yet been made. Therefore, to develop a quantifiable design criteria to show when there is "harmony and scale" with the structures of the historic district we diagramed the proportions of three typical bays.

The most important element in identifying the "harmony and scale" of a building design is identification of the building's proportions. How do the sizes of definable sections of the building relate to each other?

Normally, one can perceive two basic sets of pro-

portions in a building. The *primary proportions* deal with the size relationship of the major parts of the building (i.e., bottom to top, side to side, section to section, bay to bay). The *secondary proportions* deal with the relationship of smaller architectural elements and how they break down within the major parts (i.e., windows, doors, shutters, cornices).

Federalist architecture is pleasing and admired not for its imagination or extravagance, but because of its excellent understanding of proportions as related to the human scale. Although there were no hard and fast rules to these proportions, a certain rhythm was established and was normally only changed for some reason of functionality. The proportions of these buildings were a delicate balance controlled by the needs of flexibility and good taste.

The following figures analyze the proportions that create harmony and scale in the buildings of the Historic District and compare these to schematic elevations proposed by the developers. The X's indicate architectural treatments or dimensioning in the proposed schemes, which create proportions incompatible with the proportions of the historic buildings.

The final scheme shows a contemporary building, which, according to the guidelines for architectural treatment and proportions analysis, approaches the scale and harmony of the old commercial Federalist style.

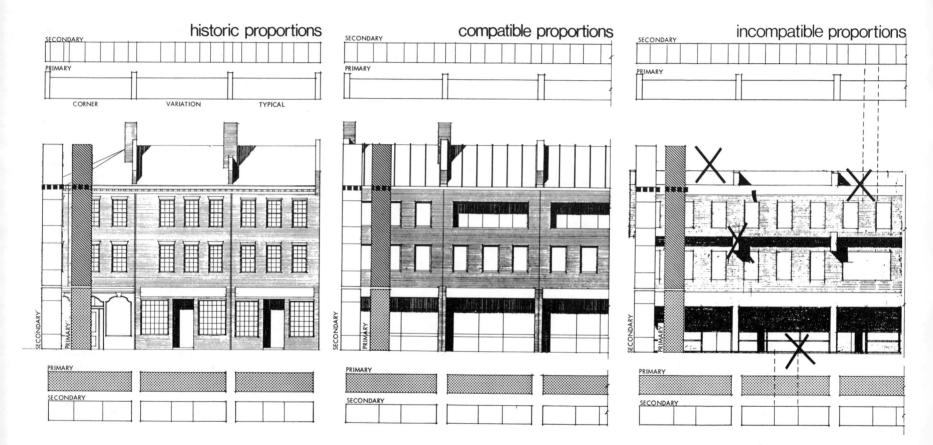

historic proportions

SECONDARY

PRIMARY

CORNER   VARIATION   TYPICAL

SECONDARY

PRIMARY

PRIMARY

SECONDARY

compatible proportions

SECONDARY

PRIMARY

SECONDARY

PRIMARY

PRIMARY

SECONDARY

incompatible proportions

SECONDARY

PRIMARY

SECONDARY

PRIMARY

PRIMARY

SECONDARY

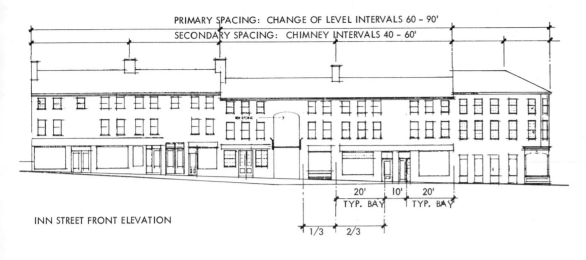

PRIMARY SPACING: CHANGE OF LEVEL INTERVALS 60 – 90'

SECONDARY SPACING: CHIMNEY INTERVALS 40 – 60'

Rhythmic compatibility

NEW OPENING

20'   10'   20'

TYP. BAY   TYP. BAY

INN STREET FRONT ELEVATION

1/3   2/3

50' TYPICAL
BUILDING WIDTH

INN STREET REAR ELEVATION

NEW WALK WAY VIOLATES
HISTORIC BAY SPACING

Historic rhythm

SECONDARY SPACING: CHIMNEY INTERVAL

Compatible rhythm

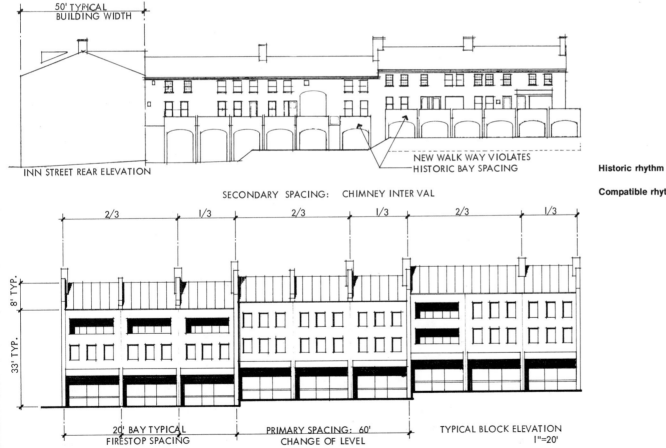

2/3   1/3   2/3   1/3   2/3   1/3

8' TYP.

33' TYP.

20' BAY TYPICAL
FIRESTOP SPACING

PRIMARY SPACING: 60'
CHANGE OF LEVEL

TYPICAL BLOCK ELEVATION
1"=20'

Retaining a Quality of Life

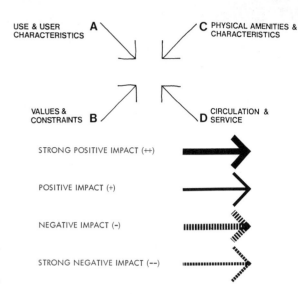

USE & USER CHARACTERISTICS **A**

C PHYSICAL AMENITIES & CHARACTERISTICS

VALUES & CONSTRAINTS **B**

D CIRCULATION & SERVICE

STRONG POSITIVE IMPACT (++)

POSITIVE IMPACT (+)

NEGATIVE IMPACT (−)

STRONG NEGATIVE IMPACT (−−)

Quality of life diagram.

What is the quality of life in a city? How can it be documented and examined?

A city or even a segment of it can be analyzed as a whole with its elements of urban form, its circulation networks, its land use and open space patterns—but the essence of its particular quality of life is something more than such large-scale abstractions. "Quality of Life" in a city is also an experience, an image, built up of a body of various experiences and images significant and meaningful to the people who regularly use the place. The problem arises as to how to describe and document not only the value of the status quo of that quality of life and experience, but in addition, to demonstrate the potential impact of a new development on the status quo, in order to retain its best qualities.

Impact in this sense, concerning quality of life, cannot be evaluated as a single, simple, economic/commercial impact, or architectural compatability impact, or traffic impact, or sociological impact, or any other special and narrow impact. The reality of a place is the conjunction and interaction of all these elements and, in its totality, it is something more. Lao Tze wrote that "the essence of a vase is the space within"; similarly, these constituent urban elements are the "walls" of the vase, and our impressions and experiences of the place are its reality. However, this synthesis can be expressed by a diagram, where the arrows represent the components of the quality of life in urban places and the arrows also represent the particular location under evaluation. The arrows can be weighted graphically to indicate the degree to which each of the components either enhances the use of the place (positive impact) or inhibits that use (negative impact). The arrows are a notational symbol which define the space and indicate the degree

to which the components define a "sense of place" conducive to the desired use. This urban quality "indicator" is an expression of the quality of life defined by the interaction of four components.

Some elements should be retained while others should be improved

---

The Urban Quality Component Evaluation chart is a device for demonstrating the strong or deficient effects of basic quality of life components and was developed at ECODESIGN to be used with Urban Quality Component Evaluation Charts to document an existing quality of life in Harvard Square, Cambridge, Massachusetts, for an Environmental Impact Statement. The urban quality "indicator" summarizes the overall impact of the components. The urban places selected for evaluation of potential impact on the charts are representative of the various types of spaces found in the Harvard Square area. These key places represent both kinds of qualities attractive to the people who use the Square and that should be retained, as well as negative qualities that should be treated or corrected to improve or enhance a given quality of life.

The components that make up the quality of life of an urban place include: 1) use and user characteristics, 2) values and constraints, 3) physical amenities and characteristics, and 4) circulation and service. While other components might also be considered in such a notational technique (such as economic considerations or municipal services), these bear less directly on the primary perceptions and experience of a visit to the place under consideration—in this case, Harvard Square—and thus are incorporated into descriptions of the four major components discussed on the charts.

Urban quality components evaluation. The following charts contain observations and descriptions of selected typical urban places in Harvard Square. The components are evaluated as strong positive to strong negative impact, in regards to the activity in the space. The schematic sections and plans graphically represent the relation of pedestrians and vehicles to the shape and size of the particular spaces. Very large spaces (i.e., Common riverbanks), where movement is not constrained or where interaction with autos is confined to numerous points around edges, are shown in section only to give a feeling for the range of scale or urban space throughout Harvard Square. Projected increase in pedestrian density is shown in black, existing use in line only. Projected auto impact, if any, would occur as back-ups outside the frame of each space, and consequently are not indicated in the plans. The impacts in the individual places are summarized on pages 226 and 227.

MBTA KIOSK / MAGAZINE STAND
URBAN QUALITY COMPONENTS EVALUATION

	A. USE & USER CHARACTERISTICS			B. VALUES & CONSTRAINTS		C. PHYSICAL AMENITIES & CHARACTERISTICS					D. CIRCULATION & SERVICE					IMPACT
	USER GROUP	USER & PEDESTRIAN ACTIVITY	COMMERCIAL ACTIVITY	LEGAL RESTRICTIONS	SOCIAL VALUES	SCALE WIDTH HEIGHT	MICRO-ENVIRONMENT	MATERIALS	STREET FURNITURE	PLANTING	PEOPLE DENSITY	VEHICLE DENSITY	SERVICE TRUCKS	ACCIDENT RATE & CONFLICT	PUBLIC TOILETS	COMPONENT INTERACTION EVALUATION
STATUS QUO	Workers, students, street people, shoppers tourist, people in transit	Circulation/ transportation exchange	Newspaper/ magazine stand, cab stand	Not applicable J-walking Double parking	Not applicable	6	Poor air quality, very noisy	Concrete, brick, wrought iron and glass kiosk	Lightpoles, signs, phone-booths, gar-bage cans	None	Heavy, congested	Heavy and constant	Bus stop @ Coop	54/yr., jaywalking crossing against sig-nal common	None	
PROJECTED	Many more tourists	Tourist cross circu-lation to Har-vard Yard.	No change	No change	No change	No change	Acceptable air quality	No change	No change	No change	Very heavy, congested	Very heavy & constant	Minimum change expected	Probable increase due to more pedestrian use	No change	
REMARKS	Major transportation link inappropriately located in center of heavy traffic flow. Harvard Square could establish pedestrian character more strongly			Implied social emphasis on vehicle predominance. Interaction here considered dynamic.		The original kiosk structure is a symbolically important element which forms a significant part of the idenity of the Square. No place to sit and wait. Image at center of Harvard Square is vehicular interchange, not people.					If Red line extended bus stop may be removed from Coop entry. Auto stopping to pick-up and to buy papers at newsstand cause some congestion.					

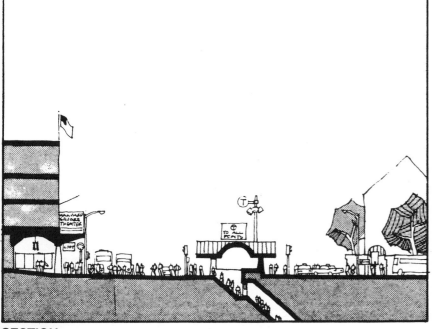

SECTION

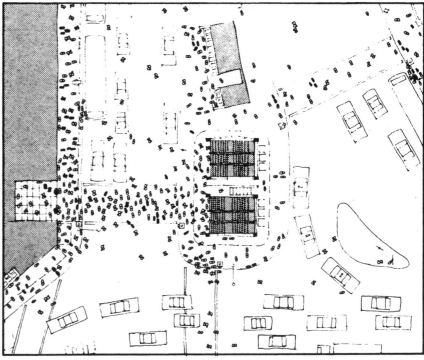

PLAN

Prepared by ECODESIGN Cambridge

FORBES PLAZA
URBAN QUALITY COMPONENTS EVALUATION

	A. USE & USER CHARACTERISTICS			B. VALUES & CONSTRAINTS		C. PHYSICAL AMENITIES & CHARACTERISTICS					D. CIRCULATION & SERVICE					IMPACT
	USER GROUP	USER & PEDESTRIAN ACTIVITY	COMMERCIAL ACTIVITY	LEGAL RESTRICTIONS	SOCIAL VALUES	SCALE WIDTH/ HEIGHT	MICRO-ENVIRONMENT	MATERIALS	STREET FURNITURE	PLANTING	PEOPLE DENSITY	VEHICLE DENSITY	SERVICE TRUCKS	ACCIDENT RATE & CONFLICT	PUBLIC TOILETS	COMPONENT INTERACTION EVALUATION
STATUS QUO	Street People, office workers, elderly men, student, street vendors	Vending, sitting meeting friends, people watching, entertainment	Handicrafts, banking, clothing, food carts	6 Street Vendors allowed (Harvard U.), daily enforcement	Vending is tolerated, not encouraged, by local merchants, enjoyed by many people	0.5 – 2	Shady, poor air quality, noisy	Brick, granite, concrete panels, show windows,	Conc. benches, raised platform under trees, lightpoles	6 large trees	Heavy @ edge, light in center, seating filled at mid-day	Heavy, constant; cab stand at curb	No major conflict	Low, 7/yr., cabstand buffers moving traffic	None	
PROJECTED	More tourists	Numbers could restrict some uses	Quality of handicraft could change	Potential increased enforcement due to increased congestion	No change	No change	Acceptable air quality	No change	No change	No change	More congestion at sidewalk, seating less adequate	Minimum increase projected	No change	increase relative to numbers	No change	
REMARKS				Harvard U. originally invited vendors – presently limits such activity. Pressure from crowds.		One of the most accommodating spaces in the area.					Increased congestion due to confluence					

SECTION

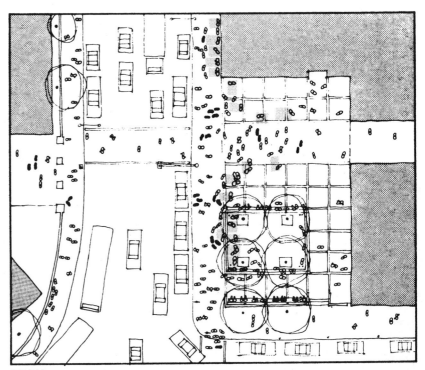

PLAN

Prepared by ECODESIGN Cambridge

MASS AVE
URBAN QUALITY COMPONENTS EVALUATION

	A. USE & USER CHARACTERISTICS			B. VALUES & CONSTRAINTS		C. PHYSICAL AMENITIES & CHARACTERISTICS					D. CIRCULATION & SERVICE					IMPACT
	USER GROUP	USER & PEDESTRIAN ACTIVITY	COMMERCIAL ACTIVITY	LEGAL RESTRICTIONS	SOCIAL VALUES	SCALE WIDTH/HEIGHT	MICRO-ENVIRONMENT	MATERIALS	STREET FURNITURE	PLANTING	PEOPLE DENSITY	VEHICLE DENSITY	SERVICE TRUCKS	ACCIDENT RATE & CONFLICT	PUBLIC TOILETS	COMPONENT INTERACTION EVALUATION
STATUS QUO	Shoppers, students, street people, office workers	Shopping, circulation	Books, clothing, restaurants	J-walking doubleparking parking meters	Not applicable	2	So. side shady, No. s ide sunny, poor air quality, very noisy	Brick sidewalks, shop windows, brick buildings	Bookstalls, lightpoles, parking meters, signs	Trees inside Harvard Yard extending over sidewalk	Heavy traffic, constricted passageway at some points	Heavy but moving	Frequently double parked	8/yr., un-controlled crossing	None	
PROJECTED	More tourists	No change	No change	No change	No change	No change	Acceptable air quality	No change	No change	No change	Very heavy	Minimum increase expected	Minimum increase expected	Probable increase due to more pedestrian use	No change	
REMARKS											Pedestrian and vehicular congestion eased if sidewalk widened and parking eliminated. Commercial side of street heavily used while Harvard side has lighter pedestrian traffic.					

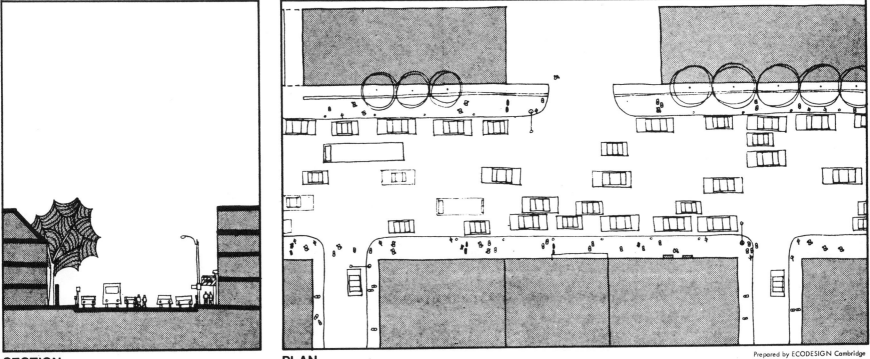

SECTION

PLAN

Prepared by ECODESIGN Cambridge

HARVARD YARD
URBAN QUALITY COMPONENTS EVALUATION

	A. USE & USER CHARACTERISTICS			B. VALUES & CONSTRAINTS		C. PHYSICAL AMENITIES & CHARACTERISTICS					D. CIRCULATION & SERVICE					IMPACT
	USER GROUP	USER & PEDESTRIAN ACTIVITY	COMMERCIAL ACTIVITY	LEGAL RESTRICTIONS	SOCIAL VALUES	SCALE WIDTH HEIGHT	MICRO-ENVIRONMENT	MATERIALS	STREET FURNITURE	PLANTING	PEOPLE DENSITY	VEHICLE DENSITY	SERVICE TRUCKS	ACCIDENT RATE & CONFLICT	PUBLIC TOILETS	COMPONENT INTERACTION EVALUATION
STATUS QUO	Students, visitors, academic personnel	Gathering, studying, sitting, sunning, promenading, circulation, sightseeing	None	Private property (Harvard U.)	Traditional inhibition of activities not conducive to academic atmosphere	2–4	Shady, quiet poor air quality	Asphalt, brick, stone, historic buildings	Lightpoles, statue of John Harvard, drinking fountain, sculpture	Large elms, hedges, grass	Low – Medium, mostly on paths	Not applicable vehicle access controled	At carefully controlled screened places	Not applicable	None, though available in Harvard buildings	
PROJECTED	More tourists	Increased sightseeing	No change	No change	No change expected	No change	Acceptable air quality	No change	No change	No change	Medium	Control	Control	No change	Controls	
REMARKS				Additional numbers might require additional supervision by Harvard Police		Additional numbers might require additional supervision and maintanence by Buildings and Grounds Department.										

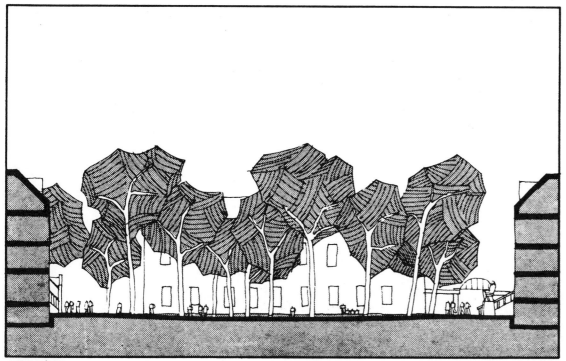

SECTION

Prepared by ECODESIGN Cambridge

BOYLSTON STREET
URBAN QUALITY COMPONENTS EVALUATION

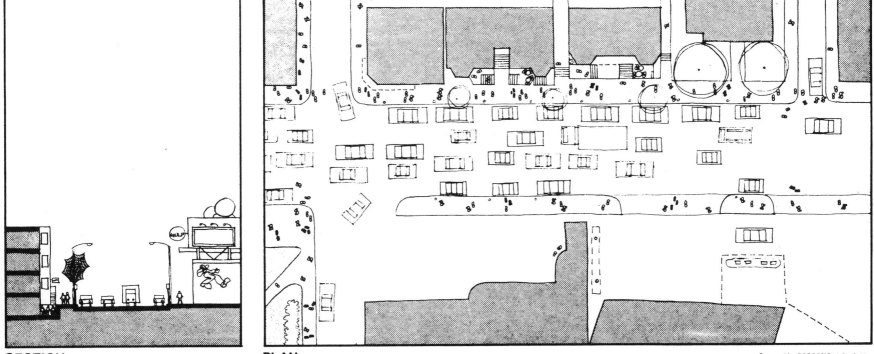

	A. USE & USER CHARACTERISTICS			B. VALUES & CONSTRAINTS		C. PHYSICAL AMENITIES & CHARACTERISTICS					D. CIRCULATION & SERVICE					IMPACT
	USER GROUP	USER & PEDESTRIAN ACTIVITY	COMMERCIAL ACTIVITY	LEGAL RESTRICTIONS	SOCIAL VALUES	SCALE WIDTH/HEIGHT	MICRO-ENVIRONMENT	MATERIALS	STREET FURNITURE	PLANTING	PEOPLE DENSITY	VEHICLE DENSITY	SERVICE TRUCKS	ACCIDENT RATE & CONFLICT	PUBLIC TOILETS	COMPONENT INTERACTION EVALUATION
STATUS QUO	Students, workers shoppers, "regulars" frequent these cafes.	Shopping, cafe sitting, circulation	Specialty shops, cafe type restaurant, car repair	Not applicable	Community concern re: change in commercial activity type	2.5	Sunny, little shade, poor air quality, noise	Brick, concrete, clapboard, shop windows, bright colors	Meter, light-pole, tables and chairs, iron fences	3 Elms	Medium, cafes fill day and evening	Heavy, jam develops every 1-1/2 minutes	Usually double parked	5/yr., jaywalking	None	
PROJECTED	More tourists	Concern of regulars, they may be forced from meeting places	Potential for tourist-oriented shops and fast food service	No change	See below	No change	Acceptable air quality	Changes on west side of street – library better use of properties adjacent	No change	Proposal for planting in front of gas stations	Heavy	No change	No change	Probable increase due to more pedestrian use	No change	
REMARKS	This area has history of business turnover, a situation conducive to increased tourist orientation of new uses. These are low overhead fledgling businesses which could not tolerate increased rents. Adjacency to library makes this area vulnerable.			Community concern that increased traffic would force widening of Boylston. Moratorium on street widenings could avoid this.		Attractive shops and cafes are concentrated on one side of the street. Widening of Boylston could further destroy the continuity and pedestrian scale of this important gateway or theme-setting street. Physical improvements to west side positive.					Pedestrian circulation is concentrated on east side of street. Library will encourage use of west side but jay-walking will probably increase. Proposed massing of Government School may deter pedestrian impacts here (see Section 4.3.2. Interaction).					

SECTION

PLAN

Prepared by ECODESIGN Cambridge

WINTHROP SQUARE
URBAN QUALITY COMPONENTS EVALUATION

	A. USE & USER CHARACTERISTICS			B. VALUES & CONSTRAINTS		C. PHYSICAL AMENITIES & CHARACTERISTICS					D. CIRCULATION & SERVICE					IMPACT
	USER GROUP	USER & PEDESTRIAN ACTIVITY	COMMERCIAL ACTIVITY	LEGAL RESTRICTIONS	SOCIAL VALUES	SCALE WIDTH/ HEIGHT	MICRO-ENVIRONMENT	MATERIALS	STREET FURNITURE	PLANTING	PEOPLE DENSITY	VEHICLE DENSITY	SERVICE TRUCKS	ACCIDENT RATE & CONFLICT	PUBLIC TOILETS	COMPONENT INTERACTION EVALUATION
STATUS QUO	Workers, students, shoppers, picnickers	Meeting, sitting, outdoor cafe, study	Office buildings, cafe/ restaurant	Not applicable	Quiet, relaxing quality of activity by unspoken agreement of users	3	Some shade, poor air quality, noisy	Grass, asphalt path; trees a ceiling	3 wooden benches, iron fencing awning; cafe tables, parking meters, street light	Rosebushes, flower plots, 1 oak, maples, hedges, short bushes	Light, casual use, all day & evening a retreat	Heavy, constant flow – noise, exhaust	None	5/yr. @ street; sq. separated from st.	None	
PROJECTED	More tourists	Increase in tourists could alter type of uses	No change expected except as described for figure 4.4.3-H	No change	Existing character possibly not appreciated or respected by increased tourists	No change	Acceptable air quality	No change	No change	No change	Light to Medium	Change in relation to numbers	No change	Probable increase due to more pedestrian use	No change	
REMARKS	Amenities of open space provided by Commonwealth Plaza, if allowing such activities as picnicking and other related facilities, could make tourist use of this park unnecessary.										Quality of a retreat from urban movement and activity potentially threatened by increased pedestrian use.					

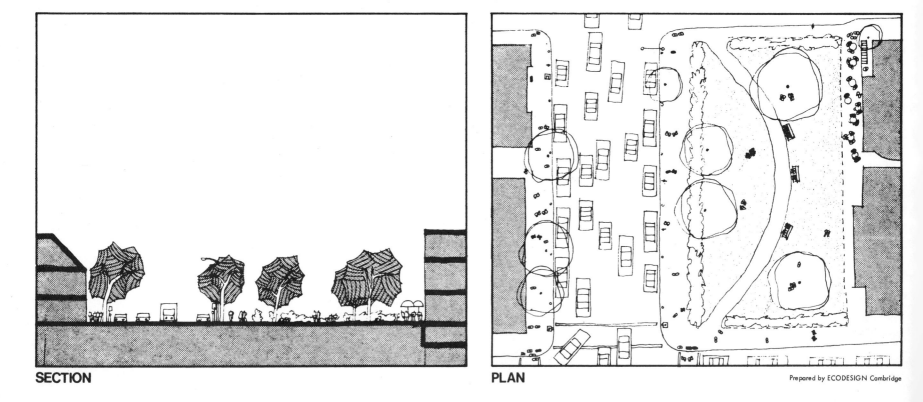

SECTION

PLAN

Prepared by ECODESIGN Cambridge

BRATTLE STREET
URBAN QUALITY COMPONENTS EVALUATION

	A. USE & USER CHARACTERISTICS			B. VALUES & CONSTRAINTS		C. PHYSICAL AMENITIES & CHARACTERISTICS					D. CIRCULATION & SERVICE					IMPACT
	USER GROUP	USER & PEDESTRIAN ACTIVITY	COMMERCIAL ACTIVITY	LEGAL RESTRICTIONS	SOCIAL VALUES	SCALE WIDTH/ HEIGHT	MICRO-ENVIRONMENT	MATERIALS	STREET FURNITURE	PLANTING	PEOPLE DENSITY	VEHICLE DENSITY	SERVICE TRUCKS	ACCIDENT RATE & CONFLICT	PUBLIC TOILETS	COMPONENT INTERACTION EVALUATION
STATUS QUO	Shoppers, students, street people, workers	Shopping, circulation, entertainment	Flower display, newsstand, restaurants, variety, banks, clothing	Occasional regulation of musicians	Not applicable	1.25	Sunny, poor air quality, noisy	Concrete paving, brick and show windows, awnings	Parking meter, lightpoles, signs, plants	Plant store display	Heavy, sporadic congestion	Very heavy traffic, double parked cars	Frequently double parked	(See MBTA kiosk), frequent jaywalking	None	
PROJECTED	More tourists	No change	Potential for tourist-oriented shops	Congestion may result in more regulation of musicians	No change	No change	Acceptable air quality	No change	No change	Congestion may prevent sidewalk display	Very heavy, increased congestion	Very heavy traffic	No change	Probable increase due to more pedestrian activity	No change	
REMARKS	Potential change in commercial due to location in critical visitor impact area, replacing existing local services (hardware, variety stores)					Textures, street elements inappropriate for pedestrian use.					pedestrian vehicular congestion eased if sidewalk widened and on-street parking eliminated. Increased congestion due to confluence must be dealt with.					

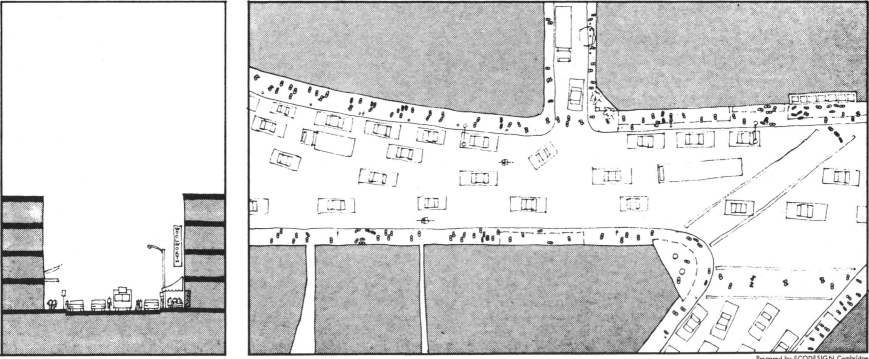

SECTION

PLAN

Prepared by ECODESIGN Cambridge

PALMER STREET
URBAN QUALITY COMPONENTS EVALUATION

	A. USE & USER CHARACTERISTICS			B. VALUES & CONSTRAINTS		C. PHYSICAL AMENITIES & CHARACTERISTICS					D. CIRCULATION & SERVICE					IMPACT
	USER GROUP	USER & PEDESTRIAN ACTIVITY	COMMERCIAL ACTIVITY	LEGAL RESTRICTIONS	SOCIAL VALUES	SCALE WIDTH/HEIGHT	MICRO-ENVIRONMENT	MATERIALS	STREET FURNITURE	PLANTING	PEOPLE DENSITY	VEHICLE DENSITY	SERVICE TRUCKS	ACCIDENT RATE & CONFLICT	PUBLIC TOILETS	COMPONENT INTERACTION EVALUATION
STATUS QUO	Shoppers, service personnel, students, workers	Circulation across and thru, service delivery parking, sitting	Sidewalk sale, Coop, coffee house, import shop	Service trucks park on curb	Not applicable	0.5	Shady, poor air quality, quiet	Paving, cobblestone and brick; walls, brick, shopwindows	Iron fencing, bollards	Small maples along street, pine hedge opp. Coop.	Heavy, sidewalk sale on Saturdays	Medium, used for illegal parking	Heavy, service alley for Coop	No data	None	
PROJECTED	Tourists	No change expected	No change expected	No change	No change	No change	Acceptable air quality	No change	No change	No change	Very heavy	no change expected	No change expected	No change expected	No change	
REMARKS				Air rights for overhead bridge		Appropriate pedestrian materials, community action culminating in suit forced transformation of this service alley into pleasant pedestrian passageway.					Overhead service and circulation bridge					

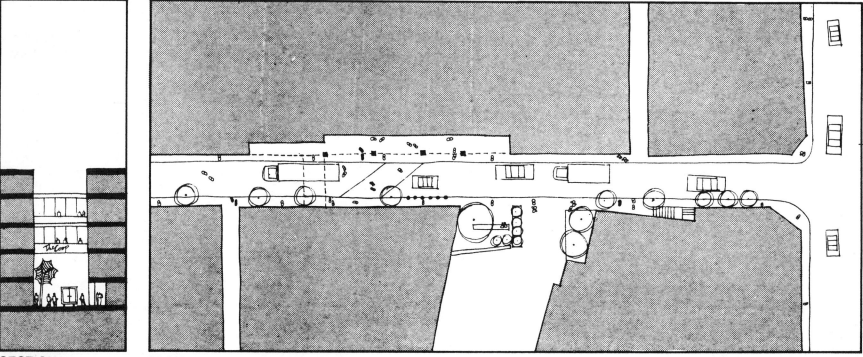

SECTION   **PLAN**

Prepared by ECODESIGN Cambridge

BRATTLE SQUARE PLAZA
URBAN QUALITY COMPONENTS EVALUATION

	A. USE & USER CHARACTERISTICS			B. VALUES & CONSTRAINTS		C. PHYSICAL AMENITIES & CHARACTERISTICS					D. CIRCULATION & SERVICE					IMPACT
	USER GROUP	USER & PEDESTRIAN ACTIVITY	COMMERCIAL ACTIVITY	LEGAL RESTRICTIONS	SOCIAL VALUES	SCALE WIDTH/ HEIGHT	MICRO- ENVIRONMENT	MATERIALS	STREET FURNITURE	PLANTING	PEOPLE DENSITY	VEHICLE DENSITY	SERVICE TRUCKS	ACCIDENT RATE & CONFLICT	PUBLIC TOILETS	COMPONENT INTERACTION EVALUATION
STATUS QUO	Street people, workers, students, shoppers	Gathering, sitting, street entertainment, circulation link	Clothing, stereos, flowers in surrounding buildings	Occasional regulation of musicians	Not applicable	4	Sunny, poor air quality, noisy	Asphalt with wood expansion joints, concrete	Heavy concrete benches, bike racks, large and small planters, street signs	Large and small evergreens, flowers	Normally light, overspill in street during perform.	Very heavy	Always double parked in surrounding sts.	16/yr., no controlled pedestrian access to plaza	None	
PROJECTED	Many tourists	No change	Potential tourist oriented shop, fast food service	No change	No change	No change	Acceptable air quality	No change	No change	No change	Medium to heavy	Very heavy	No change	Probable increase due to more pedestrian activity	No change	
REMARKS	Potential change in commercial due to location in critical visitor impact area, replacing existing local services. Properties adjacent are under consideration for development.			Traffic island taken over for park uses by pedestrian pressures.		Textures, street elements not most appropriate for pedestrian use.					North side of Brattle Street curve is already heavily congested for pedestrians due to narrow sidewalks, parking meters, etc.					

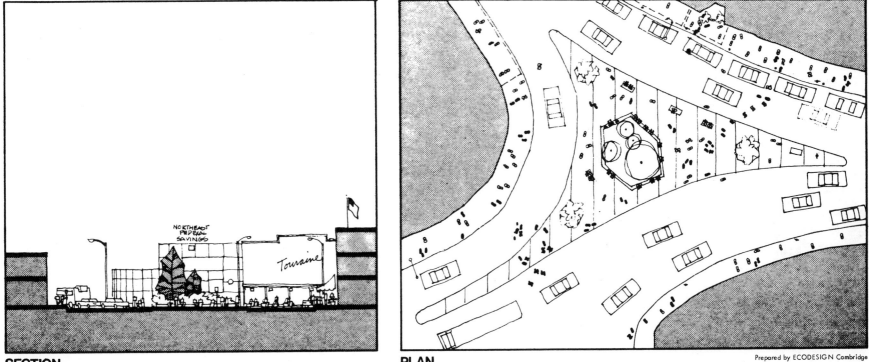

SECTION

PLAN

Prepared by ECODESIGN Cambridge

TAC COURTYARD
URBAN QUALITY COMPONENTS EVALUATION

	A. USE & USER CHARACTERISTICS			B. VALUES & CONSTRAINTS		C. PHYSICAL AMENITIES & CHARACTERISTICS					D. CIRCULATION & SERVICE					IMPACT
	USER GROUP	USER & PEDESTRIAN ACTIVITY	COMMERCIAL ACTIVITY	LEGAL RESTRICTIONS	SOCIAL VALUES	SCALE WIDTH HEIGHT	MICRO-ENVIRONMENT	MATERIALS	STREET FURNITURE	PLANTING	PEOPLE DENSITY	VEHICLE DENSITY	SERVICE TRUCKS	ACCIDENT RATE & CONFLICT	PUBLIC TOILETS	COMPONENT INTERACTION EVALUATION
STATUS QUO	Office workers, shoppers, occasional musicians	Passageway to stores, offices, sitting	Specialty shops business offices	Private property, open at all times	Professional working atmosphere	0.75	Shady, poor air quality, quiet	Brick, glass, concrete	3 benches, short wall around tree sculpture, iron railing	1 maple, several short bushes and plants	Light	Not applicable	Not applicable	Not applicable	None	
PROJECTED	Few tourists	No change expected	No change expected	No change	No change	No change	Acceptable air quality	No change	No change	No change	No change expected	No change	No change	No change	No change	
REMARKS	Tourist would probably by attracted to DR which forms street side of courtyard but courtyard is primarily used as access to professional offices.			Some quiet open spaces valued and needed.		Good example of designed exterior urban space and conscious architectual compatibility of surrounding structures.										

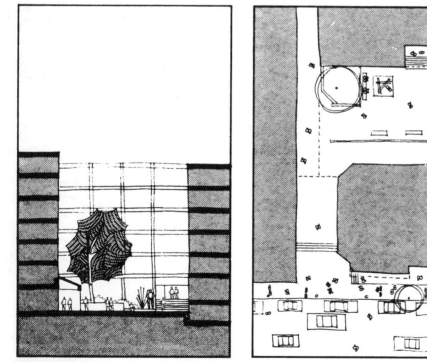

SECTION

PLAN

Prepared by ECODESIGN Cambridge

CAFE ALGIERS PASSAGEWAY
URBAN QUALITY COMPONENTS EVALUATION

	A. USE & USER CHARACTERISTICS			B. VALUES & CONSTRAINTS		C. PHYSICAL AMENITIES & CHARACTERISTICS					D. CIRCULATION & SERVICE					IMPACT
	USER GROUP	USER & PEDESTRIAN ACTIVITY	COMMERCIAL ACTIVITY	LEGAL RESTRICTIONS	SOCIAL VALUES	SCALE WIDTH/ HEIGHT	MICRO-ENVIRONMENT	MATERIALS	STREET FURNITURE	PLANTING	PEOPLE DENSITY	VEHICLE DENSITY	SERVICE TRUCKS	ACCIDENT RATE & CONFLICT	PUBLIC TOILETS	COMPONENT INTERACTION EVALUATION
STATUS QUO	Cafe clientele, chess players, musicians, writers, pedestrians from Brattle	Circulation link; outdoor cafe, chess playing, writing, music playing	Cafe, offices, restaurants, theater	Not applicable	Not applicable	0.5	Sunny, poor air quality, quiet	Asphalt, conc., gravel, paving, clapboard and brick	Cafe tables, chairs and benches, bike rack, trellis	Short bushes in alley; hedges around house, flowers and short trees inside	Cafe filled afternoon and eve.	Space separated from street & traffic by buildings & passage.	None	Not applicable	None	
PROJECTED	Few tourists	No change	No change	No change	No change	No change	Acceptable air quality	No change	No change	No change	Increased congestion in passage & cafe	No change	No change	No change	No change	
REMARKS	Potential impact from tourist may be limited by remote location.					Appropriate scale, poor texture.					Tight circulation space, does not connect major areas at this time.					

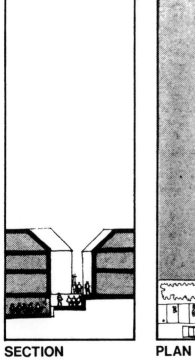

SECTION

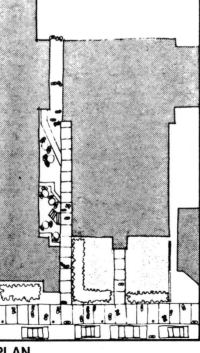

PLAN

Prepared by ECODESIGN Cambridge

MT AUBURN ST / HOLYOKE CENTER PARK
URBAN QUALITY COMPONENTS EVALUATION

	A. USE & USER CHARACTERISTICS			B. VALUES & CONSTRAINTS		C. PHYSICAL AMENITIES & CHARACTERISTICS					D. CIRCULATION & SERVICE					IMPACT
	USER GROUP	USER & PEDESTRIAN ACTIVITY	COMMERCIAL ACTIVITY	LEGAL RESTRICTIONS	SOCIAL VALUES	SCALE WIDTH/HEIGHT	MICRO-ENVIRONMENT	MATERIALS	STREET FURNITURE	PLANTING	PEOPLE DENSITY	VEHICLE DENSITY	SERVICE TRUCKS	ACCIDENT RATE & CONFLICT	PUBLIC TOILETS	COMPONENT INTERACTION EVALUATION
STATUS QUO	Office workers, students	Sitting, sunning Office workers eating lunch	Clothing Harvard Services And Health Center	Owned by Harvard, open at all times	Quiet park in transition area	1 to 3	Sunny, poor air quality, noisy	Concrete, glass, brick	Bench	Hedge, grass, 1 large tree	Light Conflict of students crossing Mt. Auburn to class	Heavy traffic buffered by hedge	Mt. Auburn is service truck route	5/yr. @ corner	None	
PROJECTED	No change expected	No change expected	No change Constant student needs should hold area stable	No change	No chaon area important for student needs and services	No change	Acceptable air quality	No change	No change	No change	No change	No change	More expected	No change	No change	
REMARKS	Distance and lack of any major shopping or tourist attraction could indicate limited numbers of tourists.			Commercial service needs forms transition between academic sector of yard and Harvard houses.		Pleasant park space , historic, club and Lampoon buildings surround.					Not heavily used park but if commercial activity increased in Square more trucks expected on Mt. Auburn service route.					

SECTION

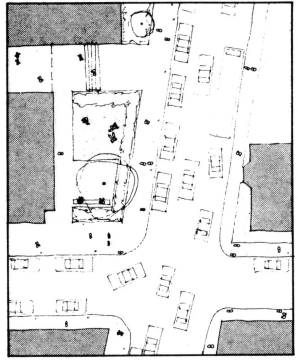

PLAN

Prepared by ECODESIGN Cambridge

These four components provide an outline for the various elements that compose Harvard Square. Paul V. Gump in *Design and Environment* observed, "Men spend their lives in one ecological unit, one behavior setting or another. . . . The quality of their existence can be markedly affected by the quality of these units." So the quality of experiences in various types of behavioral settings (urban spaces) in Harvard Square adds up to a general perception of quality of life in Harvard Square.

The evaluation of impact on these representative places will be an *internal* or user needs impact. That is, does the place work in terms of its desirable or preferred use, as is (status quo), and then what is the effect on an external phenomenon (in this case a proposed tourist attraction) on the components of such a place, and how can that proposed project be treated so that this preferred use is subsequently enhanced and retained, rather than inhibited or altered?

Use and User Characteristics

What do people want or need in their environment? What is successful accommodation? "Some common human preferences include social interaction with people, change from visual and social routines to avoid boredom, and some degree of challenge to master new problems."* In Harvard Square the use characteristics were described in the "Harvard Square Policy Plan" developed by a community task force:

People predominate in Harvard Square. The visual

*"Open Space and Psychological Functioning", Dr. Marvin J. Cline, Appendix (p. 45), from *Open Space for Human Needs*, Marcou, O'Leary & Associates.

impact is one of a large number of people moving along the sidewalks, gathered at crosswalks or congregated in such open areas as Forbes Plaza and Brattle Square. People use the Square for many different reasons and congregate there at different times of the day. Harvard Square attempts to accommodate these many diverse groups of people, but because of sheer numbers, there are space limitations and major conflicts between pedestrians and moving vehicles. Nevertheless, despite all this, it is the broad spectrum of people, as well as the individualized person congregated at one location which makes the Square unique, which gives it character as an interesting place to be and which makes it a major tourist attraction.

Harvard Square also remains basically a walking community. Despite very few pedestrian amenities, narrow streets, large amounts of vehicular traffic and almost no open space, the Square remains people-oriented and the favored modes of travel are by foot and bicycle. The commercial core is compact and concentrated and this physical fact combined with inadequate parking and a university habit to walk has resulted in fostering a pedestrian character and scale to Harvard Square."**

The particular character and quality of life in Harvard Square is to a large extent dependent on the successful accommodation of this pedestrian activity.

The use and user characteristics are evaluated in relation to the degree to which they either encourage or interfere with this desired use of a place (as evidenced in most cases by its present pedestrian

**"Users of the Square," from *Harvard Square Policy Plan*, Vol. 6, July 1973.

use or tendency toward improved pedestrian use). For example:

☐

User Group. The type of people who use Harvard Square, as they form part of the visual image and as they determine the type and level of activity, are a significant factor in an overall impression of quality of urban life and experience in Harvard Square. While some places are occupied primarily by one group or another (i.e., street people, students, professionals, etc.), a space should never inhibit other people (due to its use or users) who would like to use it. There is also a potential danger that uses accepted and generated by community residents will be supplanted or inhibited by incompatible new uses by an outside group—for example, tourists or students. The quality of life component charts developed at ECODESIGN can note this tendency in the evaluation where it is a clear possibility.

☐

User and Pedestrian Activity. When evaluating the internal impact of some facilities (such as airports or parking garages), circulation and service might be the prime component, against which all other components are evaluated; in analyzing places in Harvard Square, the prime component of urban vitality and perceived quality of life was found to be the activity of the users. The significance of this pedestrian activity is such that it is almost synonymous with the quality of life in Harvard Square.

☐

Commercial Activity. Such activity, as with the other factors of use and user characteristics, provides a distinct character. Existing facilities in Harvard Square provide a variety of services both specialized and mundane, experimental and traditional, which have evolved in response to community needs. An influence that would tend to eliminate functions and services the community requires or desires is viewed as a negative influence.

Values and Constraints

Just as there are physical shapes, textures, and provisions for certain activities, there are also *regulations and political factors* that either inhibit, encourage, or regulate particular activities and the effects of crowding. "Population concentration, by itself, is not harmful. Rather, it is social interference that is damaging."* This interference is both affected by and effects changes in the political and physical structure. Interference "might result from coordination problems, competition for resources, excessive noise and interpersonal contact or from infringements on privacy and behavioral freedom."**

In this light, then, any regulation or attitude as a result of pressures from a new use that inhibits a desirable use (either at city scale or at neighborhood scale) might constitute interference. Such evaluations obviously must take into account laws that preserve a reasonable degree of order in deference to other functions either in the particular place or in the total urban framework.

Physical Amenities and Characteristics

This component evaluates the degree to which *particular physical characteristics* can be seen to

*"A Postscript on Crowding" derived from "A Social-Psychological Model of Human Crowding Phenomena" (*AIP Journal,* March 1972) by Daniel Stokols in *Design and Environment,* Summer 1972.
**Ibid.

either enhance, encourage, or inhibit the desired activity. The various factors that determine the character of a space are interdependent. One amenity or quality can compensate for another (i.e., a building or wall material that is incompatible to a pedestrian scale could be softened and improved by growing ivy on it).

Scale. The width/height proportion describes the degree of physical enclosure and definition of space provided by the buildings around a particular space. In general, when W/H (width divided by height) is less than 1, a space is more amenable to pedestrian scale, and when it is greater than 1, toward vehicular use. This can't be taken as an absolute standard, because other variables including texture, color, planting, and symbolic or traditional significance can compensate in some cases for a low degree of spatial definition.

Micro-Environment. In a northern climate, urban places must provide for a degree of insulation from the potential types of interference to activity (shade from intense sun, noise insulation, wind breaks, rain shelters). Other deterrents, such as vehicle exhaust, smell, and smog, can only be controlled by decreasing traffic flow or by improving auto emission controls; existing air quality varies constantly in any one place, due to direction and intensity of wind, temperature, day of week, etc. Undesirable noise generated by traffic, especially trucks, can also interfere with many desirable activities.

Materials. Materials are evaluated insofar as they are sympathetic to pedestrian use and scale. Textures such as brick, wood, and stone, which provide a finer grained scale and setting are considered

more easily perceived and appreciated at a pedestrian pace, and are more desirable in defining a pedestrian precinct than smooth monolithic materials like asphalt or concrete, which are more appropriate for vehicular use spaces.

Street Furniture. Includes benches, lightpoles, parking meters, planters, and signs. In the case of a pedestrian plaza, a lack of seating areas or inadequate lighting would be viewed as a deficiency. On constricted sidewalks, too many sign poles, meter poles, and other fixtures interfere with convenient passage and therefore would inhibit the desired use of the space.

Planting. Landscaping, including grass, hedges, trees, or ivy, can provide shelter from sun, rain, wind, or noise, or can soften a building façade. Shade is desirable in spaces where people sit and relax, eat lunch. Planters and hedges serve to insulate space visually, although not acoustically, from disruptive interferences such as heavy traffic, or they can blend with and enhance a space in contrast to hard or unsympathetic building or paving materials.

Circulation and Service

The evaluation of circulation is based on a consideration of the ease of interaction of various systems. For example, if there is heavy but efficient vehicular flow and little or no pedestrian use intended or desired, the desired use would be assumed to be primarily vehicular with a strong positive impact on the fulfillment of the place. There would be negative impact if there is heavy traffic and heavy pedestrian use, and little amenity for the two to interact smoothly.

Pedestrian Density. Described as either light, medium, or heavy flow or concentration. A graphic description of pedestrian density is shown in the schematic sections and plans. Existing pedestrian density based on people counts is shown in line only. Additional pedestrian traffic generated by the proposed tourist attraction is shown in black.

Vehicle Density. This is described again as light, medium, and heavy, and is evaluated in relation to pedestrian density; again, reference is made to the Pedestrian/Vehicular Interaction maps, and to the drawings of the specific places.

Service Trucks. The lack of service access to stores and businesses results in the double-parking of service trucks and increases in traffic problems. Thus the lack of service access would be a negative impact, as it would cause increased congestion.

**Urban Quality Evaluation Summary—
Status Quo: Projected**

The composite of these component charts represents a tangible expression of the quality of life of specific places (page 226). For each place in a city it gives a clear indication of precisely what quality of life components are deficient or threatened—in need of treatment—and what that treatment should be.

The Urban Quality Evaluation Summary Maps (page 227) of urban quality "indicators" are an expression of the overall quality of life in Harvard Square as defined by the interaction of four components; the heavy outline applied to those "indicators" with more than one component arrow

registering negatively for the quality of that place is a straightforward charting of those specific areas within an urban sector that are in need of specific treatment.

This "quality of life" procedure, however, is only an effective treatment in itself when there is a strong feeling on the part of most of the community that the area *does* indeed possess a quality of life that, although not perfect, should be preserved and protected.

Such a therapeutic treatment is a fine tuning of many related elements to make for a more pleasant urban environment. The planting of trees to soften the gaping hole of a gas station, the provision of benches at bus stops, the exclusion of heavy vehicles from a street, the utilization of a remote parking area, the widening of a sidewalk— these are only a gentle massaging of urban elements compared to more dramatic and disruptive treatments such as the closing of a street to automobiles, the placing of a highway underground, the joint development of a parking garage or a raised pedestrian system with overpasses to relieve pedestrian congestion, and so on.

The composite of the component charts represents a tangible expression of the quality of life of specific places. For each place in a city it gives a clear indication of precisely which quality of life components are deficient or threatened, and what treatment should be.

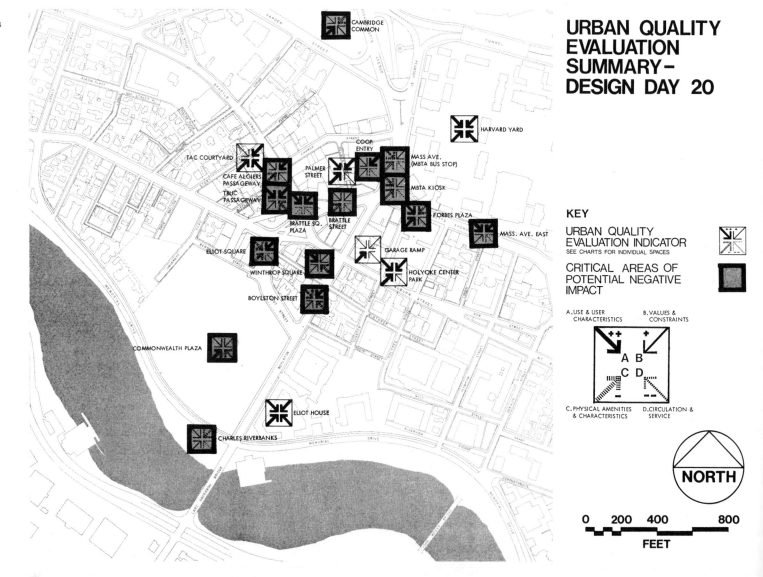

URBAN QUALITY EVALUATION SUMMARY— DESIGN DAY 20

KEY

URBAN QUALITY EVALUATION INDICATOR
SEE CHARTS FOR INDIVIDUAL SPACES

CRITICAL AREAS OF POTENTIAL NEGATIVE IMPACT

A.USE & USER CHARACTERISTICS

B.VALUES & CONSTRAINTS

A B
C D

C.PHYSICAL AMENITIES & CHARACTERISTICS

D.CIRCULATION & SERVICE

NORTH

0   200   400   800
FEET

CAMBRIDGE COMMON

HARVARD YARD

TAC COURTYARD

CAFE ALGIERS PASSAGEWAY

TRUC PASSAGEWAY

COOP ENTRY

PALMER STREET

MASS AVE. (MBTA BUS STOP)

MBTA KIOSK

BRATTLE SQ. PLAZA

BRATTLE STREET

FORBES PLAZA

MASS. AVE. EAST

ELIOT SQUARE

WINTHROP SQUARE

GARAGE RAMP

HOLYOKE CENTER PARK

BOYLSTON STREET

COMMONWEALTH PLAZA

ELIOT HOUSE

CHARLES RIVERBANKS

227

The Urban Quality Evaluation Summary Maps of urban quality ''indicators'' are also an expression of the overall quality of life in the area studied as defined by the interaction of four components. The heavy outline applied to those indicators with more than one component arrow registering negatively for the quality of that place is a straightforward means of charting those specific areas within an urban sector that are in need of treatment.

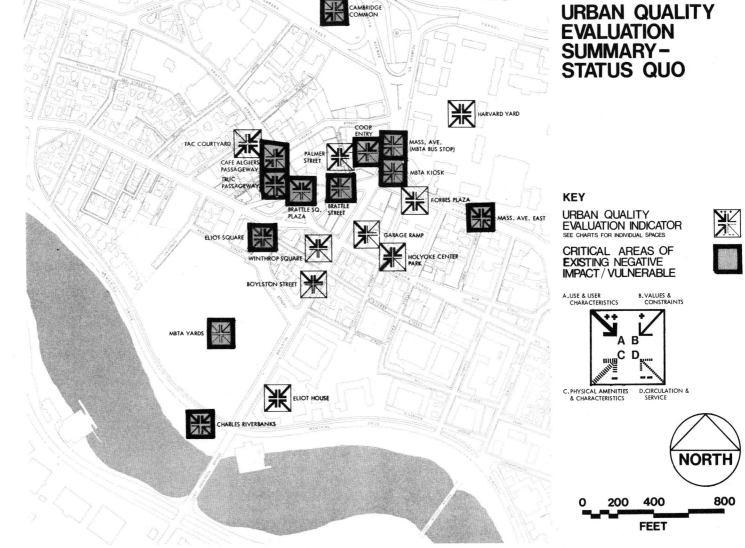

URBAN QUALITY EVALUATION SUMMARY– STATUS QUO

CAMBRIDGE COMMON

HARVARD YARD

TAC COURTYARD

COOP ENTRY

MASS. AVE. (MBTA BUS STOP)

PALMER STREET

CAFE ALGIERS PASSAGEWAY

TRUC PASSAGEWAY

MBTA KIOSK

FORBES PLAZA

BRATTLE SQ. PLAZA

BRATTLE STREET

MASS. AVE. EAST

ELIOT SQUARE

GARAGE RAMP

WINTHROP SQUARE

HOLYOKE CENTER PARK

BOYLSTON STREET

MBTA YARDS

ELIOT HOUSE

CHARLES RIVERBANKS

KEY

URBAN QUALITY EVALUATION INDICATOR
SEE CHARTS FOR INDIVIDUAL SPACES

CRITICAL AREAS OF EXISTING NEGATIVE IMPACT / VULNERABLE

A. USE & USER CHARACTERISTICS

B. VALUES & CONSTRAINTS

A B
C D

C. PHYSICAL AMENITIES & CHARACTERISTICS

D. CIRCULATION & SERVICE

NORTH

0   200   400   800

FEET

BRATTLE SQUARE
EXISTING

MASSACHUSETTS AVENUE
EXISTING

Simple, direct attempts to minimize adverse impacts. Widen sidewalks—eliminate curb parking.

Often the simple, most direct solution is more effective than the grand gesture

The simple, sensitively applied treatment sometimes grand gesture, and should be considered as a first alternative. For example, what if Urban Quality Component Evaluations and Summaries show the effects of a substantial increase in pedestrian use to be that people might begin to bypass and avoid the precise thing they came to experience and enjoy? What if the simple experience of ''window shopping'' is inhibited by an increased crowd of people in front of the displays? What if street musicians attract a crowd that fills streets and sidewalks so much so that enforcement of vending laws, now fairly relaxed, might be tightened up in the interest of improving traffic circulation?

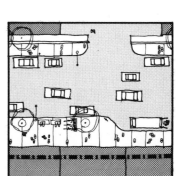

BRATTLE SQUARE
PROPOSED

MASSACHUSETTS AVENUE
PROPOSED

Widening sidewalks by eliminating on-street parking could be a way to soften such adverse impacts. This would provide room for all the varied sidewalk activities such as sidewalk cafés, and street sales, to occur freely. Those activities would be the first thing affected by increased pedestrian congestion. Such a straightforward action would contribute to a solution of several problems at once:

1

Traffic flow through the area in question (in this case, Harvard Square) would be improved by the removal of parking maneuvers. Normal impediments to efficient circulation such as opening doors, cars driving slowly searching for parking places, and double-parked service trucks would all be either eliminated or controlled. The wider sidewalk space could have special turnoff spaces for service trucks. incorporated in its design. A bicycle path could be provided, which would reduce bicycle and vehicle

conflicts. As no traffic lanes would be eliminated, auto circulation could continue with its own particular brand of excitement that the auto/pedestrian mix is said to bring to an urban area, such as Harvard Square.

2

The pedestrian emphasis now present in Harvard Square would be enhanced with sufficient space to avoid having to walk in the street in order to avoid sidewalk congestion. The extended sidewalk space could incorporate brick paving materials, planting and street furniture to increasingly assert a pedestrian-scaled domain in the Square. The projected increase in pedestrian activity due to the new project could be absorbed, at least on the sidewalks, by thus almost doubling the width of the existing sidewalks. This would still allow space for normal street activities such as newspaper hawkers, street musicians, store displays and signs. As park-

ing meters and many parking signs also could be removed, numerous impediments to pedestrian passage would be eliminated. Façade easements could be adapted to regulate signage or storefront treatment.

But even the simple solution becomes complex when its implementation is thought through in detail. Such an action would have to be coincident with a parking plan for Harvard Square to accommodate the on-street parking thus eliminated. The action would have to be developed on a cooperative basis by the city government and local interest groups and developers. The city and its citizens might demand some reparation by the developer of the attraction bringing the increase in pedestrian traffic that made such expenses necessary. The complications could be worth it if the result is an image of ''people spaces'' rather than parked cars.

A Peace Settlement

Sometimes people just can't seem to agree about what to do with their cities; the goals of individuals seem to be in conflict with either the urban environment or with the goals of the urban community as a whole.

In some cases, an action or a project is, in fact, basically incompatible with a city's goals, while in others it is really a disagreement as to the effects of an action, or in still others, it is simply that no attempt has been made to identify and resolve the areas of incompatability. It is at this stage that such disagreements can often be blown out of proportion and begin to fragment a city and its resources—resulting in loss of objectivity, loss of community spirit in the city, a dispersement and waste of valuable energies.

Measuring a risk taken

If the disagreements are over the physical effects of a project such as air or water quality, there are standards already developed and in use in the Environment Impact Statement process that can identify acceptable or unacceptable emissions of toxic material or industrial wastes. The impact of a project on a city's sanitary waste systems or energy supply systems can also be measured and actions can be taken to accommodate it. But how do you measure a risk that is taken—or the effects of a project on an existing quality of life? At ECODESIGN we designed the Urban Quality Evaluation Chart (pages 211–222) to attempt to enumerate and evaluate these qualities. These charts can identify situations where existing conditions in a particular area are so severe that any increase in congestion or in other adverse effects (although slight when taken separately) could constitute a major negative impact.

They cannot, however, demonstrate for an entire area the dramatic cumulative effects of a great number of minor impacts—a little more traffic, a little more pedestrian congestion, taking a risk that wasn't there before, or a growing antagonism between city factions. . . . All of these individually minor effects can begin to build to a critical mass that, if not untangled, can constitute collectively a major adverse impact on an area.

Checking for overlapping and accumulative impacts

To enable a community to confront each of these limitations and problems directly, to classify its problem area, and to check for possible steps that could be taken to avoid or minimize these impacts we developed the matrix shown on page 230.

The matrix is divided into six major Impact Areas:
I
Response to Goals and Objectives
II
Risks taken/By whom
III
Project Physical Program and Plans
IV
Project Operations and Use
V
Urban Functions and Urban Frame
VI
Urban Quality of Life Components

Problems or adverse impacts are identified as relating to one or more of these areas, and then summarized briefly on the matrix. Then, item by item, a city, its urban designers, and its citizens can consider what actions or alternatives would serve to avoid or to minimize these impacts.

Sometimes minor problems develop to a critical mass

Some impact items and some measures to minimize adverse impacts eventually end up being discussed under two or more of the Impact Areas as there are critical overlappings and variations of those considerations. These recurring items must not be regarded as duplication, but rather as a means of illustrating how some apparently "minor impacts" become major factors when they overlap and affect several impact areas. In the same way, many of the measures to avoid or minimize adverse impacts tend to avoid or minimize more than one impact. The initial purpose of the matrix was in fact to illustrate the cumulative effects of this repetition and overlapping.

To illustrate how the matrix works, let us take an example of a broad interpretation of an "adverse impact" and assume that an action or a project that subjects a city to the total and unmodified risk of the unknown effects of a project would constitute an adverse impact.

This impact would be charted under Impact Area II, Risks Taken/By Whom, with summaries of the specific risk problems—the fallibility of facts and figures, the unpredictability of people, who ultimately take these risks, and so on. At the same time, any mechanism proposed or inherent in the project or in the city to minimize the risks and/or the expenses of ameliorating the consequences of them would be noted under Measures to Minimize Adverse Impacts II—Risk Reduction: responsibility, cooperation, communication.

ADVERSE IMPACTS AND MEASURES TO AVOID OR MINIMIZE THEM

Legend (MEASURES TO MINIMIZE):
- ● VERY EFFECTIVE MEASURE
- ◍ EFFECTIVE SUPPLEMENTARY MEASURE
- ○ RELATED MEASURE
- ☐ NOT EFFECTIVE
- ▦ VERY EFFECTIVE FOR 2 COMMUNITY IMPACTS

Column groups (left to right):
- **I. RESPONSE TO GOALS & OBJECTIVES** — columns 1–6
- **II. RISK REDUCTION: RESPONSIBILITY, COOPERATION, COMMUNICATION** — columns 7–12
- **III. PROJECT PHYSICAL PROGRAM & PLANS** — columns 13–17
- **IV. PROJECT OPERATIONS PROGRAM & USE** — columns 18–21
- **V. URBAN FUNCTION & FRAME** — columns 22–27
- **VI. URBAN QUALITY OF LIFE COMPONENTS** — columns 28–34

Column headers:
1. Define or redefine and reinforce clear mutual goals and objectives
2. Set economic objectives to provide or increase city tax base
3. Set social objectives to maximize user cost-benefits
4. Return to an original concept of project such as space or functional program
5. Locate facility at more compatible alternative site
6. Make all discussion public and publicized
7. Make all discussions and policies comprehensible
8. All efforts should take comprehensive view of project area as a totality
9. Structure interaction between all concerned parties to cooperatively implement measures to minimize
10. Developer should recognize responsibility for their corporation interface and effect on project area
11. Structure or restructure task force groups to represent community directly
12. Give stronger implementation and enforcement powers
13. Provide for physical expansion, flexibility, and program growth
14. Increase area for specific functions – i.e. parking, commercial, office, housing, etc.
15. Relocate main access points and revise circulation or expand traffic flow area
16. Meet code recommendations – ie. exits, stairs, toilets, ramps, barrier–free design, fire codes
17. Develop physical program alternatives to reduce impact from over crowding or other impacts
18. Determine and maintain optimal balance between program and capacity
19. Increase operating hours – i.e. Sundays, evenings
20. Require reservations as per some national parks to preserve resources
21. Reduce or enlarge building cost in order to re-establish original program and building size
22. Program firms management response to responsibility to community
23. Zone facility as Conditional Use – requiring support, involvement, and assistance to community
24. Establish Environmental Review Board or Zoning Overlay District
25. Incentive Zoning or direct reparations to go toward new improvements
26. Reroute, grade separate circulation or close area to traffic
27. City plan to make adjustments to accommodate new growth directions
28. Widen sidewalks, eliminate parking, and provide pedestrian amenities
29. Zone as Special District to counter incompatible commercial development pressures
30. Institute Special Assessment District to provide pedestrian amenities
31. Fast food regulations with definite policy or enforcement
32. Improve and redirect pedestrian activities to relieve development pressures and sprawl
33. Acquire Federal/State funding and political commitments to implement parking changes
34. All participant–developer/city–local institutions to program budgets within Environmental Strategy.

ADVERSE IMPACTS — Columns 1–12 (Sections I & II)

Adverse Impact	1	2	3	4	5	6	7	8	9	10	11	12
VI. URBAN QUALITY OF LIFE COMPONENTS												
Increased vehicular/pedestrian conflict – beyond tolerable or adoptable level.					●	●		●			●	
Decreasing resident use of area as rents increase and existing specialty shops leave or change merchandise.	○		◍		●	●	◍	◍	●		○	
Potential commercial pressure contrary to unique size, quality and character of existing commercial areas.	○				●			○		◍	◍	○
Existing undesirable noise and odor pollution will increase due to increased bus and auto traffic.					◍				◍			
Litter will increase – pickup cost borne by City		●					○			○	○	
V. URBAN FUNCTION & FRAME												
Lack of existing City planning policy has made assessment of potential impacts and alternative proposals difficult.	●	○	◍	○	●	●	●	●				
Pressure for more intensive commercial development in neighborhood adjacent to site will bring secondary traffic		○			◍		◍	●	●	◍	●	
Pressure for full use of permitted zoning is contrary to existing scale in residential areas							◍	◍	●	◍	●	
Precedents indicate City will be unable to respond to impacts expeditiously and implement means to minimize	●	◍		◍		◍	◍	○				
IV. PROJECT OPERATIONS PROGRAM & USE												
Peak attendance may exceed functional capacity of building – overload controls entail extra operating costs	○	●		◍		◍	●	◍	●	●		
Current scheme includes no plans for expansion or flexibility, no management structure for use controls.	○		○	◍		◍	●	◍	◍	●		
Impacts in uncontrolled peak years may result in lasting damage to area character and business		○			●							
Visitor overflow from undersized facility will adversely impact already critically congested areas.	▦		◍		▦	◍	▦	◍	▦	◍	○	
Existing functional problems in urban frame are so critical that any increase in traffic constitutes negative impact					●	◍					●	
III. PROJECT PHYSICAL PROGRAM & PLANS												
Minor inconsistencies with building standards – stair landings, toilet distribution, drinking fountains, etc.												
Program and plan eliminates several hundred parking spaces presently available for city use.		◍	●									
No new tax base for City from related facilities or any par of prime large downtown site		●				○			●	●	◍	
Parking is inappropriate land use for approximately 1/3 of CBD site adjacent a river and park amenity					○			◍		◍		
II. RISKS TAKEN & BY WHOM												
Risks due to difficulty of pin-pointing attendance and possible over or under projections	▦			◍		◍	◍	◍	○	○		
No legal mechanism compels implementation of measures to minimize adverse impacts. E.I.S. not legally binding							◍	○	●	●	◍	
City alone will bear burden of loss of amenities related to the totality of the risks noted above.						○	●	●	●	●	●	
I. RESPONSE TO GOALS & OBJECTIVES												
Curtailment of original dynamic goals for project because of costs and constraints of site and location.		●	●	●								
Not responsive to cities' goal of related facilities for tax base and commercial core expansion	●	●		●		◍	○	●				
Lack of flexibility in new separated plan – a rigid program would not be responsive to problems			●	●		◍	○					
Non maximization of numbers of possible visitors and public exposure to a national cultural resource.	●		◍	●		○	◍					

ADVERSE IMPACTS — Columns 13–34 (Sections III, IV, V, VI)

Adverse Impact	13	14	15	16	17	18	19	20	21	22	23	24	25	26	27	28	29	30	31	32	33	34
Increased vehicular/pedestrian conflict – beyond tolerable or adoptable level.																						
Decreasing resident use of area as rents increase and existing specialty shops leave or change merchandise.	○																					
Potential commercial pressure contrary to unique size, quality and character of existing commercial areas.						◍		◍	◍													
Existing undesirable noise and odor pollution will increase due to increased bus and auto traffic.							◍	●														
Litter will increase – pickup cost borne by City																						
Lack of existing City planning policy has made assessment of potential impacts and alternative proposals difficult.						◍	◍	◍											◍	◍		
Pressure for more intensive commercial development in neighborhood adjacent to site will bring secondary traffic						●	●	●														
Pressure for full use of permitted zoning is contrary to existing scale in residential areas						●		●														
Precedents indicate City will be unable to respond to impacts expeditiously and implement means to minimize						○		○														
Peak attendance may exceed functional capacity of building – overload controls entail extra operating costs					◍	◍	●	●											◍	●	◍	
Current scheme includes no plans for expansion or flexibility, no management structure for use controls.	○				●															○		●
Impacts in uncontrolled peak years may result in lasting damage to area character and business																						
Visitor overflow from undersized facility will adversely impact already critically congested areas.	◍																					
Existing functional problems in urban frame are so critical that any increase in traffic constitutes negative impact					◍																	
Minor inconsistencies with building standards – stair landings, toilet distribution, drinking fountains, etc.				●																		
Program and plan eliminates several hundred parking spaces presently available for city use.						◍																●
No new tax base for City from related facilities or any par of prime large downtown site					◍																○	
Parking is inappropriate land use for approximately 1/3 of CBD site adjacent a river and park amenity																						
Risks due to difficulty of pin-pointing attendance and possible over or under projections					◍	○	●	●		▦	◍	◍				◍	●		◍			
No legal mechanism compels implementation of measures to minimize adverse impacts. E.I.S. not legally binding											◍	○										
City alone will bear burden of loss of amenities related to the totality of the risks noted above.					◍						○						◍	◍	○			
Curtailment of original dynamic goals for project because of costs and constraints of site and location.					◍		●	●														
Not responsive to cities' goal of related facilities for tax base and commercial core expansion											○											
Lack of flexibility in new separated plan – a rigid program would not be responsive to problems					◍																	
Non maximization of numbers of possible visitors and public exposure to a national cultural resource.					○		◍	◍														

Identifying problems and solving them. Problems or adverse impacts are identified as relating to one or more of the six impact areas and summarized briefly on the matrix. Then, item by item, a city, its urban designers, and its citizens can consider what actions would most directly solve specific problems, would relate beneficially to the greatest number of adverse impacts and would be most concurrent with the cities' goals and objectives. This matrix is a sample condensed from twelve charts dealing with many detailed EIS considerations of a proposed project.

Discussion relevant to risks then might consider:

1
How accurate are existing demographic, planning, socioeconomic, and other projection methodologies, especially with respect to a proposed site and a specific project.

2
How consistent or inconsistent is that site? Is it fixed and predictable or of a transitional and changing character that is difficult to predict.

3
What is the margin of accuracy that can be guaranteed or even expected under the conditions above? And given that margin of error, who takes the risk? Who lives with the problems, who supervises the conditions, who engineers the solutions and who pays for the expense?

When these questions are all answered, the consideration then becomes one that was always presented by Supreme Court Justice Warren at the conclusion of each verdict: "but is it fair?" Are there responsibilities and a part of the burden of the risks taken that might, and should, be assumed by the developers as opposed to the citizens? Are there inherent obligations in return for the right to be located in a particular area? Or obligations inherent in the position of a tax-free institution? Do these obligations include a responsibility for consequences that is even more requisite in an area where conditions are vulnerable and changing, and therefore the risks are higher and more unpredictable? Are there, in fact, sufficient measures available to avoid or minimize adverse effects? Are there legal mechanisms to assure their implementation?

Checking for corrective actions of means to minimize

This type of discussion could be carried on by task forces in each of the impact problem areas, and measures to avoid or minimize are noted in the matrix by dots that are keyed to indicate the degree to which they are effective. A measure effective in avoiding or minimizing three or more adverse impacts is highlighted by a tone on the chart and regarded as a recommended measure to be implemented.

Measures "to reduce risk" might be listed under any one of the six Impact Areas, whereas other impacts such as a building code violation could only show as being avoided by a corrective action under Impact Area III—Project Physical Program and Plans.

Some "measures taken" to treat a problem are attitudinal or administrative

In some cases measures to minimize will be definitive and physically concise actions such as "meet code requirements for stair and toilets," "increase on-site parking," "provide benches and bike racks," or "widen sidewalks." In other cases, they are attitudinal or administrative measures such as "develop set of mutual goals and objectives," "structure interaction among all participating parties," "make all discussion public and publicized," "make all discussions and policies comprehensible to general citizenry," "give stronger implementation or enforcement powers to a citizens group."

Other measures taken are legal or quasi-legal

A legal measure such as a zoning mechanism, on the other hand, might be charted under Urban Function & Frame, but still be effective in avoiding or minimizing areas of impact, especially in the areas of Response to Goals and Objectives and Risk Reduction. Zoning codes, regulations, and legal measures are often the peacemakers—the only way of affecting, implementing, and enforcing a settlement. Many variations of these important tools have evolved including the following:

Land use zoning	Nuisance laws
Floor area ratio	Restrictive covenants
Cluster zoning	Subdivision control
Bonuses	Special use permits
Preferential tax schemes	Billboard regulations
Incentive zoning	Height regulations
Planned unit development	Building codes
Special assessment district	Public health standards
Loading zones	Business districts
Spot zoning	Parking plans & requirements
Mobile home zoning	Defensible space concepts
Architectural control & compatibility	Multiple dwellings
Environmental impact statement	Nonconforming uses
Environmental impact review board	Parcel rezoning
Performance standards & specifications	Commercial zoning
Conditional use & contract zoning	Exclusionary zoning
Floating zones	Fast food regulations
Development rights transfer	Filling stations regulations
Protection of aesthetics	Historic sites & districts
Residential density control	Landmarks preservation
	Special district zone
	Land use controls
	Industrial zoning
	Subdivision deed restrictions

Lot size regulations

Yard regulations

Façade easements

Mandatory inclusionary land use

Land banking

Agri-zoning

Each zoning measure must be viewed in light of the nature of the particular controversy to be resolved. Often the developer has stated his goals and presented his plans; the community has voiced its objections; then both sides retreat into rhetorical defensive positions, polarizing all sides and creating a confrontation where any gesture at cooperation on either side would be interpreted as concession rather than compromise. While in many ways each new project is a unique facility with unique problems and potentials, in other respects they are not unique. For example, although a new tourist attraction may be a very special place, even if proposed by a non-profit corporation, it is no different from other corporations that seek to locate in a community. To define possible areas of negotiation and agreement between municipalities and corporations seeking to enter a community, one can review previous examples of negotiations that were worked out when a corporation's project was felt to be in conflict with goals and objectives of a community.

□

One simple case is a McDonald's restaurant in Philadelphia that was required to have one employee pick up litter in the area around the site for five minutes every hour. A fast-food seafood restaurant in New Haven/Woodmont, Connecticut, was compelled to eliminate its take-out service when it failed to adequately control the litter problem generated by its customers.

□

Perhaps one of the most thorough examples of community/corporation cooperation is the Polaroid Corporation entering the community of Norwood, Massachusetts. Polaroid took the stance that, unless all concerned were satisfied with the project from all standpoints, they would not build. With this as a criterion, the process was complex and lengthy, but in the end, worked.

Polaroid's strategy was to meet communities and residents on an equal footing, with respect for their positions, and to invite and implement their ideas and suggestions for specific projects, problems, and community volunteer programs. Polaroid paid for all utilities and services in the site, reduced the building height by one story, and altered exterior lighting. Parking was moved behind the building out of sight, and (before the transportation plan) a scheme was worked out where buses were used to consolidate worker traffic into the site and reduce the number of cars on city streets and reduce the size of the parking lot. Public recreation areas were developed on the site. Finally, the neighbors of the project designed the landscaping themselves and Polaroid installed it.

In other instances, Polaroid loaned carpenters to community settlement house rehabilitation projects, was involved in prison programs, neighborhood family care centers, and other projects. This sets an example of developer/community cooperation and definition of mutual goals, which has been contrary to general experience.

By the intent of an Environmental Impact Statement as spelled out by the Environmental Protection Act, it is clear that responsibility for off-site traffic or pollution conditions rests with the organization seeking to enter the community for its own interests. It is imperative that this attitude of concern be extended to other areas such as landscaping, improvement of pedestrian conditions off-site, or participation in organizations of merchants, institutions, and other groups. Once the community or or city settles on its criteria for development, there are many ways it can enforce compliance with the prerequisites it sets for development. While these prerequisites may either be derived from existing statutes or by negotiated arrangements, the mechanisms for controlling the intent of the developer could be the same.

Based on legal or extra-legal agreements and review measures (described below), a proposed project can be seen as a "conditional use." Construction could only proceed if certain conditions are met or agreed to beforehand, including adequate measures to minimize adverse impacts. While the burden of concern for how the project will fit into the community is on the developer, this doesn't preclude a division of responsibility for some actions or measures to other involved bodies (the city, its government, a merchant's association, local tax-free institutions, a community group, and so on). The various ordinances or controls that follow, for instance, would compel adherence to the conditions of use.

□

Overlay District. Normal zoning districts have requirements concerning placement of buildings, floor/area ratios, parking requirements, etc. An overlay district would be a specially defined area, overlapping standard zoning boundaries, defining special requirements within that area. Such requirements could deal with many things, including stricter requirements than the standard zoning, compliance with cooperative development efforts in the areas of parking or pedestrian amenity. There could also be provisions for negotiated arrangements of actions—benefiting the community and services provided by the community.

☐

Environmental Impact Review Board. This could be a way to require conformance by the developer with requisite conditions for construction. The Review Board would be instituted by the city and it would have the power to examine all aspects of the design from physical appearance to circulation and environmental impact (including noise and odors), to evaluate compatability with surrounding land uses. The Review Board, in the case of an incompatible proposal or design, could describe specific conditions or measures that would make it acceptable to the Board and the community.

The previous explanations of various zoning or review procedures are concerned essentially with ensuring conformance with specific conditions or requisites established elsewhere; the following measures both define specific actions and include the means (by statute of zoning review) to enforce the criteria.

☐

Incentive Zoning. Incentive zoning is one of the standard ways in which cities can encourage businesses to attend to particular community needs. For example, if a business provides more than the minimum amount of parking required, there could be other incentives like a more generous floor-area ratio and less restrictive setback requirements. In this way, a company is encouraged to provide something the community needs. The developer whose project will have a significant impact on the pedestrian activity level might be cooperative and contribute toward amelioration of pedestrian amenities in the area with perhaps a trade-off in other areas. The "other areas" must be carefully defined through negotiation so that the developer cannot avoid meeting essential responsibilities for parking, alignment, bounding, or other measures to minimize adverse impacts that might be cited.

☐

Special Assessment District. Special Assessment is a means of implementing and financing physical measures to minimize adverse impacts, such as tree planting, new sidewalk paving, street furniture, lighting, and widening sidewalks. The city government could implement the proposed improvements while the work could be financed by various parties with interests in the district on a proportional basis; for example, the more street frontage or land area devoted to a particular business, institution, or commercial facility, the larger their share of the total cost. The special assessment district could be a committee instituted by a city ordinance to oversee proposed improvements and changes, and the proportional distribution of the costs. Such a scheme is presently in operation in Los Angeles (the "City Beautiful Committee") and Atlanta.

Much precious time, money, and energy can be saved by avoiding conflicts

---

Policy review committees, environmental impact studies, community task forces, are just some means by which disagreements in areas can be judged. But when the settlement is of a nonphysical nature, it is usually voiced in some form of zoning or code. But much precious time, money, and energy would be saved if it were possible to avoid such conflicts. The spirit of an Environmental Impact Statement is essential to protect resources for the community or the citizenry at large against encroachments on or usurpation of those resources (physical or qualitative) by special interests (whether governmental or private). Although the Environmental Impact Statement process presently applies primarily to government-funded projects and although it is rendered somewhat ineffective by an accumulation of red tape, the process as a concept is a valid one. Much should be discussed about the basic fallacy of the present EIS process—such a procedure should be made an integral part of the entire design process, not simply a review made after the project has been proposed, designed, presented, and community reaction concerning it has already been polarized.

The process of Urban Design with environmental assessment returns us to the roots of urban evolution. It is the actions of citizens, their leaders, and advisors testing a "what if?" series of alternatives against shifting contexts and circumstances.

A Glossary for Recycling Cities

This glossary contains many of our own personal definitions of technical or semi-obscure words or terms used in this book and in general in urban planning. It also has a heavy sprinkling of adaptations from Charles Abrams' *The Language of Cities: A Glossary of Terms,* The Viking Press, New York, 1971, which contains as complete a glossary as is available in any published document.

Abandonment
The relinquishment of ownership and control of property.

Accessibility
The quality of admitting entrance, access, or approach.

Acquisition or Taking
The process of obtaining right-of-way.

Air Rights
The right to the use of space over property owned by another.

Amenities
The pleasurable or aesthetic, as distinguished from the utilitarian, features of a plan, project, or location.

Beautification
The act of improving the aesthetic attributes of the physical environment.

Bikeway
A thoroughfare reserved for bicycles either exclusively or during specially assigned periods.

Blight
A metaphor from the plant world used to describe that concentration of forces which puts a building or a neighborhood on its way to becoming a slum.

Budget
An itemized statement of proposed expenditures and anticipated receipts of any government, person, or corporation for a defined period, usually a year.

Builder: Developer
One whose occupation is to erect buildings.

Capital improvement
Any substantial physical facility built by the public or any major nonrecurring expenditure of government.

CBD
Abbreviation for "Central Business District."

Central Business District
That center or core within the embracing region in which is concentrated the most intensive commercial activity.

Central city — The urbanized area surrounding and including the central business district. A large and densely populated center of economic, social, and political activity.

City — Any large or important human settlement.

City-linear — A concept of city form with commercial and service facilities strung out in a narrow belt along a main traffic route.

City planning — The guidance and shaping of the development, growth, arrangement, and change of urban environments with the aim of harmonizing them with the social, aesthetic, cultural, political, and economic requirements of life.

City, satellite — A smaller city on the outskirts of a larger city, independent of its jurisdiction but within its economic and social orbit.

Cityscape — The urban equivalent of a landscape.

Client — The group that is to be the beneficiary (or victim) of planners' work.

Code, building — A body of legislative regulations or by-laws that prescribes the materials, minimum requirements and methods to be used in the construction, rehabilitation, maintenance, and repair of buildings.

Community — A group of people living together in some identifiable territory and sharing a set of interests embracing their lifeways.

Community facilities — Facilities used in common by a number of people and often owned by the public.

Community participation — The theory that the local community should be given an active role in programs and improvements directly affecting it.

Conservation — The protection of the resources of man's environment against depletion or waste and the safeguarding of its beauty.

Cost-benefit analysis — An analytic method designed to evaluate alternative programs in terms of their potential benefits and likely costs, and to aid decision-makers in choosing among them.

Coverage — The proportion of the net or gross land area of a site taken up by a building or buildings.

Cul-de-sac — A passage or place with only one outlet.

Decentralization — The transference of authority from a higher level of government to a lower one or to the people.

Demography — The study of population and population changes.

Density — The average number of persons, families, or dwellings per unit area (acre, square mile, etc.).

Design speed — A speed determined for design and correlation of the physical features of a highway that influence vehicle operation. It is the maximum safe speed that can be maintained over a specified section of highway when conditions are favorable.

Developed area — An area of land on which site improvements such as grading and utility installation have been made and buildings erected.

Developer — *See* "Builder."

Easement	An acquired right of use, interest, or privilege (short of ownership) in lands owned by another.	Goal; Objective; Plan; Program; Project; Scheme	The end result or ultimate accomplishment toward which an effort is directed.
Eco	The habitat or environment.	Grade separation	The separation at different levels of two intersecting roads, by bridge, tunnel, or underpass, so as to permit the roads to cross without obstructing free traffic movement in either.
Ecology	The study of the interrelationships among living organisms and their environments.		
Economic base	The sum of all activities that result in the receipt of income in any form by a city's inhabitants.	Grading	The activity of moving and shaping the earth.
Ecosystem	Dynamic unit undergoing change while all organisms and factors are interacting in different ways.	Highest & best use	The most productive use, reasonable but not speculative or conjectural, to which property or resources may be put in the near future.
Effluent	Liquid sewage discharged by a collection network or a treatment plant.	Holistic	Emphasizing the organic or functional relationship between parts and wholes.
EIS	Environmental Impact Statement.	Human factors	The physiological and psychological capacities and requirements of man and his ecosystem.
Eminent domain	The right of a government to acquire private property for public use or benefit upon payment of just compensation.	Human scale	That combination of qualities that gives man's work an appropriate relationship to man's size and feelings.
Empirical	Relating to or based upon direct experience or actual observation.		
Environment	The sum of all external conditions influencing the growth and development of an organism.	Infrastructure	The basic utilities, enterprises, installations, and services essential for the development, operation, and growth of a city, state, or country.
Exurbia	The area beyond the heavily settled suburbs of a city, distinguished by higher-income commuters, class consciousness, and exclusiveness.	Interchange	The point or system of roadways where two or more roads cross and where allowance is made for the interchange of traffic between them.
Floor-Area Ratio (FAR)	A formula for regulating building volume using an index figure that expresses the total permitted floor area on the lot.	Joint development	The cooperative use of a highway or other transportation corridor for residential, institutional, industrial, and commercial development to humanize the highway itself and so that it fits into the urban fabric.

Laissez faire	A theory of government in which almost all economic activities are left to the play of private operation with as little government interference as possible.
Land	Generally the solid portion of the earth's surface.
Land bank	A stockpile of publicly owned land which is being held for future use as needed.
Land, improved	Raw land that has been provided with sidewalks, water, sewers, and other basic facilities in preparation for residential or industrial development.
Landlord	One who owns and leases real property to a tenant.
Land use	The employment of a site or holding so as to derive revenue or other benefit from it.
Land-use plan	The official formulation of the future uses of land, including the public and private improvements to be made on it and the assumptions and reasons for arriving at the determinators.
LDC	Less Developed Country
Legibility	The ease with which the parts of a city can be recognized and organized into a coherent pattern by a person conceiving of the city as a whole.
Linkage	A relationship between two or more establishments that is characterized by frequent interaction, particularly the movement of persons or goods.
Master Plan, City Plan	A comprehensive, long-range plan intended to guide the growth and development of a city, town, or region.

Maximize	To increase to the highest possible degree.
Megalopolis	The greater urbanized area resulting from the gradual merging of many cities into one great urban agglomeration.
Megastructure	An unusually large structure; a great construction of related parts organized into a whole.
Metropolis	The chief city of a country, state, or region.
Metropolitan area	An area in which economic and social life is predominantly influenced by a central city, to which it is linked by common interests though not often by common policies.
Migration	Movement from one place of abode to another, usually with the intention to settle.
Modal split	The relative breakdown in the use of particular modes of travel for a specific type of traffic.
Mode of transportation	The type of transportation used by a traveler or for a commodity in transit.
Model	A synthetic representation, patterned after an actual or proposed product or system, created to test alternate formats or predict behavior. It may be in physical form, as in an architectural model or a computer model.
Morphology	The form and structure of an organism regarded as a whole—when referring to cities meaning the understanding of the growth and development of the city-form.
Municipality	A town, city, or other district having powers of local self-government. Its powers are generally provided either by specific charter or by state statute.

Neighborhood	A local area whose residents are generally conscious of its existence as an entity and have informal face-to-face contacts and some social institutions they recognize as their own.
New Town	Any new, large-scale development planned to provide housing, work, places, and related facilities within a more or less self-contained environment.
New-Town-in-town	A development on acreage located within a city, as distinguished from a new community developed on open suburban or rural land.
Nodes	The central points, intersection, or "joints" in any complex or system.
Open Space	That portion of the landscape which has not been built over and which is sought to be reserved in its natural state or for agricultural or outdoor recreational use.
Optimum	The best or most favorable.
Option	The exclusive right, for an agreed period, to purchase or lease a property at a stipulated price or rent.
Origin-Destination Survey (O & D Survey)	A traffic-study technique that systematically samples the movement of people, vehicles, and goods in a given area with a view to determining where they begin and end their journeys, the purpose of the journeys, the modes of travel, the elapsed time, and the land use at origin and destination.
Parameter	A variable that can be kept constant while the effect of shifting other variables is investigated.

Park	An open area, usually landscaped or left in its natural state, intended for outdoor recreation and the general enjoyment of nature.
Parking	The temporary storage of vehicles between trips.
Pedestrian	One who walks to negotiate distances.
Planned-Unit Development (PUD)	A residential development in which the subdivision and zoning regulations apply to the project as a whole rather than to its individual lots.
Plat	A map of a city, town, or subdivision that indicates the location and boundaries of individual properties.
Pollution	The fouling of the air, water, or soil, by the introduction of injurious or corrupting elements.
Population	The total number of people living in a given locality.
PRT	Personal Rapid Transit—a people mover.
Public Use	Objects for which public powers or funds may be employed for the benefit of the public.
Radial street pattern	A design in which the streets run from a center outward or from circumference inward along a radius.
Recreation	Any activity voluntarily undertaken for pleasure, fun, relaxation, exercise, or release from boredom, worry, or tension.
Region	A portion of the earth's surface defined and distinguished from adjacent areas by some homogeneity in its natural features, its climate, people, interests, involvements, and administrative controls.

Rehabilitation	The restoration or improvement of deteriorated structures, public facilities, or neighborhoods.	Superblock	A consolidation of a number of smaller blocks and the interior streets into one large block.
Relocation	Settlement of households or businesses in new locations, particularly as applied to persons displaced by governmental action.	System	1) A complex unity formed of many diverse parts. 2) An aggregation of objects jointed in regular interaction or interdependence. 3) Any set of objects or events with relationships between them or their attributes.
Reparcelation	Pooling of uneconomic or fragmented plats to achieve a workable holding.		
Right of Way	Legal right to pass through the grounds of another.	Systems analysis	1) A term often used almost synonymously with "operations research" to describe a research or decision-making process by which alternative approaches to overall design, or to a problem, are considered in order to arrive at a system that provides optimum performance with respect to established criteria. 2) Sometimes described as a phase of systems studies following systems synthesis in which consequences are deduced from alternative systems on costs, performance, and so on.
Riparian rights	The rights accruing to a landowner on the bank of a natural watercourse, lake, or ocean to enjoy access to it for power, fishing, irrigation, swimming, skating, or building piers or wharves.		
Setback regulations	The requirements of building laws that a building be set back a certain distance from the street or lot line either on street level or at a prescribed height.		
Standard	A prescribed criterion of acceptable, usually minimum-dimension, quality or performance.	Systems approach	1) Loosely, looking at the overall situation rather than at the narrow implications of the task at hand; particularly, looking for interrelationships between the task at hand and other functions related to it. 2) The methods used by systems analysis and "operations research" people in solving problems.
Standard Metropolitan Statistical Area (SMSA)	As defined by the Bureau of Census in 1960, a county or group of contiguous counties that contains at least one city of 50,000 inhabitants or more, also contiguous counties essentially metropolitan in character and socially and economically integrated with the central city.	Task force	A committee or group of experts appointed to investigate and report on a specific problem.
Street furniture	Municipal equipment including benches, lights, signs, shelters, kiosks, plantings, and so on.	Town	An urban settlement larger than a village, but smaller than a city—but functioning as a political subdivision of a state.
Suburb	A district, usually residential, on the outskirts of a city.	Transitional area	An area in process of change from one use or type of occupancy to another.

Transit, mass	The act or means of conveying masses of people from place to place along a given right-of-way system; routes are usually prearranged, and service is operated according to prescribed schedules.	Zoning	In general, the demarcation of a city by ordinance into zones and the establishment of regulations to govern the use of the land and the location, bulk, height, shape, use and coverage of structures within each zone.
Transportation	The act or means of moving people or objects from place to place.	Zoning, cluster	A form of zoning that allows a developer to reduce his minimum lot size below the zoning ordinances' requirements if the land thereby gained is preserved as permanent open space for the community.
Transportation terminal	A facility where transfer between modes of transportation takes place.		
Urban design	The discipline concerned with, and the process of giving form and function to, ensembles of structure, to whole neighborhoods or to the city at large.		
Urban renewal	The improvement of urban environments through public initiative and assistance in demolishing slums, rehabilitating or conserving existing structures, providing for better housing, commercial, industrial, and public buildings, as well as greater amenities pursuant to comprehensive plans.		
Utilities	The basic service systems required by a developed area—water supply, sanitary and storm sewers, electricity, gas, and telephone service.		
Village	A settlement that is larger than a hamlet or "junction," but smaller than a town and not truly urban, but incorporated.		
Volume	The number of vehicles, pedestrians, or shoppers passing a given point during a specified period of time.		

Selected Bibliography

Abrams, Charles — *Man's Struggle for Shelter in an Urbanizing World,* MIT Press, Cambridge, Mass., 1964.

Alexander, Christopher — *Notes on the Synthesis of Form,* Harvard University Press, Cambridge, Mass., 1964.

"The City As a Mechanism for Sustaining Human Contact," in Ewald, J., *Environment for Man: The Next 50 Years,* Indiana University Press, Bloomington, 1968.

Appleyard, Donald, Kevin Lynch, and John R. Myers — *The View from the Road,* MIT Press, Cambridge, Mass. 1965.

Ardrey, R. — *The Territorial Imperative,* Delta-Dell, New York, 1968.

Arnheim, Rudolf — *The Dynamics of Shape,* complete issue of *Design Quarterly* 64, 1966.

Visual Thinking, University of California Press, Berkeley, 1969.

Asihara, Yoshinabu — *Exterior Design in Architecture,* Van Nostrand Reinhold, New York, 1970.

Bacon, Edmund N. — *Design of Cities,* Viking Press, New York, 1967.

Banz, George — *Elements of Urban Form,* McGraw-Hill, New York, 1970.

Barnett, Jonathan — *Urban Designs as Public Policy—Practical Methods of Improving Cities,* Architectural Record, McGraw-Hill Pub., New York, 1974.

Berlyne, D. E. — "The Motivational Significance of Novelty," *New Society,* May 1964

Blumenfeld, Hans — *The Modern Metropolis,* Paul D. Spreiregen (ed.), MIT Press, Cambridge, Mass., 1967.

Borgstrom, G. — *Too Many, A Study of Earth's Biological Limitations,* Macmillan, New York, 1969.

Boulding, Kenneth E. — *The Meaning of the 20th Century,* Harper & Row, New York, 1969.

Economic Analysis, 2 Vols.; Vol 1, *Microeconomics;* Vol. 2, *Macroeconomics,* Harper & Row, New York, 1966.

Boyarsky, William & Nancy — *Backroom Politics—How Your Local Politicians Work, Why Your Government Doesn't, and What You Can Do About It,* T. P. Tarcher, Hawthorne Books, New York, 1974.

Britt, S. — "Pedestrian Conformity to a Traffic Regulation," in *Journal of Abnormal and Social Psychology,* 1960.

Buchanen Report — *Traffic in Towns,* Her Majesty's Stationery Office, London, 1963.

Burns, W. — *New Towns for Old: The Technique of Urban Renewal,* Leonard Hill, London, 1963.

Caldwell, William — *How To Save Urban America,* Signet, New York, 1973.

Carson, Rachel — *Silent Spring,* Crest, New York, 1969.

Carver, Humphrey — *Cities in the Suburbs,* University of Toronto Press, Toronto, 1962.

Caudill, W. W., F. D. Lawyer, and T. A. Bullock — *A Bucket of Oil: A Humanistic Approach to Building Design for Energy Conservation,* Cahners Books, Boston, 1974.

Chermayeff, S. and C. Alexander — *Community and Privacy,* Doubleday & Co., Garden City, New York, 1963.

Ciriacy-Wantrup — *Resource Conservation,* University of California Press, Berkeley, 1952.

A Scientific American Book — *Cities,* Alfred A. Knopf, New York, 1965.

The Citizens' Advisory Committee on Recreation and Natural Beauty — *Community Action for National Beauty,* U.S. Government Printing Office, Washington, 1966.

Clark, Samuel D. — *The Suburban Society,* University of Toronto Press, Toronto, 1966.

Clay, Grady — *Close-Up: How to Read the American City,* Praeger Publishers, New York, 1973.

Committee on Resources and Man — *Resources and Man,* San Francisco, W. H. Freeman, 1969.

Commoner, B. — *Science and Survival,* New York, Viking Press, 1966.

Costonis, John J. — *Space Adrift—Saving Urban Landmarks Through the Chicago Plan,* University of Illinois Press, Urbana, Chicago, London, 1974.

Cox, G. (ed.) — *Readings in Conservation Ecology,* New York, Appleton, 1969.

Craik, K. H. — "Environmental Psychology," in *New Directions in Psychology,* ed. by K. H. Craik, et al., 4, 1–121, Holt, Rinehart & Winston, New York, 1970.

Cullen, Gordon — *Townscape,* Architectural Press, London, 1964.

Cutler, Laurence S. and Sherrie Stephens Cutler — *Handbook of Housing Systems for Designers and Developers,* Van Nostrand Reinhold, New York, 1974.

DeChiara, Joseph and John Hancock Callender — *Time Saver Standards for Building Types,* McGraw-Hill, New York, 1973.

DeChiara, Joseph and Lee Koppelman — *Planning Design Criteria,* Van Nostrand Reinhold, New York, 1969.

DeJonge, D. — *Images of Urban Areas—Their Structure and Psychological Foundations,* in Gutman, 271–290.

Dober, Richard — *Environmental Design,* Van Nostrand Reinhold, New York, 1969.

Domhoff, G. W. — *Who Rules America,* New York, Prentice-Hall, 1967.

Douglas, W. — *Wilderness Bill of Rights,* Boston, Little, Brown, 1965.

Doxiadis, C. A. — *Urban Renewal & the Future of the American City,* Public Administration Service, Chicago, 1966.

Editors of *Fortune* — *The Exploding Metropolis,* Anchor, New York, 1957.

Ehrlich, P. — *The Population Bomb,* Ballantine, New York, 1968.

Ehrlich, Paul R. and Anne H. Ehrlich — *Population, Resources, Environment: Issues in Human Ecology,* San Francisco, W. H. Freeman, 1970.

Eldredge, H. — *Taming Megalopolis,* 2 vols, Anchor, New York, 1967.

Ewald, William R., Jr. (ed.) — *Environment for Man,* Indiana University Press, Bloomington, 1967.

Faltermayer, E. — *Redoing America,* Collier, New York, 1969.

Fitch, James Marston — *American Building—The Historical Forces That Shaped It,* 2nd ed., Houghton Mifflin, Boston, 1966.

Franklin Institute — "New Concepts in Urban Transportation," *Journal of the Franklin Institute,* Vol. 286, No. 5, November, 1968, Franklin Institute of the State of Pennsylvania.

Fruin, J. J. — *Pedestrian Planning and Design,* Metropolitan Association of Urban Designers & Environmental Planners, New York, 1971.

Galbraith, John Kenneth — *The Affluent Society,* Boston, Houghton Mifflin, 1969.

The New Industrial State, Houghton Mifflin, Boston, 1969.

Gans, H. J. — *The Levittowners: Ways of Life and Politics in a New Suburban Community,* Pantheon, New York, 1967.

The Urban Villagers: Group and Class in the Life of Italian-Americans, Free Press, New York, 1962.

"Urbanism and Suburbanism as Ways of Life: A Reevaluation of Definitions," in Arnold M. Rose (ed.), *Human Behavior and Social Processes,* Houghton Mifflin, Boston, 1962.

Gibson, J. J. — *The Perception of the Visual World,* Houghton Mifflin, Boston, 1950.

Giedion, Sigfried — *Space, Time & Architecture* (5th ed.), Harvard University Press, Cambridge, Mass., 1968.

Ginzberg, Eli (ed.) — *Technology and Social Change,* Columbia University Press, New York, 1965.

Goffman, E. — *The Presentation of Self in Everyday Life,* Doubleday Anchor, Garden City, 1959.

Relations in Public, Basic Books, New York, 1971.

Behavior in Public Places, Free Press, New York, 1963.

Gottman, Jean — *Megalopolis,* Twentieth Century Fund, New York, 1961, MIT Press, paperback ed., 1964.

Gregory, R. L. — *Eye and Brain,* New York, McGraw-Hill, 1966.

Gutkind, E. A. — *The Twilight of Cities,* Free Press, New York, 1962.

Gutman, R. (ed.) — *People and Buildings,* New York: Basic Books, 1972.

Hall, E. — *The Hidden Dimension,* Anchor, New York, 1966. (Doubleday, Garden City, New York)

The Silent Language, Doubleday, Garden City, New York, 1959; Fawcett, Premier Books, New York, 1966.

Halprin, L. — *Cities,* MIT Press, Cambridge, Mass., 1972.

Hanlin, Oscar and John Burchard (eds.) — *The Historian and the City,* Harvard University Press, Cambridge, Mass., 1963.

Hardin, G. (ed.) — *Population, Evolution, and Birth Control,* W. H. Freeman, San Francisco, 1969.

Heimer, M. — *Contemporary Approaches to Creative Thinking,* Atherton, New York, 1964.

Hilberseimer, L. — *The Nature of Cities,* Paul Theobald, Chicago, 1955.

The New Regional Pattern, Paul Theobald, Chicago, 1949.

Hommann, Mary — *Wooster Square Design,* New Haven Redevelopment Agency, New Haven, 1965.

Hosken, Fran P. — *The Language of Cities,* Schenkman, Cambridge, Mass., 1972.

The Function of Cities, Schenkman, Cambridge, Mass., 1973.

244

Hoyt, Homer — *World Urbanization—Expanding Population in a Shrinking World,* Urban Land Institute Technical Bulletin No. 43, Urban Land Institute, Washington, 1962.

Jacobs, Jane — *The Death and Life of Great American Cities,* New York, Random House, 1961.

Jarrett, H. (ed.) — *Environmental Quality in a Growing Economy,* Johns Hopkins, Baltimore, 1966.

Jeffers, R. — *Not Man Apart,* Sierra Club, Ballantine, New York, 1969.

Jencks, Charles — *Architecture 2000 Predictions and Methods,* Praeger, London, 1971.

Johnson-Marshall, Percy — *Rebuilding Cities,* University of Edinburgh Press, Edinburgh, Scotland.

Jones, Martin V. — ''The Methodology of Technology Assessment,'' *The Futurist,* February 1972.

Kahn, Louis I. — ''Design with the Automobile: The Animal World,'' *Canadian Art,* Vol. 19, No. 1, Jan./Feb. 1962.

Kepes, Gyorgy (ed.) — Vision & Value Series I: *Education of Vision; Structure in Art and in Science; The Nature and Art of Motion;* George Braziller, New York, 1965.

Series II: *The Man-made Object; Sign, Image, Symbol; Module, Proportion, Symmetry, Rhythm;* George Braziller, New York, 1966.

Klose, Dietrich — *Metropolitan Parking Structures,* Praeger, New York, 1965.

Kormondy, E. — *Concepts of Ecology,* Prentice-Hall, New York, 1969.

Langer, Susanne — *Philosophical Sketches,* Johns Hopkins, Baltimore, 1962; Mentor Books, New York, 1964.

Lansing, J., R. Marans, and R. Zehner — *Planned Residential Environments,* Ann Arbor: Survey Research Center, I.S.R., Univ. of Michigan, 1970.

Le Corbusier — *Oeuvre Complete 1910—1965,* 7 Vols. Editions de l'Architecture, Zurich, 1937–1965.

The Radiant City, original French ed., 1933; Orion Press, New York, 1964.

Creation is a Patient Search, Praeger, New York, 1960.

Lenz-Romeiss, F. — *The City—New Town or Home Town?* (translated by E. Kunster and F. A. Underwood) Praeger, New York, 1973.

Lowry, William P. — ''The Climate of Cities,'' *Scientific American,* Vol. 217, No. 2, August 1967.

Lynch, Kevin — *The Image of the City,* MIT Press, Cambridge, Mass., 1960.

Maki, Fumihiko — *Investigations in Collective Form,* School of Architecture, Washington University, St. Louis, Mo., 1964.

Movement Systems in the City, Harvard Urban Design Program, November 1965.

Manheim, Marvin L. — *Hierarchical Structure: A Model of Design and Planning Processes,* MIT Press, Cambridge, Mass., 1966.

''Problem-solving Processes in Planning and Design,'' *Design Quarterly,* 66/67, 1966.

Manuel, Frank E. — *Utopias and Utopian Thought,* Houghton Mifflin, Boston, 1967; paperback ed., Beacon Press, Boston.

Marine, G. — *America the Raped,* Simon and Schuster, New York, 1969.

Massachusetts Institute of Technology — *Survey of Technology for High Speed Ground Transport,* Cambridge Mass., June 1965.

McHale, J. — *The Future of the Future,* George Braziller, New York, 1969.

McHarg, I. — *Design with Nature,* Natural History Press, New York, 1969.

Mead, Margaret — *Continuities in Cultural Evolution,* Yale University Press, New Haven, 1964.

Meier, Richard L., and Richard D. Duke — ''Gaming Simulation for Urban Planning,'' *Journal of the American Institute of Planners,* Vol. 32, January 1966.

Michelson, W. H. — *Man and His Urban Environment: A Sociological Approach,* Reading, Mass., Addison-Wesley, 1970.

Milgram, S. — ''The Experience of Living in Cities,'' *Science,* 1970.

Miller, Brown, Neil J. Pinney and William S. Saslow — MIT Report #23, *Innovation in New Communities,* MIT Press, Cambridge, Mass. and London, England, 1972.

Miller, G. A. — *Psychology: The Science of Mental Life,* New York, Harper & Row, 1962.

Mills, C. Wright — *The Power Elite,* Oxford University Press, New York, 1956; Galaxy Books paperback ed., 1959.

Power, Politics, and People, Oxford University Press, New York, 1963.

Moholy-Nagy, Sibyl — *Matrix of Man,* Praeger, New York, 1968.

Moody, Walter D. — *What of the City?* A. C. McClurg & Co., Chicago, 1919.

Moore, Gary T. (ed.) — *Emerging Methods in Environmental Design Planning,* MIT Press, Cambridge, Mass., 1970.

Moore, R. L. — "Pedestrian Choice and Judgment" in *Operation Research Quarterly,* 1954.

Morris, D. — *The Naked Ape,* Dell, New York, 1969.

Mumford, Lewis — *The City in History,* Harcourt Brace & World, New York, 1961.

Techniques and Civilization, Harcourt Brace & World, New York, 1961.

Nader, Ralph (Study Group) — *Politics of Land,* Grossman, New York, 1973.

Nairn, Ian — *The American Landscape: A Critical View,* Random House, New York, 1965.

National Committee on Urban Transportation, Public Administration Service — "Standards for Street Facilities," *Procedure Manual 7A,* Chicago, 1958.

Newman, O — *Defensible Space,* Macmillan, New York, 1972.

Odum, E. — *Ecology,* Holt and Rinehart, New York, 1969.

Owen, Wilfred — *The Accessible City,* Brookings Institute, Washington, 1972.

The Metropolitan Transportation Problem, Brookings Institute,

Paddock, W. — *Famine Nineteen Seventy-Five,* Boston, Little, Brown, 1968.

Passoneau, Joseph R., and Richard Wurman — *Metropolitan Atlas: 20 American Cities,* MIT Press, Cambridge, Mass., 1966.

Peckham, Morse — *Man's Rage for Chaos,* Chilton, Philadelphia, 1965.

Perin, C. — *With Man in Mind: An Interdisciplinary Prospectus for Environmental Design,* MIT Press, Cambridge, 1970.

Perloff, Harvey S. — *Planning and the Urban Community,* University of Pittsburgh Press, Pittsburgh, 1961.

Perloff, Harvey S., and Lowdon Wingo, Jr. — *Issues in Urban Economics,* Johns Hopkins, Baltimore, 1968.

Perry, Brian J. L. — *The Human Consequences of Urbanization: Divergent Paths in the Urban Experience of the 20th Century,* St. Martin's Press, New York, 1973.

Greater London Council — *The Planning of a New Town,* London, 1961.

Platt, John — "World Transformation: Changes in Belief Systems," *The Futurist,* June 1974.

Porter, E. — *In Wildness is the Preservation of the World,* New York, Sierra Club/Ballantine, 1967.

Rasmussen, Steen Eiler — *Experiencing Architecture,* Wiley, New York, 1959.

Towns and Buildings, Harvard University Press, Cambridge, Mass., 1951.

Regional Plan Association — *Urban Design Manhattan,* Viking Press, New York, 1969.

Report of the National Advisory Commission on Civil Disorders — E. P. Dutton, New York, 1968.

Reps, John W. — *The Making of Urban America: A History of City Planning in the United States,* Princeton University Press, Princeton, New Jersey, 1964.

Ricci, Leonardo — *Anonymous (20th Century),* George Braziller, New York, 1962.

Rienow, R. and L. Rienow — *Moment in the Sun,* Ballantine, New York, 1969.

Riesman, David — *The Lonely Crowd,* Yale University Press, New Haven, 1950; paperback ed., 1961.

Robinette, Gary O. — *Plants/People/and Environmental Quality,* U.S. Department of the Interior, Washington, D.C., 1972.

Rodwin, Lloyd — *The Future Metropolis,* George Braziller, New York, 1961.

Rudofsky, B. — *Architecture Without Architects,* Doubleday, New York, 1969.

Safdie, Moshe — *Beyond Habitat,* MIT Press, Cambridge, Mass., and London, England, 1970.

Schaller, L. E. — *The Impact of the Future,* Abingdon Press, Nashville, 1969.

Schmertz, Mildred F. (ed.) — *Open Space for People—Acquisition, Conversation, Creation. and Design,* American Institute of Architects, New York, 1970.

Schwartz, William (ed.) — *Voices for the Wilderness,* from the Sierra Club Wilderness Conferences, Ballantine, New York, 1969.

Sekler, Eduard F. — "The Visual Environment," in *The Fine Arts and the University,* Macmillan, Toronto, 1965.

Sharp, D. (ed.) — *Planning and Architecture,* Barrie and Rockcliff, London, 1967.

Sitte, Camillo — *City Planning,* Random House, New York, 1965.

Smithson, Alison (ed.) — *Team 10 Primer 1953–1962,* special issue of *Architectural Design,* Vol. 32, No. 12, December 1962.

Sommer, R. — *Personal Space,* Prentice-Hall, Englewood Cliffs, New Jersey, 1969.

Stanford Research Institute — *Future Urban Transportation Systems: Impacts on Urban Life and Form,* HUD Contract No. H-776, Menlo Park, Calif., March 1968.

Storer, J. — *Man in the Web of Life,* Signet, New York, 1968.

Suttles, G. D. — *The Social Order of the Slum,* University of Chicago Press, Chicago, 1968.

Tandy, Cliff (cons. ed.) — *Handbook of Urban Design,* Crane, Russack & Co., Architectural Press, New York, 1971.

Thomas, W. — *Man's Role in Changing the Face of the Earth,* University of Chicago Press, 1956.

Tunnard, C. — *The City of Man: A New Approach to the Recovery of Beauty in American Cities,* Charles Scribner's Sons, New York, 1970.

U.S. Department of Transportation — *Center City Transportation Project,* DOT-UT,32, September 1970.

Van Ettinger, Jan — *Towards a Habitable World,* Elsevier, Amsterdam, 1960.

Vayda, A. — *Environment and Cultural Behavior,* Natural History Press, Garden City, New York, 1969.

Vernon, M. D. — *The Psychology of Perception,* Penguin, Baltimore, 1962.

Villee, Claude A. — *Biology,* 3rd ed., W. B. Saunders Co., Philadelphia, London, 1957.

Von Hertzen, H. and P. D. Spreriegen — *Building A New Town: Finland's New Garden City Tapiola,* MIT Press, Cambridge, Mass., 1971.

A. M. Vorhees & Associates — *Urban Design and Development Study,* Vol. 1, March 1970.

Weber, Max — *The City,* original German ed., 1921; Free Press, New York, 1958; Collier Books paperback ed., New York, 1962.

White, Morton and Lucia White — *The Intellectual Versus the City,* Joint Center for Urban Studies, Cambridge, Mass., 1962; Mentor Books paperback ed., New York, 1964.

Whittick, Arnold (ed.) — *Encyclopedia of Urban Planning,* McGraw-Hill, New York, 1974.

Whyte, W. — *Last Landscape,* Doubleday, New York, 1968.

Wittlin, Alma — *Museums in Search of Usable Future,* MIT Press, Cambridge, Mass., 1970.

Wohlwill, J. F. — *The Physical Environment: A Problem for the Psychology of Stimulation,* in Gutman, 83–93. [See Gutman Entry].

Wright, Frank Lloyd — *The Living City,* Horizon Press, New York, 1958.

Wurster, Catherine Bauer — "Can Cities Compete with Suburbia for Family Living?" *Architectural Record,* Vol. 136, December 1964.

Zucker, Paul — *Town and Square,* Columbia University Press, New York, 1959.

Illustration
Credits

80 (*bottom*)
Courtesy of Westinghouse Electric Corporation

81, 82
Courtesy of Atlantic Richfield Company

83
Courtesy of Forrest Wilson

88
Reproduced from an engraving by Andrea Pozza, *Prospettiva de Pittori et Architetti,* 1723

101
Courtesy of Mark Robson, Filmakers Production, Universal Pictures

104
Courtesy of Whiz Bang Quick City Citizens

116 (*left*)
Courtesy of Metrex Aerial Surveys Company

118 (*top left*)
Reproduced from National Committee of Urban Transportation

118 (*right*)
Courtesy of Sherrie Stephens Cutler for Perry, Dean, Hepburn, and Stewart for the master plan of Franklin Park Zoo, Boston, 1966

127
Reprinted, with permission, from *Rebuilding Cities,* Percy Johnson-Marshall

128
Reproduced from an engraving by Bigelow and Hazan

139
Reproduced from an old steel engraving, circa 1820

202
ECODESIGN, Inc. as advisory consultants to Cambridge Planning Department

Index